PASS the

CompTIA

Network+

Exam

N10-008

Hazim Gaber, B.Sc. (ENG), CSSBB,

PMP

Published By

HSM Press

HSMG Services & Consulting Inc.

34th Floor

10180 101 ST NW

Edmonton, AB T5J 3S4

Canada

Phone: 1-800-716-8955

www.hsmglobal.ca

books@hsmglobal.ca

Foreword

I am delighted to have the opportunity to help you improve your security skills and to obtain the prestigious & internationally-recognized Network+ designation.

This book has been organized to make it easier to absorb and understand the information. I have included practical examples where appropriate.

This is a work in progress. If you have any suggestions to improve this book, or if you see any errors, or if you need help, I would be grateful if you contacted me. My e-mail address is hazim@hsmservices.ca

Visit the Network+ Page at hsmpress.ca/comptia

Regards,

Hazim

September 2021

Table of Contents

Contents

Part A: Introduction

What is the CompTIA Network+?

CompTIA Network+ is an entry level credential for IT Professionals to identify issues and solve problems with computer networks.

CompTIA Network+ allows you to do the following

- Detect security threats
- Install and configure network components that protect critical systems & infrastructure
- Design security network architecture
- Install and configure identity and access systems
- Implement best practices for risk management and business continuity
- Install and configure public key cryptography infrastructure

You should have

- At least two years experience in IT administration and security
- Day-to-day knowledge of technical security information
- Broad knowledge of security threats
- Experience with computer networks

CompTIA overlaps with

- Networking certifications (Cisco CCNA for example)
- Virtualization certifications (VMWare)
- Storage certifications

What can you do with a CompTIA Network+ Certification?

- System Engineer
- Systems Administrator
- Network Administrator
- Network Field Technician
- Network Analyst

CompTIA is "vendor neutral"

The beauty of networks is that when they work, they all work together regardless of the manufacturers of the underlying equipment. Network protocols are designed to be open. Manufacturers implement these open protocols into their hardware. So, a Cisco router can talk to a Netgear or HP switch or an Aruba Wireless Access Point.

Having said that, each manufacturer has specific commands, best practices, and features implemented into their devices. For example, Cisco devices use the Cisco Discovery Protocol, which allows the Cisco devices to discover neighboring Cisco devices. This feature is not available on products made by other manufacturers.

Each manufacturer has their own set of network certifications. These certifications cover the basics, but also focus on troubleshooting and configuring the manufacturer's devices. For example, Cisco offers the Cisco Certified Network Associate certification, which covers many of the same topics as the Network+. It also teaches you how to configure Cisco Switches and Routers.

What should you do? You must remember that the Network+ certification is only a basic certification and has no sequel. There is no certification that builds on Network+. Manufacturer certifications can get more advanced.

For example, Cisco offers the Cisco Certified Network Professional certification, the Cisco Certified Internetwork Expert Certification, and the Cisco Certified Architect certification. Each of these certifications covers more advanced topics and are available in many tracks such as "routing and switching", "collaboration",- "voice over IP", "security", and "cloud". Each of these certifications require a basic understanding of the network. It would take a lifetime to become an expert in every track. Many network experts are experts in a single area like VoIP, cloud, or security. Once you know the basics, you can choose a route that interests you.

When you are in the field, you might encounter network hardware belonging to many different manufacturers. Cisco is the most popular, but Netgear, HP, Dell, Brocade, Juniper, Ubiquiti, and Fortigate make similar equipment. If you know how they all work, you may just need to look up the appropriate commands when performing troubleshooting.

I decided when writing this book, to keep it vendor-neutral, but to use examples of popular technologies. What's new and popular?

- SD-WAN devices including VeloCloud, Meraki, and Viptela

- Cloud managed Wi-Fi and network devices such as Meraki, Ubiquiti, Aruba, and Mist

- VoIP as a Service such as Phone.com and Ring Central

CompTIA Network+ consists of one 90-minute exam

CompTIA Network+ N10-008 has been updated in September 2021 by adding:

- Cloud computing
- Virtualization technology
- A larger focus on security

It will probably be updated again in 2024.

How do I obtain the Network+ Certification?

You must pass the exam, N10-008. The passing score is 720 (out of a possible score from 100 to 900). The exam is 90 minutes long and contains a maximum of 90 questions. The actual number of questions will depend on the difficulty. If you receive an exam with more difficult questions, there may be fewer questions.

About the Exam

- You can register online to take the exam. The online system will show you the dates and times that are available.
- You may be able to write the exam on a Saturday or Sunday, depending on the Prometric Test Center.
- You may reschedule the exam for free, if you do so at least 30 calendar days before the exam.
- You may reschedule the exam for USD$70, if you do so at least 2 calendar days before the exam.
- You may not reschedule the exam if there are less than 2 calendar days before the exam.
- If you do not show up to the exam or are more than 15 minutes late to the exam, you will not be allowed to write the exam, and will forfeit the entire fee.

- At the exam center, you are required to show a piece of government-issued photo ID.
- You will be required to empty your pockets and place the contents in a locker.
- If you are wearing eyeglasses, they will be inspected.
- You may be checked with a metal detector.
- You can only bring your photo ID and locker key into the exam room.
- The test center will provide you with scratch paper, a pencil, and a basic calculator.

- While you write the exam, you will be monitored via audio and video surveillance.
- Each exam is up to 90 multiple-choice questions, and you have 90 minutes to complete the exam.
- You can take a break at any time, but the time on the exam will continue to elapse.

- It goes without saying that cheating will not be tolerated!

- The questions are
    - Multiple-choice (single, and multiple responses)
    - Drag & Drop
    - Performance Based (you are provided with a scenario, which you must explore; you are required to correct the issue)

About this Book

- The Exam has 5 Main Topics
- We're going to cover each topic in order
- This is the best way because some readers have advanced knowledge and just need to brush up on specific topics, while other people are starting from the very beginning
- Sometimes that won't make sense because we are explaining an advanced concept before explaining a basic concept, but I will explain concepts as necessary
- Keep everything in the back of your mind; you might choose to go back and re-read a section

Sample Performance based Question

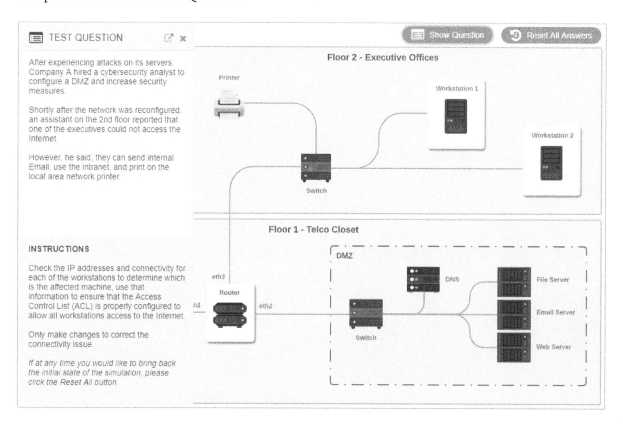

TEST QUESTION

After experiencing attacks on its servers, Company A hired a cybersecurity analyst to configure a DMZ and increase security measures.

Shortly after the network was reconfigured, an assistant on the 2nd floor reported that one of the executives could not access the Internet.

However, he said, they can send internal Email, use the intranet, and print on the local area network printer.

INSTRUCTIONS

Check the IP addresses and connectivity for each of the workstations to determine which is the affected machine, use that information to ensure that the Access Control List (ACL) is properly configured to allow all workstations access to the Internet.

Only make changes to correct the connectivity issue.

If at any time you would like to bring back the initial state of the simulation, please click the Reset All button.

Show Question | Reset All Answers

Floor 2 - Executive Offices

Printer
Workstation 1
Workstation 2
Switch

Floor 1 - Telco Closet

DMZ
eth3
Router
h1
eth2
Switch
DNS
File Server
Email Server
Web Server

Coverage Amount	Coverage Details

24% · **1.0 Network Fundamentals**

- Compare and contrast the Open Systems Interconnection (OSI) model layers and encapsulation concepts
- Explain the characteristics of network topologies and network types
- Summarize the types of cables and connectors and explain which is the appropriate type for a solution
- Given a scenario, configure a subnet and use appropriate IP addressing schemes
- Explain common ports and protocols, their application, and encrypted alternatives
- Explain the use and purpose of network services
- Explain basic corporate and datacenter network architecture
- Summarize cloud concepts and connectivity options

19% · **2.0 Network Implementations**

- Compare and contrast various devices, their features, and their appropriate placement on the network
- Compare and contrast routing technologies and bandwidth management concepts
- Given a scenario, configure and deploy common Ethernet switching features
- Given a scenario, install and configure the appropriate wireless standards and technologies
-

16% · **3.0 Network Operations**

- Given a scenario, use appropriate statistics and sensors to ensure network availability
- Explain the purpose of organizational documents and policies
- Explain high availability and disaster recovery concepts and summarize which is the best solution

29%   **4.0 Network Security**
- Explain common security concepts
- Compare and contrast common types of attacks
- Given a scenario, apply network hardening techniques
- Compare and contrast remote access methods and security implications
- Explain the importance of physical security

22%   **5.0 Network Troubleshooting**
- Explain the network troubleshooting methodology
- Given a scenario, troubleshoot common cable connectivity issues and select the appropriate tools
- Given a scenario, use the appropriate network software tools and commands
- Given a scenario, troubleshoot common wireless connectivity issues
- Given a scenario, troubleshoot general networking issues

Recommended Tools, Hardware & Software

Every job requires tools, and the Network+ is no different. You won't need the tools for your exam, but you will need them for your job.

I recommend

- Buy high quality tools that will last a long time. Cheap tools are more expensive in the long term. They break down and cause frustration.
- Ask for advice, read reddit reviews, read reviews on Amazon, watch YouTube videos, until you find the tools that are best for you. Ask me!

Recommended Tools, Supplies, & Equipment

Some of these are recommended by CompTIA and some are recommended by me!

Laptops & Smartphones

Apple Tablet/Smartphone
Android Tablet/Smartphone
Windows Tablet/Smartphone

Software

Some of the software may also be incorporated into hardware

Packet Sniffer
Protocol Analyzer
Terminal Emulation Software such as PuTTy
Linux/Windows OS
Software Firewall
Software IDS/IPS
Network Mapper
Hypervisor Software
Virtual Network Environment
Wi-Fi Analyzer
Spectrum Analyzer
Network Monitoring Tools
DHCP Service
DNS Service
TFTP Server
Knowledgebase / Ticket Management Software such as AutoTask or Service Now

Equipment

Layer 2/3 Switch

Router
Firewall
VPN Concentrator
Wireless Access Point
Laptop that supports virtualization
Media Converter
Configuration Terminal (with Telnet and SSH)
VoIP System (including a phone)
SOHO Router/Switch
Surge Suppressor
Power Distribution Unit (PDU)
Uninterruptable Power Supply (UPS)
Managed Switch
Hub

Tools

RJ-11/RJ-45 Crimper
Cable tester
Punchdown Tools with Cutting and Non-
Cutting 110, 66, BIX, and Krone Blades
Cable Stripper
Coaxial Crimper
Wire Cutter
Tone Generator and Probe
Fiber Termination Kit
Optical Power Meter
Butt Set
Multimeter
Power Supply Tester
Screwdriver, Drill, or Screw Gun and Assorted
Bits

Spare Parts

Optical and Copper Patch Panels
Punchdown Blocks – 66, 110, and BIX
NICs
Power Supplies
GBICs
SFPs
Patch Cables – cat5e, cat6, fiber
RJ-45 Connectors
RJ-45 Jacks
RJ-11 Connectors

Unshielded Twisted Pair Cable Spool or Box
Coaxial Cable Spool or Box
F-Connectors / BNC Connectors
Fiber Connectors
Antennas
Bluetooth Wireless Adapters
Console Cables and RS-232 to USB Serial
Adapter
Rack Screws
Assorted Sheet Metal, Wood, & Drywall Screws
Velcro
Zip Ties
Grounding Cable and Lugs

Acronyms Used in This Book

AAA	Authentication, Authorization, and Accounting
AAAA	Authentication, Authorization, Accounting, and Auditing
ACL	Access Control List
ADSL	Asymmetric Digital Subscriber Line
AES	Advanced Encryption Standard
AH	Authentication Header
AP	Access Point
APC	Angle Polished Connector / Angled Physical Contact
APIPA	Automatic Private Internet Protocol Address
APT	Advanced Persistent Tool
ARIN	American Registry for Internet Numbers
ARP	Address Resolution Protocol
AS	Autonomous System
ASIC	Application Specific Integrated Circuit
ASP	Application Service Provider
ATM	Asynchronous Transfer Mode
AUP	Acceptable Use Policy
BCP	Business Continuity Plan
BERT	Bit-Error Rate Test
BGP	Border Gateway Protocol
BLE	Bluetooth Low Energy
BNC	British Naval Connector / Bayonet-Niell-Concelman
BootP	Boot Protocol/Bootstrap Protocol
BPDU	Bridge Protocol Data Unit
BRI	Basic Rate Interface
BSSID	Basic Service Set Identifier
BYOD	Bring Your Own Device
CaaS	Communication as a Service
CAM	Content Addressable Memory
CAN	Campus Area Network
CARP	Common Address Redundancy Protocol
CDMA	Code Division Multiple Access
CSMA/CA	Carrier Sense Multiple Access/Collision Avoidance
CSMA/CD	Carrier Sense Multiple Access/Collision Detection
CHAP	Challenge Handshake Authentication Protocol
CIA	Confidentiality, Integrity, and Availability
CIDR	Classless Inter-Domain Routing
CNAME	Canonical Name
CoS	Class of Service
CPU	Central Processing Unit
CRAM-MD5	Challenge-Response Authentication Mechanism-Message Digest 5

CRC	Cyclic Redundancy Checking
CSMA/CA	Carrier Sense Multiple Access/Collision Avoidance
CSU	Channel Service Unit
CVE	Common Vulnerabilities and Exposures
CVDM	Course Wave Division Multiplexing
DaaS	Desktop as a Service
D B	Decibel
DCS	Distributed Computer System
DDoS	Distributed Denial of Service
DHCP	Dynamic Host Configuration Protocol
DLC	Data Link Control
DLP	Data Loss Prevention or Data Leak Prevention
DLR	Device Level Ring
DMZ	Demilitarized Zone
DNAT	Destination Network Address Translation
DNS	Domain Name System/Domain Name Server/Domain Name Service
DOCSIS	Data-Over Cable Service Interface Specification
DoS	Denial of Service
DR	Designated Router
DSCP	Differentiated Services Code Point
DSL	Digital Subscriber Line
DSSS	Direct Sequence Spread Spectrum
DSU	Data Service Unit
DWDM	Dense Wavelength Division Multiplexing
E1	E-Carrier Level 1
EAP	Extensible Authentication Protocol
EDNS	Extension Mechanism for DNS
ECP	Exterior Gateway Protocol
EIA/TIA	Electronic Industries Association/Telecommunication Industries Association
EIRP	Effective Isotropic Radiated Power
EMI	Electromagnetic Interference
ESD	Electrostatic Discharge
ESP	Encapsulated Security Payload
ESSID	Extended Service Set Identifier
EUI	Extended Unique Identifier
FC	Fibre Channel
FCoE	Fiber Channel Over Ethernet
FCS	Frame Check Sequence
FDM	Frequency Division Multiplexing
FHRP	First Hop Redundancy Protocol
FHSS	Frequency Hopping Spread Spectrum
FM	Frequency Modulation
FQDN	Fully Qualified Domain Name

FTP	File Transfer Protocol
FTPS	File Transfer Protocol Security
GBIC	Gigabit Interface Converter
Gbps	Gigabits per second
GLBP	Gateway Load Balancing Protocol
GPG	GNU Privacy Guard
GRE	Generic Routing Encapsulation
GSM	Global System for Mobile Communications
HA	High Availability
HDLC	High-Level Data Link Control
HDMI	High-Definition Multimedia Interface
HIDS	Host Intrusion Detection System
HIPS	Host Intrusion Prevention System
HSPA	High-Speed Packet Access
HSRP	Hot Standby Router Protocol
HT	High throughput
HTTP	Hypertext Transfer Protocol
HTTPS	Hypertext Transfer Protocol Secure
HVAC	Heating, Ventilation, and Air Conditioning
Hz	Hertz
IaaS	Infrastructure as a Service
IANA	Internet Assigned Numbers Authority
ICA	Independent Computer Architecture
ICANN	Internet Corporation for Assigned Names and Numbers
ICMP	Internet Control Message Protocol
ICS	Internet Connection Sharing/Industrial Control System
IDF	Intermediate Distribution Frame
IDWS	Intrusion Detection System
IEEE	Institute of Electrical and Electronics Engineers
IGMP	Internet Group Message Protocol
IGP	Interior Gateway Protocol
IGRP	Interior Gateway Routing Protocol
IKE	Internet Key Exchange
IMAP	Internet Message Access Protocol
IMAP4	Internet Message Access Protocol Version 4
InterNIC	Internet Network Information Center
IoT	Internet of Things
IP	Internet Protocol
IPS	Intrusion Prevention System
IPSec	Internet Protocol Security
IPv4	Internet Protocol Version 4
IPv6	Internet Protocol Version 6
ISAKMP	Internet Security Association and Key Management Protocol
iSCSI	Internet Small Computer Systems Interface

ISDN	Integrated Services Digital Network
IS-IS	Intermediate System to Intermediate System
ISP	Internet Service Provider
IT	Information Technology
ITS	Intelligent Transportation System
IV	Initialization Vector
Kbps	Kilobits per second
KVM	Keyboard Video Mouse
L2TP	Layer 2 Tunneling Protocol
LACP	Link Aggregation Control Protocol
LAN	Local Area Network
LC	Local Connector
LDAP	Lightweight Directory Access Protocol
LDAPS	Lightweight Directory Access Protocol (secure)
LEC	Local Exchange Carrier
LED	Light Emitting Diode
LLC	Logical Link Control
LLDP	Link Layer Discovery Protocol
LSA	Link State Advertisements
LTE	Long Term Evolution
LWAPP	Light Weight Access Point Protocol
MaaS	Mobility as a Service
MAC	Media Access Control/Medium Access Control
MAN	Metropolitan Area Network
Mbps	Megabits per second
MBps	Megabytes per second
MDF	Main Distribution Frame
MDI	Media Dependent Interface
MDIX	Media Dependent Interface Crossover
MGCP	Media Gateway Control Protocol
mGRE	Multipoint Generic Routing Encapsulation
MIB	Management Information Base
MIMO	Multiple Input, Multiple Output
MU-MIMO	Multiuser – Multiple Input, Multiple Output
MLA	Master License Agreement/Multilateral Agreement
MMF	Multimode Fiber
MOA	Memorandum of Agreement
MOU	Memorandum of Understanding
MPLS	Multiprotocol Label Switching
MS-CHAP	Microsoft Challenge Handshake Authentication Protocol
MSA	Master Service Agreement
MSDS	Material Safety Data Sheet
MT-RJ	Mechanical Transfer Registered Jack
MTU	Maximum Transmission Unit
MTTR	Mean Time to Recovery

MTBF	Mean Time Between Failures
MT-RJ	Mechanical Transfer – Registered Jack
MTTR	Mean Time to REpair
MU-MIMO	Multiuser Multiple Input, Multiple Output
MX	Mail Exchanger
NAC	Network Access Control
NAS	Network Attached Storage
NAT	Network Address Translation
NCP	Network Control Protocol
NDA	Non-Disclosure Agreement
NDR	Non-Delivery Receipt
NetBEUI	Network Basic Input/Output Extended User Interface
NFC	Near Field Communication
NFS	Network File Service
NFV	Network Function Virtualization
NGFW	Next Generation Firewall
NIC	Network Interface Card
NIDS	Network Intrusion Detection System
NIPS	Network Intrusion Prevention System
NIU	Network Interface Unit
Nn	Nanometer
NNTP	Network News Transfer Protocol
NS	Name Server
NTP	Network Time Protocol
OCSP	Online Certificate Status Protocol
OCx	Optical Carrier
OID	Object Identifier
OS	Operating System
OSI	Open Systems Interconnect
OSPF	Open Shortest Path First
OTDR	Optical Time Domain Reflectometer
OUI	Organizationally Unique Identifier
PaaS	Platform as a Service
PAN	Personal Area Network
PAP	Password Authentication Protocol
PAT	Port Address Translation
PC	Personal Computer
PCM	Phase-Change Memory
PDoS	Permanent Denial of Service
PDU	Protocol Data Unit
PGP	Pretty Good Privacy
PKI	Public Key Infrastructure
PoE	Power over Ethernet
POP	Post Office Protocol
POP3	Post Office Protocol version 3

POTs	Plain Old Telephone Service
PPP	Point-to-Point Protocol
PPPoE	Point-to-Point Protocol over Ethernet
PPTP	Point-to-Point Tunneling Protocol
PKI	Primary Rate Interface
PSK	Pre-Shared Key
PSTN	Public Switched Telephone Network
PTP	Point-to-Point
PTR	Pointer
PUA	Privileged User Agreement
PVC	Permanent Virtual Circuit
QoS	Quality of Service
QSFP	Quad Small Form-Factor Pluggable
RA	Router Advertisements
RADIUS	Remote Authentication Dial-in-User Service
RAID	Redundant Array of Inexpensive (or Independent) Disks
RARP	Reverse Address Resolution Protocol
RAS	Remote Access Service
RDP	Remote Desktop Protocol
RF	Radio Frequency
RFC	Request for Comment
RFI	Radio Frequency Interface
RFP	Request for Proposal
RG	Radio Guide
RIP	Routing Internet Protocol
RJ	Registered Jack
RPO	Recovery Point Objective
RSA	Rivest, Shamir, Adelman
RSH	Remote Shell
RSTP	Rapid Spanning Tree Protocol
RTO	Recovery Time Objective
RTP	Real-Time Protocol
RTSP	Real-Time Streaming Protocol
RTT	Round Trip Time or Real Transfer Time
SA	Security Association
SaaS	Software as a Service
SAN	Storage Area Network
SC	Standard Connector/Subscriber Connector
SCADA	Supervisory Control and Data Acquisition
SCP	Secure Copy Protocol
SDLC	Software Development Life Cycle
SDN	Software Defined Network
SDP	Session Description Protocol
SDSL	Symmetrical Digital Subscriber Line
SDWAN	Software-Defined WAN

SFP	Small Form-Factor Pluggable
SFTP	Secure File Transfer Protocol
SGCP	Simple Gateway Control Protocol
SHA	Secure Hash Algorithm
SIEM	Security Information and Event Management
SIP	Session Initiation Protocol
SLA	Service-Level Agreement
SLAAC	Stateless Address-Auto Configuration
SLIP	Serial Line Internet Protocol
SMB	Service Message Block
SMF	Single-Mode Fiber
SMS	Short Message Service
SMTP	Simple Mail Transfer Protocol
SNAT	Static Network Address Translation/Source Network Address Translation
SNMP	Simple Network Management Protocol
SNTP	Simple Network Time Protocol
SOA	Start of Authority
SOHO	Small Office Home Office
SONET	Synchronous Optical Network
SOP	Standard Operating Protocol
SOW	Statement of Work
SPB	Shortest Path Bridging
SPI	Stateful Packet Inspection
SPS	Standby Power Supply
SQL	Structured Query Language
SRV	Service Record
SSH	Secure Shell
SSID	Service Set Identifier
SSL	Secure Sockets Layer
SSO	Single Sign-On
ST	Straight Tip or Snap Twist
STP	Spanning Tree Protocol/Shielded Twisted Pair
SVC	Switched Virtual Circuit
SYLOG	System Log
T1	Terrestrial Carrier Level 1
TA	Terminal Adapter
TACAS	Terminal Access Control Access Control System
TACAS+	Terminal Access Control Access Control System+
TCP	Transmission Control Protocol
TCP/IP	Transmission Control Protocol/Internet Protocol
TDM	Time Division Multiplexing
TDR	Time Domain Reflectometer
Telco	Telecommunications Company
TFTP	Trivial File Transfer Protocol

TIA/EIA	Telecommunications Industry Association/Electronic Industries Association
TKIP	Temporal Key Integrity Protocol
TLS	Transport Layer Security
TMS	Transportation Management System
TOS	Type of Service
TPM	Trusted Platform Module
TTL	Time to Live
TTLS	Tunneled Transport Layer Security
TX/RX	Transmit and Receive
UC	Unified Communications
UDP	User Datagram Protocol
UNC	Universal Naming Convention
UPC	Ultra Polished Connector
UPS	Uninterruptible Power Supply
URL	Uniform Resource Locator
USB	Universal Serial Bus
UTM	Unified Threat Management
VDSL	Variable Digital Subscriber Line
VIP	Virtual IP
VLAN	Virtual Local Area Network
VNC	Virtual Network Connection
vNIC	Virtual Network Interface Card
VoIP	Voice over IP
VPN	Virtual Private Network
VRF	Virtual Routing Forwarding
VRRP	Virtual Router Redundancy Protocol
VTC	Video Teleconference
VTP	VLAN Trunk Protocol
WAF	Web Application Firewall
WAN	Wide Area Network
WAP	Wireless Application Protocol/Wireless Access Point
WDM	Wavelength Division Multiplexing
WEP	Wired Equivalent Privacy
WLAN	Wireless Local Area Network
WMS	Warehouse Management System
WPA	Wi-Fi Protected Access
WPS	Wi-Fi Protected Setup
WWN	World Wide Name
XDSL	Extended Digital Subscriber Line
XML	eXtensible Markup Language
Zeroconf	Zero Configuration

Part B: N10-008 1.0 Networking Fundamentals

1.1 Compare and contrast the Open Systems Interconnection (OSI) model layers and encapsulation concepts

- *OSI Model*
  - *Layer 1 – Physical*
  - *Layer 2 – Data Link*
  - *Layer 3 – Network*
  - *Layer 4 – Transport*
  - *Layer 5 – Session*
  - *Layer 6 – Presentation*
  - *Layer 7 - Application*
- *Data encapsulation and decapsulation within the OSI model context*
  - *Ethernet Header*
  - *Internet Protocol (IP) Header*
  - *Transmission Control Protocol (TCP) / User Datagram Protocol (UDP) headers*
  - *TCP Flags*
  - *Payload*
  - *Maximum Transmission Unit (MTU)*

In my previous book, I had an introduction about how networks function, but now that the order of the material has changed, we are going to jump right in. I will introduce background material as needed.

The question we want to ask is: how does data on a network (or on the Internet) get from one point to another? How is it that when you plug a computer into an ethernet jack or connect to the Wi-Fi in a building, things just work (usually)? How do devices understand each other?

Well, manufacturers create devices according to established standards. Devices communicate with each other based on specific protocols (languages) that are defined by the international community. If you get into the business of making ethernet adapters, patch panels, fiber optic cables, switches, routers, etc., you will also have to follow those standards and protocols so that your devices can communicate with all the existing devices.

To create these standards and protocols, we had to create a model of the network. The **OSI (Open Systems Interconnection) model** is the single most important concept you will need to know (to pass the exam). OSI is just a concept.

There are seven layers:
- **Layer 1 – Physical**
- **Layer 2 – Data Link**
- **Layer 3 – Network**
- **Layer 4 – Transport**
- **Layer 5 – Session**
- **Layer 6 – Presentation**
- **Layer 7 – Application**

We are going to see some examples of communications that allows this model to make sense. But each layer carries data for the layers below it. Or in other words, each layer packages (encapsulates) the data from the layer below it. So, a device or program on the Application layer creates content and addresses it to a device on the Application layer at the other side. It gives this content to a device Presentation layer, which packages it, addresses it to the device in the Presentation layer on the other side, and sends it a device on the Session layer. This goes on until we get to the Physical layer.

When the data is received by the Physical layer on the other side, it is unpackaged and sent up the devices on each layer until it is received by the Application layer.

We need to understand the layers so that

- We can design a network and make sure that all the devices are connected and that they can communicate with each other properly

- We can identify which layer is affected when something goes wrong. This way, we can properly troubleshoot the software or configuration that is causing the issue

- We can start troubleshooting at the bottom layer and work our way up, or start at the top layer and work our way down, or figure out what is the highest layer that is working and then troubleshoot the next layer above it

Let's look at an example. You want to send an e-mail. The Layer 7, Application Layer is the software that a user sees (Microsoft Word, Google Chrome, etc.). You type up the e-mail in Microsoft Outlook and send it off. But what is really happening? You only saw the seventh layer.

Well, Layer 6 is the Presentation Layer. It takes the data from Layer 7 and makes sure that the Application layer of the recipient can understand it. What if the recipient's computer has a Mac or Unix operating system? What if the user doesn't use HTML to display e-mails? What if the user's computer is in a different language?

Idea: If you type up a document in Microsoft Word and then open it in Notepad, it will look like gibberish. Why? Because Microsoft Word has its own internal language that keeps track of things like fonts, formatting, layout, highlights, etc.. This language is useless to humans. Humans just want to see the properly formatted Word document or e-mail. So, the Presentation layer takes this gibberish that the computer understands and converts it into something that a human understands. If you open the same e-mail on your phone, or tablet, or 24" monitor, it will look different. The Presentation Layer on each device understands the capabilities of that device and translates the gibberish into a format that is suitable for its Application layer.

Layer 5 is the Session Layer. What is a Session? A Session is when two devices agree to communicate with each other for a period. When you send the e-mail, your computer calls up the receiving computer and says, "hey, I want to send you an e-mail". The two computers use the session to exchange data and keep it open until one or both decide to close it. *Technically (as we will find out layer), your computer wouldn't directly contact the recipient's computer. It would call up the e-mail server of its own service provider and send the e-mail there. That e-mail server would call the e-mail server of the recipient and send the e-mail there. The receiving e-mail server would call up the recipient's device and further transport the e-mail. We just tried to make it simple for this example.*

Layer 4 is the Transport Layer. Layer 4 takes the data from the Session Layer and packages it or breaks it into pieces. So, it might cut up your e-mail into chunks, give each one a number, and send each chunk separately to the recipient. The recipient has already agreed to receive these chunks because it has an established session. The Transport Layer on the other side would put them back together in the correct order. If some of those chunks don't show up, the sending Transport Layer can send them again. The Transport Layer also puts the IP address of the recipient on each chunk. Later, we are going to look more specifically at a transport protocol known as TCP/IP.

Layer 3 is the Network Layer. Say you are in New York City and you are sending an e-mail to a device in Los Angeles. Layer 4 put the IP address of the recipient on each "chunk". How does the data get to the destination? Throughout the internet are many routers and many cables. So, there are many pathways for data to get from NYC to LA. The router in your office looks at the destination IP address and decides about the next router to send the e-mail to (probably the main NYC router for your ISP). That router receives the data and makes its own decision sending it to a router in California. A main router in California sends the data to a router in LA. Finally, a router in LA forwards that e-mail to the recipient's office router. Routers have algorithms that make these decisions efficient (as we will learn about later).

In the Layer 3, we call each "chunk" of data a **packet**. We will find out later that a packet has a very specific format so that routers can understand them. The size of the packet is known as the **Maximum Transmission Unit**. The sender and recipient agree on the largest size of packet that they can handle.

You can think of this layer like the mail. If you send a letter from NYC to LA, a mailman isn't going to pick up the letter and drive straight to LA with it. Instead, that letter will go to the local NYC post office no matter the destination (just like your local office router must process all of the outgoing data no matter the destination). The local post office sorts mail going to California and ships them off to a main post office in California. That post office sorts the mail going to LA and ships them to the main LA post office. The main LA post office sorts the mail into routes for trucks and letter carriers, and those trucks and letter carriers deliver your letter to the recipient.

Layer 2 is the Data Link Layer. Layer 2 allows two directly devices to communicate. Every network device has a unique address called a MAC address. This address is burned in to the device from the factory and is unique regardless of the manufacturer. Layer 2 uses MAC addresses to forward traffic.

Remember those chunks called packets? Well, your computer doesn't send packets. It creates the packet and puts the destination IP address on it, but your computer doesn't know how to get it to California. So, the destination IP address is kind of useless to your computer.

Instead, your computer thinks about the next destination of the packet. It might be the same office, an office across the street, or an office in another country. As we will find out later, your computer just needs to think about whether the destination is within the office or outside the office (or in other words, whether it is behind the router or past the router).

Your computer finds out the MAC address of the packet's destination. Then the computer packages this packet into a **frame** and adds the destination MAC address. If the destination is within your office, your computer puts the destination MAC address of the actual recipient. If the destination is somewhere else, your computer won't be able to figure out the destination MAC address, so it puts the destination MAC address of the router as the recipient. The router receives this frame and removes the packet. Then it figures out the MAC address of the next destination (probably the next router). It puts the packet into a new frame with a new MAC address as the destination.

Your computer might be connected directly to your office router, but most likely it will connect to a switch. The switch understands and forwards frames based on the MAC address. We will find out more about how switches work later. When you send a frame to a device within your office, the switch can deliver that frame without having to talk to the router. When you send a frame addressed to the router (i.e. a frame containing a packet that has a destination outside of your office), the switch delivers that frame to the router.

In the case of our e-mail example, your computer encapsulates the packets containing pieces of your e-mail into frames. It puts the MAC address of your office router as the destination. The office switch delivers those frames to the router. The router removes the packet from the frame. The router finds the MAC address of the next router and packages the packet into a new frame. It puts the MAC address of the next router into the destination field on the new frame and sends it along. This process continues until the frame is finally delivered to the destination.

Layer One is the Physical Layer. It is the actual transmission layer and contains the wiring. Layer One also deals with directly connected devices. When your computer tries to send data to the switch, your computer and the switch must agree on a speed. What if your computer or the switch can't handle a speed that is too high? Thus, two directly connected devices must agree on the speed to use on the line. If the line supports only a one-way transmission, they must also agree who will talk and who will listen at each time.

Now let's think about the router in the receiving office. The Physical Layer receives the data (0's and 1's as an electronic or fiber transmission). That data is eventually recorded into a frame on Layer Two. The router's Layer Two receives the frame. The router's Layer Three technology removes the packet from the frame and figures out the destination MAC address of the device in the office that is entitled to it. It repackages the packet into a frame with the new destination MAC address and forwards the frame.

The switch in the office receives the frame and forwards it to the correct computer. The receiving computer removes the packet from the frame and sends it to the Transport Layer. The Transport

Layer waits until all the associated packets are received and reassembles them. It also asks for missing packets to be resent (if any). The Transport Layer sends this assembled data to the Session Layer. The Session Layer sends the data to the Presentation Layer, which understands that the data is an e-mail. The Presentation Layer thinks about the best way to translate the content for the Application Layer. The Application Layer displays the e-mail in the recipient's web browser or e-mail application.

When the router puts a packet into a frame, it is called **encapsulation**. When a router removes a packet from a frame, it is called **deencapsulation**. We are going to use those words more often throughout the book.

A frame has the following format

Preamble	Delimiter	MAC Destination	MAC Source	Tag	Length	Payload	Check Sequence	Interpacket Gap
FRAME (ETHERNET) HEADER						PAYLOAD	ETHERNET TRAILER	

You don't need to worry too much about these now but

- **Preamble**. This lets the devices know that this is an Ethernet frame. It is a bunch of 0's and 1's that let the two devices sync so that they don't miss or misinterpret any of the following data and looks like this - 10101010 10101010 10101010 10101010 10101010 10101010 10101010 10101011.

- **Delimiter**. Basically, just a space to say "pay attention, the preamble is finished, and the real data is starting. We need the delimiter because the receiving device may have missed a portion of the preamble and won't know how long until it ends.

- **MAC Destination**. The MAC address of the destination device.

- **MAC Source**. The MAC address of the source device.

- **Tag**. The tag is optional but tells us some information about the frame and its priority.

- **Length**. The length of the frame.

- **Payload**. The actual data we are sending.

- **Check Sequence**. A check digit that is mathematically computed from the frame data. It is used by the recipient to verify that the data was received correctly.

- **Interpacket Gap**. A space we make before sending the next frame.

Remember that the router strips the headers from the frame to look at just the Payload. It can add new headers if necessary. Well, the Payload is actually a Packet with its own Header and Payload.

Length	Protocol	Check Sequence	Source IP	Destination IP	Payload
IP HEADER					PAYLOAD

Notice that in the IP world, we only have headers and no trailer.

You don't need to worry too much about these now but

- **Length**. The length of the packet.

- **Protocol**. The protocol that the packet will use.

- **Check Sequence**. A check digit that is mathematically computed from the packet header data. It is used by the recipient to verify that the data was received correctly.

- **Source IP**. The IP address of the destination device.

- **Destination IP**. The IP address of the source device.

- **Payload**. The actual data we are sending.

There are actually many more fields in the header, but they are less important.

If we take the Payload from an IP packet, we can further dig inside it to find that it has its own header. This Payload is known as a **Segment**. If we were using TCP or UDP as our protocol for sending data, our Segment might look like this:

Source Port	Destination Port	Flag	Payload
IP HEADER			PAYLOAD

You don't need to worry too much about these now but

- **Source Port**. The port that the data originated from.
- **Destination Port**. The protocol that the data is travelling to.
- **Flag**. A flag tells us whether the segment was sent to establish a connection or to acknowledge receipt of some other data.
- **Payload**. The actual data we are sending.

In summary, an ethernet frame looks like this

<table>
<tr><th>Ethernet Header</th><th>IP Header</th><th>TCP Header</th><th>Payload</th><th>Ethernet Trailer</th></tr>
<tr><td></td><td></td><td colspan="2">TCP Segment</td><td></td></tr>
<tr><td></td><td colspan="3">IP Packet</td><td></td></tr>
<tr><td colspan="5">Ethernet Frame</td></tr>
</table>

We can further summarize the contents and group them by OSI Layer.

<table>
<tr><th colspan="5">Contents</th><th>What It's Called</th><th>OSI Model Layer Name</th></tr>
<tr><td></td><td></td><td></td><td>Raw Data</td><td></td><td></td><td>Application
Presentation
Session</td></tr>
<tr><td></td><td></td><td>TCP Header</td><td>Raw Data</td><td></td><td>Segment</td><td>Transport</td></tr>
<tr><td></td><td>IP Header</td><td>TCP Header</td><td>Raw Data</td><td></td><td>Packet</td><td>Network</td></tr>
<tr><td>Ethernet Header</td><td>IP Header</td><td>TCP Header</td><td>Raw Data</td><td>Ethernet Trailer</td><td>Frame</td><td>Data Link</td></tr>
<tr><td colspan="5"></td><td></td><td>Physical</td></tr>
</table>

Now that we understand the model, we will revisit each topic in more depth.

1.2 Explain the characteristics of network topologies and network types

- *Mesh*
- *Star / Hub-and-Spoke*
- *Bus*
- *Ring*
- *Hybrid*
- *Network types and characteristics*
    - *Peer-to-Peer*
    - *Client-Server*
    - *Local Area Network (LAN)*
    - *Metropolitan Area Network (MAN)*
    - *Wide Area Network (WAN)*
    - *Wireless Local Area Network (WLAN)*
    - *Personal Area Network (PAN)*
    - *Campus Area Network (CAN)*
    - *Storage Area Network (SAN)*
    - *Software-Defined Wide Area Network (SD-WAN)*
    - *Multiprotocol Label Switching (MPLS)*
    - *Multipoint Generic Routing Encapsulation (mGRE)*
- *Service-Related Entry Point*
    - *Demarcation Point*
    - *Smartjack*
- *Virtual Network Concepts*
    - *vSwitch*
    - *Virtual Network Interface Card (vNIC)*
    - *Network Function Virtualization (NFV)*
    - *Hypervisor*
- *Provider links*
    - *Satellite*
    - *Digital Subscriber Line (DSL)*
    - *Cable*
    - *Leased Line*
    - *Metro-Optical*

There are several types of network topologies

- **Star** – the star shaped network consists of a central hub and branches that connect to it. Most local ethernet networks are star-shaped. A central switch connects to multiple client devices such as computers and printers. A star network is also known as a **hub-and-spoke**.

- **Ring** – a ring network is one where each device connects to two neighbors, and no device is central. A ring network provides redundancy because the devices can continue to communicate even when one link fails. The ring network is common with large routers on the internet, which may have multiple routes.

- **Bus** – a bus network is where multiple devices share the same physical cable. Ethernet does not function with a bus network, but some forms of industrial communication do.

- **Mesh** – a mesh network is where each device has direct links to several other devices. A mesh network provides the most redundancy because the devices can continue to communicate even when multiple links have failed.

  A mesh network is not possible with client devices such as computers and printers, because each typically has only one network interface. The mesh network exists for the backbone of the internet.

- **Hybrid** – a hybrid network is a combination of the above types.

When you plan out your network, you should think about

- The size of your facility or campus

- The types of devices that you plan to connect

- The bandwidth that is required in each portion of your facility or campus

- The bandwidth that is required between portions of the facility or campus

- Whether fiber or copper connections are required

- The cost to acquire and maintain each network device

- The future needs of the organization and the expected growth

- The level of redundancy required

Some ideas

- The backbone of the internet is a mesh network in that every major ISP network is connected to several other ISP networks. This offers redundancy by providing multiple pathways for data transmission.

- A small office or home might have a star network where all the devices connect to a central modem/router.
- A larger office might have a star or hybrid star network with multiple layers. For example, a core switch in the main server room will feed smaller switches on each floor. Each client device will connect to one of these smaller switches.

- A corporate or university campus with multiple buildings will have a star or hybrid star network. A core switch will be in the main server room and will feed a smaller aggregation switch at each building. Depending on the size of the building, it may have multiple edge switches, or devices may connect directly to the aggregation switch.

  The campus may also have a fiber optic ring network that surrounds the entire campus. A ring provides additional redundancy. One benefit of the ring is that it can be constructed in the early stages of the campus. As more buildings are added, the ring can be cut and new buildings can be spliced onto it without having to install additional fibre.

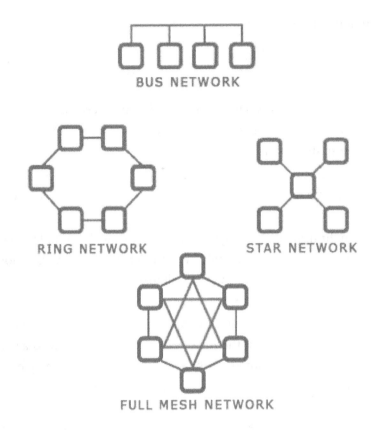

BUS NETWORK

RING NETWORK

STAR NETWORK

FULL MESH NETWORK

In the following example, in yellow, we have a fiber optic backbone connected as a ring to the existing buildings – A, B, and C. We can add additional buildings onto the same backbone.

Each building has an aggregation switch that connects to the core switch. Building A has edge switches that connect to the aggregation switches. User devices in Building A can connect directly to each edge switch. User devices in Building B and C can connect directly to the aggregation switches.

We could draw the core switch as being on the backbone instead of being directly connected to each aggregation switch. If the fiber has enough capacity, we can directly connect the core switch to each aggregation switch without any issues.

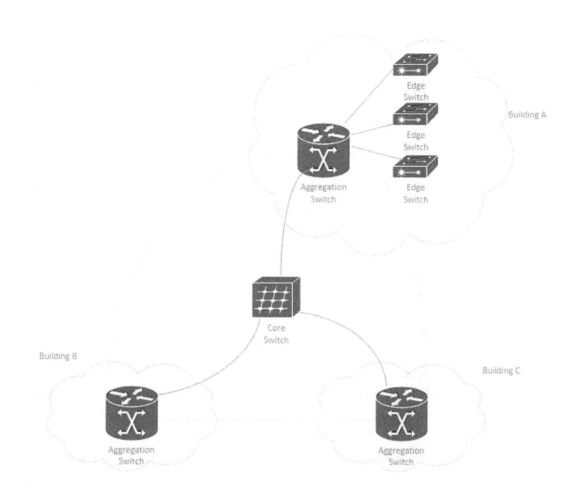

Let's look at some network types.

- **Peer-to-Peer**. You might recognize this from file sharing applications. Peer to Peer is a distributed architecture where every computer acts as a server to the other computers. A peer makes some of its resources available to the other peers without the use of an intermediate server.

  Peer-to-Peer networks are used by file sharing applications, cryptocurrencies, Microsoft Windows update, and some other applications. In general, the devices on the P2P network do not have direct physical connections to one another and instead operate on top of another network. For example, you can set up a P2P network using devices on your office LAN.

- **Client-Server**. A Client-Server network is one where multiple devices request content or communicate with a central server.

  Examples of Client-Server networks include corporate file sharing, websites, and e-mail systems. For example, when you visit a website, that website is hosted on a server and your computer is the client. Multiple clients can connect to the same web server.

  The Client-Server network also operates on top of another network such as a LAN or WAN.

- **Local Area Network (LAN).** A LAN is the network in your office or home. It consists of devices connected behind a router (a router separates the LAN from the WAN).

- **Wide Area Network (WAN).** A WAN connects multiple networks together across long distances. It allows devices in multiple locations to act like they're on the same network. An organization with offices spreads all over the country might connect them through a WAN. An internet service provider (or multiple ISPs) will own the backbone infrastructure that makes the WAN possible. Essentially, the company is paying the ISP a large amount of money to prioritize the traffic between its offices. If the ISP doesn't own the entire backbone, then it negotiates with other ISPs to also prioritize the traffic in exchange for a portion of the fees.

  WAN may also refer to standard internet connections such as DSL, Cable, Fiber, Broadband, etc. (i.e. connections that introduce your network to the outside world).

- **Wireless Wide Area Network (WWAN).** A WWAN is a WAN but delivered over a cellular modem. WWANs are increasingly popular as back up connections and also for remote sites where the cost of extending a fiber optic cable would be prohibitive.

- **Software-Defined Wide Area Network (SD-WAN).** An SD-WAN is new technology that allows a company to connect multiple offices without the expense of a traditional WAN. It does so by connecting standard internet connections to an SD-WAN router at each office.

  The SD-WAN router uses the internet connections to connect to cloud service providers and route traffic just as a traditional WAN would do. Since cloud service providers have data centers throughout most of the world now, and own the backbone infrastructure between those centers, the only slow portion of the SD-WAN will be between the office and the cloud. The result is the performance that is similar to a standard WAN without the cost.

- **Metropolitan Area Network (MAN).** A MAN is larger than a LAN and can link multiple LANs together in a geographic area like a city. An organization with multiple offices in the same city might use a MAN.

- **Wireless Local Area Network (WLAN).** A WLAN is a portion of the LAN that is wireless. When wireless access points are connected to the LAN, they connect wireless clients with the rest of the LAN.

- **Personal Area Network (PAN).** A PAN is a small network formed by a user and his devices (such as a cell phone, tablet, and laptop). PANs are typically wireless and may use technologies like Bluetooth.

- **Campus Area Network (CAN).** A CAN is a network at a campus like a university or hospital. It may connect multiple LANs together. A CAN might be considered a LAN if no routers are involved. A CAN is different from a WAN in that the campus owns the infrastructure between the LANs.

- **Storage Area Network (SAN).** A SAN is a network that connects storage appliances to servers. A storage appliance is a type of hardware that is dedicated to storing large amounts of data. SANs could use ethernet or Fiber Channel.

- **Multiprotocol Label Switching (MPLS).** MPLS is an ISP technology that allows data packets to be routed from point to point across any type of transport medium (copper, fiber, or antenna), and via any protocol.

  An ethernet packet is transported from the customer site to the ISP over the MPLS. The ISP uses ethernet (its own internal LAN) to transport the packet to its destination. From there, it exits and uses the MPLS to get to the destination customer site.

- **Multipoint Generic Routing Encapsulation (mGRE).** mGRE was developed by Cisco. It allows a company with multiple sites to establish a VPN connection between them. A VPN allows a company to establish a "tunnel" between two or more sites. The traffic between the two sites is packaged and encapsulated over the tunnel. A VPN allows the sites to act like they are on the same network.

  A VPN has poor performance compared to a WAN, but is less expensive, and can be established over standard internet connections.

  Normally, a VPN must be manually configured on the router at each customer site. When the customer sites have public IP addresses that change, the routers must be manually reconfigured each time that the IP address changes.

  When there are many VPN sites, the VPN is created as a "hub and spoke", so that there is a central VPN server that connects to many branch offices. This way, each branch is not attempting to establish dozens of connections with other offices (which would overload the routers). But a large number of VPN connections can overload the VPN server as well.

  mGRE allows the VPN tunnels to be created dynamically as required using **Next Hop Resolution Protocol (NHRP)**. When the addresses of the spoke sites change, mGRE can use NHRP to find the new ones. Effectively, when a spoke site realizes that its IP address has changed, it calls up the hub and lets it know.

How does internet get into your building?

In legal terms, the **Demarcation Point** is where the ISPs equipment stops, and the customer's equipment starts. It may also be known as the **demarc, DMARC, MPOE, main point of entry, MPOP**, or **minimum point of presence**. It might also be called the Service-Related Entry Point.

The customer may own some or all the customer premises equipment (CPE) or the ISP may own some or all of it.

A demarcation point may be a termination block (such as a 66-block or 110-block), where wiring from the ISP is terminated. Or it may consist of a **NID** (**Network Interface Device**) such as the one below. Note that this NID has two sides – an ISP side and a customer side. The NID is usually installed outside a house or building. In a large office building or shopping mall, the demarcation point may be a large room with thousands of pairs of wiring.

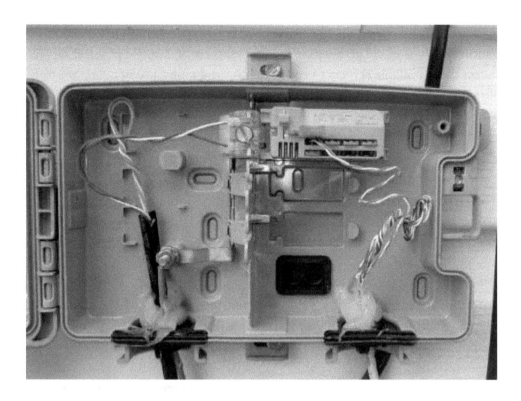

What if the customer's equipment is too far from the demarcation point? The ISP must then supply a **demarcation extension**. This is also known as a **Service Interface Extension** or **inside wiring**. The customer must typically pay for the cost of the extension.

An ISP may install a **CSU/DSU (channel service unit/data service unit)** at the demarcation point. The CSU/DSU converts the customer's digital signal into an analog signal that travels over the telephone network.

Another device is called a **Smart Jack**. Where did the Smart Jack come from? In the past, to reduce competition, ISPs supplied and owned all the Customer Premises Equipment. ISPs used proprietary protocols to prevent customers from connecting their own CPE (such as modems). Eventually, the US federal government made it illegal and required each ISP to provide the customer with a physical wire connection, known as an RJ48. The problem was that the ISPs preferred to install their own equipment so that it could run diagnostic tests on the circuit. What if the customer complained that the internet wasn't working? If the ISP owned the equipment, it could connect to it and perform diagnostic tests. If the customer owned the equipment, it couldn't.

The solution was to create a Smart Jack. The smart jack is an electronic device with an RJ48 handoff that the customer could connect to. On the ISP side of the smart jack, they can monitor the connection and perform diagnostic tests. On the customer side, there is a standard RJ48 customer connection that satisfies the requirement of the federal government.

The ideas behind the network delivery (especially the LAN) have been expanded to virtualization technologies. Virtualization allows us to create multiple "virtual" servers on a single physical server. But when we try to connect those multiple servers to each other or to the physical network, we must employ network virtualization. This is related to Software Defined Networking (SDN). We will explore this topic in more details later.

But we have four ideas

- **Hypervisor**. The Hypervisor is a software application that runs as the base operating system on a physical server. It allows the user to create multiple virtual servers, which run inside the hypervisor. The hypervisor tricks the virtual servers into believing that each of them has separate physical hardware.

  The advantage of a virtual machine is that we can maximize the resources of our hardware. We can run multiple servers on the same physical hardware instead of having separate servers for each application.

  We can also run the same virtual server across multiple physical servers. This provides redundancy in case one of the physical servers were to experience a hardware failure. It also allows us to increase the resources of a high-demand virtual server so that it can have the computing power of multiple physical servers.

- **vSwitch**. The vSwitch is a virtual switch that runs inside the Hypervisor and connects the multiple virtual servers. There can be multiple vSwitches if required.

- **Virtual Network Interface Card (vNIC)**. Each virtual server can have one or more vNICs that allow the server to connect to the switch.

- **Network Function Virtualization (NFV)**. NFV takes this a step further and virtualizes load balancers, routers, and firewalls, which used to require dedicated hardware.

  Consider in a network that each function must be performed by a proprietary device, such as a load balancer, a firewall, a router, etc. For example, you may have a Cisco router or Cisco firewall. Now, what if we want to increase the capacity of the physical router? We would have to buy a larger router. What if we want to install a physical router in a cloud infrastructure, or inside a virtual machine? It is not possible.

  With NFV, we can take the software component of the proprietary router, firewall, or load balancer and install it on a server (inside a hypervisor) virtual machine. The manufacturer of the proprietary hardware will create an "image" of the operating system on their router/firewall/load balancer, which we would then install as a separate virtual machine and virtually connect it to the other components. The virtualized infrastructure would run on generic physical hardware, which can be scaled up or down as required. It also requires less space in some cases.

Remember that the physical hardware must still physically connect to the internet, so there will always be a need for some physical infrastructure.

When I buy an internet connection, how is it delivered?

ISDN or **Integrated Services Digital Network** was an older type of internet connection. It delivered data, voice, video, or fax over the same physical telephone line. ISDN supported connection speeds of up to 128 kbit/s. At least two simultaneous connections were possible over a single ISDN line. ISDN was a circuit-switched network (between the user and the ISP) that provided subscribers with access to a packet-switched network.

ISDN technology was later used to develop the **PRI**, or **Primary Rate Interface**. PRI is a technology that can transmit multiple analog phone lines over a single pair of wires. Previously, each phone line required a separate pair of wires. The PRI delivers 23 "channels" of voice traffic and one overhead channel. That is, a PRI can handle up to 23 simultaneous phone calls on a single pair of wires. A phone call coming in over a PRI is tagged with the number that was dialed. This way, an organization could have hundreds of phone numbers on a single PRI, if they do not have more than 23 simultaneous phone calls.

A PRI is delivered over a **T1** line, or **Transmission System 1** line. The total bandwidth carried by a T1 is 1.544 Mbit/s. Each channel is 64 kbit/s. The different channels are separated with a time-division multiplexing algorithm. In other words, each channel receives a separate time slot for when its data is transmitted.

Who decided that T1 should be 1.544 Mbit/s as opposed to some other number? AT&T did. They invented T1 in the 1960s because they were trying to send telephone traffic long distances without the use of expensive equipment.

I need to go off on a tangent. Think of water flowing from a garden hose. It is continuous. It never stops. I could measure the flow rate every 10 seconds, or every second, or every $1/10^{th}$ of a second, or every $1/100^{th}$ of a second, etc.. This is known as my "sample rate". What if the flow rate is 1 gallon/second at my first measurement and 1.1 gallons/second at my second measurement? Did it instantly jump from 1 gallon/s to 1.1 gallons/s? No. Between measurements it might have been 1.01, 1.02, 1.03 g/s, etc.. The point is, we can't take an infinite amount of measurements. It's physically impossible.

When you're talking on the phone, the phone isn't listening to you all the time. It's taking samples of your voice and sending them to the network. If the samples are taken at short enough time intervals, the call can be reconstructed on the other side without any noticeable loss of quality. Our brains fill in the blanks.

A phone measures your voice 8000 times per second (8000 Hz). Each measurement is 8 bits in size. If I have 24 channels, then I need 8 bits x 24 channels = 192 bits/measurement. I must add one extra bit called the "framing" bit, which is used in error handling. So, I have 193 bits per measurement. Since there are 8000 measurements per second, 193 x 8000 = 1544000 bits/s or 1.544 Mbit/s.

Why did they choose 24 channels and not some other number? Rumor has it that AT&T performed some tests on cables they had installed underground in Chicago. They increased the transmission rate until the quality was just barely unacceptable. They had to stop at 24 channels.

Eventually other phone companies figured out a way to increase the bandwidth on a wire, and other T's were developed. Another common T system is **T3**, which carries 44.736 Mbit/s.

Another system competing with the T1 is the **E1**, which carries up to 32 channels, for a total of 2.048 Mbit/s. Only 30 channels are useful, because E1 uses one channel for synchronization, and one for management. The E1 system uses time-division multiplexing just like the T1 system.

Other phone companies found ways to increase the bandwidth of the E1 system, resulting in the **E2** (8 Mbit/s), **E3** (34 Mbit/s), and **E4** (140 Mbit/s) systems.

What if we need to transmit data long distances, and the copper wiring just won't cut it? That's where fiber comes in. Across large ISPs, **Optical Carrier transmission rates** have become standardized. The standard transmission rate is OC-1, which carries 51.84 Mbit/s. We can measure the transmission rate of a line in multiples of the standard rate. We can give this line a name in the format of OC-#, where # is the multiple. For example, if a line has a transmission rate of 103.88 Mbit/s, that is double the standard rate. We would call this line an OC-2 line.

Three common OC lines are the **OC-3**, which has a rate of 155.52 Mbit/s, **OC-48**, which has a rate of 2488.32 Mbit/s, and the **OC-192** line, which has a rate of 9953.28 Mbit/s. The OC-48 line is used by many ISPs. OC-192 can work with 10 Gigabit Ethernet. Some undersea fiber optic cables use transmission rates of OC-768 (approximately 39 Gbit/s).

OC uses a system called **SONNET**, or **synchronous optical networking protocol**. Remember that data is broken up into packets, and that each packet has a header. The difference between a SONNET transmission and other types of transmissions is that the packet and header are sent at the same time. The header is mixed up with the rest of the packet.

In a smaller organization, the type of internet connection delivered may be **DSL**, **Metropolitan Ethernet**, **Cable Broadband**, or even **Dial-Up**.

DSL or **Digital Subscriber Line** is delivered over a phone line. It may provide speeds of up to 150 Mbit/s. A subscriber will require a **DSL modem** to convert the signal from a phone line to an ethernet cable. The same phone line can be used to transmit voice simultaneously. Internet traffic is transmitted at a different frequency from voice traffic. At the ISP's network, these are filtered and sent to different types of equipment. Voice traffic is routed to a telephone switch, while data traffic travels to an internet router. The device that performs this filtering is called **a digital subscriber line access multiplexer** or **DSLAM**. Each DSL modem must synchronize with the DLSAM so that they can filter out noise and errors. A DSL modem will typically have a "link" or "DSL" light that shows its synchronization status. Below is a photo of a common DSL modem.

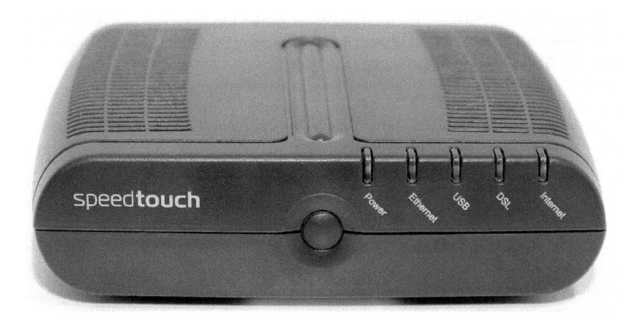

Cable Broadband is a product competing with the DSL. While DSL is typically provided by a phone company Cable Broadband is provided by a cable television provider and is delivered over a coaxial cable. A subscriber requires a **cable modem** to connect to the network. At the provider's facility, a device known as a **cable modem termination system** is installed. This device synchronizes with the subscriber cable modems and transfers their data to the internet.

It's called **broadband** because multiple signals travel over a single wire at the same time, each occupying a different frequency. This is compared with other types of connections, which are known as **baseband**. On a baseband connection, a single signal travels over the wire.

The slowest form of internet is **Dial-Up**, but Dial-Up is generally available anywhere a phone line is. A **Dial-Up modem** converts an analog phone signal to and from a digital internet signal. The modem first calls a number dedicated by the ISP. The modem and ISP's equipment synchronize and then transmit/receives data. An ISP does not require additional special equipment to maintain a Dial-Up service. A Dial-Up connection works at speeds of up 56 Kbit/s.

Many of these technologies are being replaced by **Metropolitan Ethernet**, also known as **metro Ethernet, Ethernet MAN**, or **metropolitan-area Ethernet**. How does it work? An ISP builds a large ethernet network in a city (or in a downtown area) and allows subscribers to connect to it. Why use metro Ethernet? It's cheaper to maintain an ethernet network because it does not require special equipment at the subscriber's side (modems) or at the ISP's side (multiplexers and termination systems). The ISP already owns all of the backbone cables in the city.

The ISP may connect to the customer site via a router or switch. Traffic from different customer sites is aggregated with larger switches. Multiple MANs can be aggregated via an IP-MPLS system.

An ISP may provide MPLS over its metro ethernet. An ethernet packet is transported over MPLS from the customer to the ISP. The ISP uses ethernet to transport the packet to its destination. Why use MPLS? The ISP can handle traffic from any type of medium or protocol. It is easy to perform end-to-end troubleshooting of an MPLS network than a pure ethernet network.

A new alternative to metro Ethernet is **metro optical** (although nobody calls it this). It is basically metro Ethernet delivered over a fiber optic cable.

A **leased line** is a dedicated circuit between two offices. It is permanently connected. It may also be called an **Ethernet leased line**. A company that wants to connect two offices with the same LAN can rent a leased line from an ISP (subject to availability). The leased line may have an unlimited bandwidth or be limited to a specific speed.

In rural areas, internet may be delivered over a satellite modem. Satellite has a high latency and is expensive, but in some areas, it is the only choice.

An internet connection can be transported via Copper, Fiber, Satellite, or Point-to-Point antenna.

Copper is the oldest transmission medium. Traditionally, the phone and cable companies owned copper cable for transmitting phone calls and cable television. They later began using them for transmitting internet. DSL, Dial-Up, cable, T1, E1, T3, and E3 are transmitted over copper.

Fiber is quickly replacing copper, even in residential neighborhoods. Most fiber is being installed by the phone companies, which own the right to install additional wiring. Cable companies and cellular providers own some fiber as well. Metro Ethernet is typically delivered over fiber, although it could be delivered over copper.

A **satellite** internet connection is suitable for rural areas that have no physical wiring. The biggest problem with satellite internet is that it has high latency. It takes a long time for a signal to travel from a subscriber's satellite dish to a satellite in the earth's orbit (up to 120 ms). The total latency can be up to 1000 ms, whereas the latency of a broadband connection may be only 40 ms. A subscriber must have a "line of sight" between their satellite antenna and the satellite in the sky. If it is blocked by trees or clouds, the signal will suffer.

A traditional satellite dish can only receive data. Since the internet is two ways, a satellite internet connection requires a transmitter that points back at the satellite in the sky. Sometimes, the satellite connection is combined with a dial-up connection. Data that requires low latency is transmitted over the dial up connection.

Satellite internet can also be transmitted over a portable modem. These transmit with a speed of about 500 kbit/s but cost up to $5 per megabyte of data transmitted.

A **Point-to-Point antenna** is another less common way to provide internet service without wiring. A service provider installs a transmitter at the top of a large tower in the center of a city. Each subscriber installs an antenna on their rooftop, pointed towards the tower. The internet is transmitted over a radio signal. The subscriber connects his antenna to network equipment (typically provided by the ISP), which then connects to his network.

How can you decide which internet connection you need? We will discuss this in more detail, but in general

- What bandwidth do you require? Think about the performance of the internet connection.

- How many offices do you have and where are they located? This will affect the types of internet connections available.

- Do you need to connect the offices together over a WAN or SD-WAN, or will a VPN be suitable?

- What is the budget and what is the cost of the different options?

- Do you need redundant connections? Consider some common scenarios

  o A single office might have one broadband connection and one back up cellular connection.

o A business with multiple offices across many states/provinces will have a WAN (although many businesses are switching to SD-WAN). Rural offices connect back to the main offices over a VPN since the cost of a WAN in those areas may be too expensive.

o An office may route normal internet traffic over a broadband connection and inter-office traffic over a WAN. This allows them to purchase a lower-capacity WAN.

o Some remote offices may connect via satellite or cellular.

1.3 Summarize the types of cables and connectors and explain which is the appropriate type for a solution

- *Copper*
    - *Twisted Pair*
        - *Cat 5*
        - *Cat 5e*
        - *Cat 6*
        - *Cat 6A*
        - *Cat 7*
        - *Cat 8*
    - *Coaxial/RG-6*
    - *Twinaxial*
    - *Termination Standards*
        - *TIA/EIA-568A*
        - *TIA/EIA-568B*
- *Fiber*
    - *Single-Mode*
    - *Multimode*
- *Connector Types*
    - *Copper*
        - *RJ-45*
        - *RJ-11*
        - *BNC*
        - *DB-9*
        - *DB-25*
        - *F-Type*
    - *Fiber*
        - *Local Connector (LC)*
        - *Straight Tip (ST)*
        - *Subscriber Connector (SC)*
        - *Mechanical Transfer Registered Jack (MTRJ)*
            - *Angled Physical Connector (APC)*
            - *Ultra Physical Connector (UPS)*
    - *Transceivers/Media Convertors*
    - *Transreceiver Type*
        - *Small Form-Factor Pluggable (SFP)*
        - *Enhanced Form-Factor Pluggable (SFP+)*
        - *Quad Small Form-Factor Pluggable (QSFP)*
        - *Enhanced Quad Small Form-Factor Pluggable (QSFP+)*
- *Cable Management*
    - *Patch Panel/Patch Bay*
    - *Fiber Distribution Panel*

- o *Punchdown Block*
  - ▪ *66 Block*
  - ▪ *110 Block*
  - ▪ *Krone*
  - ▪ *BIX*
- • *Ethernet Deployment Standards*
  - o *Copper*
    - ▪ *10Base-T*
    - ▪ *100Base-TX*
    - ▪ *1000Base-T*
    - ▪ *10GBASE-T*
    - ▪ *40GBASE-T*
  - o *Fiber*
    - ▪ *100BASE-FX*
    - ▪ *100BASE-SX*
    - ▪ *1000BASE-SX*
    - ▪ *1000BASE-LX*
    - ▪ *10GBASE-SR*
    - ▪ *10GBASE-LR*
    - ▪ *Coarse Wavelength Division Multiplexing (CWDM)*
    - ▪ *Dense Wavelength Division Multiplexing (DWDM)*
    - ▪ *Bidirectional Wavelength Division Multiplexing (WDM)*

Now we have an idea of how our network will work, we can look at the types of cables we can use to connect it. There are two main choices: copper or fiber.

There are two types of network cable: Copper and Fiber. When do we use copper and when do we use fiber?

Most of the copper wiring in use is **Unshielded Twisted Pair (UTP)**. This is a standard ethernet cable that contains eight wires, twisted into four pairs. The twists are designed to cancel out most forms of electromagnetic interference (from radio waves and nearby power lines). UTP can be run up to 100 meters.

For more advanced applications, we can use a **Shielded Twisted Pair (STP)** cable. This is also known as F/UTP cable. The difference is that the STP cable contains a foil around the wires. The foil blocks out even more electromagnetic interference than the twists. The foil connects to the termination point on each end of the cable and acts as an electrical ground. STP cable is used in applications such as video transmission and in areas where there is a large amount of interference. If we peel back a cable, we can see the difference.

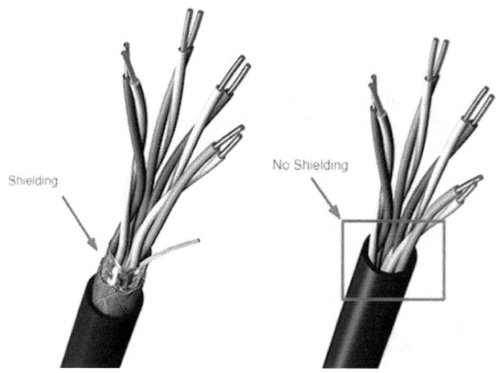

If we went crazy, we could buy a cable that had a separate shield around every pair. The shield protects the wires from electromagnetic interference. It also protects individual wire pairs from cross-talk (interference from a neighboring wire pair).

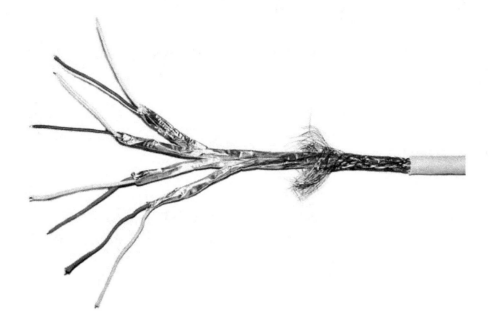

Most device network interfaces accept a copper (UTP or STP) connection. That includes switches, IP cameras, computers, and VoIP phones.

Another form of copper wiring is **coaxial**. Coaxial wiring can be run up to 500 meters. It consists of a central conductor with a braid wrapped around it. The braid shields the central conductor from electromagnetic interference that could disrupt the signal.

Coaxial cable can be run up to 500 meters. It is used to connect older analog cameras, satellite systems, antennas, and cable modems.

Fiber optic cable can be run longer distances than copper. It also has a larger bandwidth. But fiber is more difficult to install than copper. It requires specialized equipment to test and terminate. A fiber optic cable uses light to transmit data.

We can't connect a fiber optic cable to standard host devices. For example, a VoIP phone or computer will not have a fiber optic connector. If we ran a fiber optic cable to a far away computer, we would need a device called a media converter to convert the fiber to copper.

Fiber comes in two forms: **single-mode**, and **multimode**. Single mode cable can be run upwards of 200 km. The light signal travels down the center of the cable as a single signal. Multimode cable can be run up to 1 km. The light bounces up and down inside the cable.

A single copper cable contains eight wires. When connected, the copper cable carries data in multiple directions. But a single fiber optic cable can contain multiple strands. A single strand carries data in only one direction. When we peel back the fiber optic cable, we find multiple strands, which can be color coded. We need at least two strands to make a circuit and carry data. Most common sized fibers have six or twelve strands.

Some of the most common copper standards are outlined in the table below.

Cat3	Cat3 was an old cabling system that is now considered obsolete. It supported network speeds of up to 10 Mbit/s.
	Cat3 was used by analog phone systems and digital phone systems (Nortel, Panasonic, Avaya).
	Cat3 is still used by telecommunication companies for cross-connecting analog phone lines.

The cable is available as 3-pairs, 10-pairs, 25-pairs, 50-pairs, 100-pairs, or 200-pairs.

The wires follow a standard color code. The color code repeats every 25 pairs.

Cat5	Cat5 was an older system for ethernet. It is also considered obsolete, but still in use at some buildings. It supported speeds of up to 1000 Mbit/s. The maximum length of a single cable is 100m.
Cat5e	Cat5e is the current ethernet standard. It supports speeds of up to 1000 Mbit/s. The maximum length of a single cable is 100m.
Cat6	Cat6 is another current ethernet standard. It supports speeds of up to 1000 Mbit/s. The maximum length of a single cable is 100m. Cat6 cable is more expensive than cat5e, but has less noise and interference

Cat6A	Cat6A is a new ethernet standard. It supports speeds of up to 10 Gbit/s. It is more difficult to install than cat6 because bends and kinks to the cable can reduce its capacity. To help reduce damage to the cable, the pairs may be glued together.
Cat7	Cat7 is a new ethernet standard that was developed and never adopted. It was replaced with Cat6A. It is not recognized by existing regulations.
Cat8	Cat8 is a new ethernet standard that is still under development. It is limited to 30m. It is intended for speeds of up to 40 Gbit/s and is intended for data centers only.

There are two methods for terminating a cat5e/cat6/cat6A cable. The methods are known as **568A** and **568B**. Remember that the ethernet cables contain 4 pairs of wires (colored as blue, orange, green, brown). The difference between 568A and 568B is that the position of the orange and green wires is swapped.

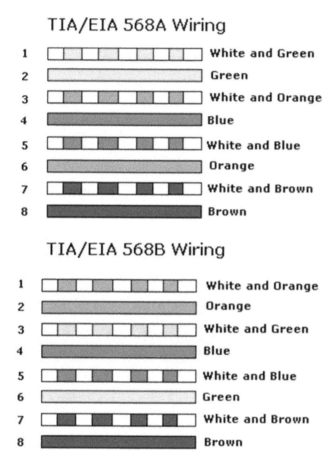

If we look at the side of a cat5e jack, we can see that the manufacturer has marked a color code for "A" style terminations and "B" style terminations. On the other side of the jack, we would see similar markings. The color order may vary from manufacturer to manufacturer.

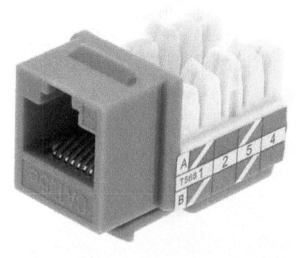

We should insert the wire into the correct colored slot on the jack or patch panel and then terminate it with a punch-down tool of the appropriate size.

We could also terminate the cable to a male connector. The male connectors follow the same color code as the female connectors. We use a tool called a crimper to secure the wires inside the connector.

Both 568A and 568B are acceptable termination methods. A cable should be terminated with the same method on both sides. An organization may require the cable to be terminated using a specific method. Most organizations prefer 568B, and most governments prefer 568A.

If we terminate the cable in the same order on both ends, we call it **a straight through cable**. If we terminate the cable as 568A on one end and 568B on the other end, the orange and green pairs become crossed. This is called a **crossover cable**.

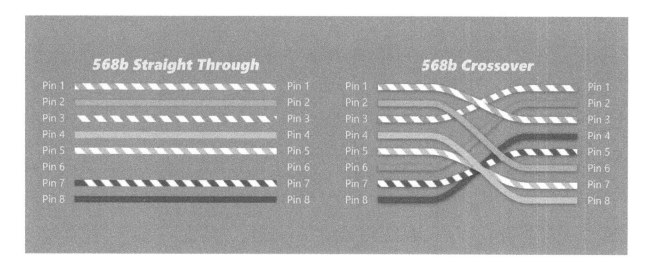

Why would we make a cross-over cable? Network devices usually use the orange and green pairs to communicate. A device like a switch transmits over the orange pair and listens on the green pair. A device like a computer transmits on the green pair and listens on the orange pair. If we connect a computer to a switch, collisions do not take place.

If we want to connect two computers together or two switches together, they will try to talk on the same pair and listen on the same pair. No data will get through. The device doesn't know the color of the wire; it only knows the position of the wire. If you punched the blue wire in the orange wire's spot, the device would communicate over the blue wire.

So, if we use a cross-over cable, then one switch will transmit over the orange pair (wires 1 and 2) and listen over the green pair (wires 3 and 6). The other switch will transmit over the green pair (wires 3 and 6) and listen over the orange pair (wires 1 and 2).

We don't need crossover cables to connect switches anymore. If two modern switches are connected via a straight through cable, they will immediately detect the collision and agree on who will use which wire pairs.

The coaxial cable is available in many sizes. The number relates to the thickness of the core conductor in the center. The two most common RG-59 and RG-6. Coaxial cable is used for satellite systems, surveillance cameras, cable modems, and other analog systems. Your ISP may install it, but I do not recommend it unless absolutely required.

RG-59	RG-59 is used for short lengths and is cheaper than RG-6.
RG-6	RG-6 is used for satellite systems and surveillance cameras. It can provide a better-quality signal than RG-59

Twinaxial cable or **Twinax** is a coaxial cable with two internal conductors. Twinax can be used for 10GB or 40GB Ethernet. A 100GB version is being developed. The maximum length of a Twinax is 10 meters. Twinax is being used to connect servers, switches, and storage appliances in data centers, where a high bandwidth, low latency connection is required.

After we install the cable, we must terminate it somehow. We must put a connector on the end so that we can plug it into something. A copper connector can be male or female.

Name	Male	Female
RJ-11 Used for analog phone lines Contains 4 pins but is 6 pins wide. Also known as 6P4C. A similar connector called RJ-12 contains 6 pins. It is also known as 6P6C. You can attach a connector to a cable with a crimper. A male connector costs about $0.50 and a female connector costs about $2.00.		
RJ-45 Used for Ethernet (UTP cable or STP cable). It contains 8 pins – one for each wire. The pin out is standard.		

The female RJ-45 jack is available in many colors and types, such as cat5e, cat6, or cat6A.

Both the male and female connectors are available in shielded and unshielded.

A male connector costs about $0.50 and a female connector costs between $2.00 and $10.00 depending on the manufacturer.

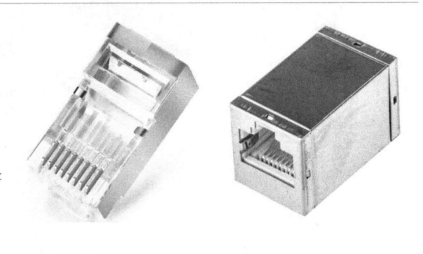

BNC

We can terminate a coaxial cable to a BNC connector.

The male BNC connector twists on to lock to a female connector. BNC connectors are available in different formats for different cable thicknesses.

BNC connectors are used for commercial AV applications.

A BNC connector costs about $5.00.

F-connector

We can terminate a coaxial cable to an F-connector.

The male F connector screws on to lock to a female connector. F connectors are available in different formats for different cable thicknesses. F connectors are used by residential cable companies.

An F connector costs about
$5.00.

DB-9

A DB-9 connector (or serial
connector) has nine pins. We
can connect an STP or UTP
cable to it. The pin out can
vary from manufacturer to
manufacturer.

Some older network
equipment uses the DB-9
connector.

We can also use a DB-9 to RJ-
45 adapter.

DB-25

A DB-25 connector is like the
DB-9, but it has 25 pins. Only
nine of the pins are used.

We can connect an STP or
UTP cable to it. The pin out
can vary from manufacturer to
manufacturer.

We also have connectors for fiber optic cables. We can purchase adapters for any type of fiber
connector. Notice that fiber cables do not have female connectors, only male. We can convert a
male connector to a female connector by connecting it to a coupler.

LC

Most popular for network equipment,
especially SFPs.

SC

ST

Used by telecommunications companies for fiber distribution.

MTRJ

After a fiber connector is manufactured, it is polished. The angle at which it is polished affects its data transmission. Two fiber connectors must be mated together so that they can transmit data.

Originally, we made connectors that were flat and touched each other. You can see that the fiber is only a tiny part in the center of the connector.

These connectors didn't perform well because the surface area was large.

Eventually, we started making connectors that were highly polished, leaving just the fiber portion at the tip of the connector. These are called **Ultra Physical Contact Connectors (UPC)**.

There is less back reflection, but it increases over time.

Each time we remove and reinsert the connector, it wears a little bit, which scratches its surface. Over time, the wear results in transmission errors.

Finally, we started making the **Angled Physical Contact Connector (APC)**. We polish the connector at an angle of 8°.

This connector does not have any back reflection, even after repeated connections and disconnections.

We use this angle on SC connectors only, because they can only be inserted in one way. The other connectors can be rotated, so they will not maintain the correct angle.

Look at this Cisco switch. On the left are 48 copper ports. Each one can accept a single RJ-45-terminated cable. On the right are four additional ports – the bottom two are copper and the top two are "**SFP**", or **small form-factor pluggable transceiver**.

You can't plug a cable into an SFP port.

So, what's the point? Well, there are many types of cables and available speeds – copper, single-mode fiber, multi-mode fiber, 10Gbit speeds, 1Gbit speeds, etc. The manufacturer of the switch can't sell a different type of switch for every possible connector. It would result in too many switch combinations. Instead, the manufacturer adds some "SFP" ports.

Look at this switch. Almost all its ports are SFP ports.

You figure out what kind of connections you require – copper or fiber (single-mode or multi-mode). And you decide the speed that you require – 1GB, 10GB, or 40GB. And if you're using fiber, you decide what kind of connector you're using LC, SC, etc.. Then you buy the right SFPs and insert them into the switch. An SFP could cost between $10 and $2000 depending on the speed and cable types. You can mix and match SFPs on a single switch.

An example of a copper SFP is below. You insert the SFP into an SFP port and then you insert the cable into the SFP. SFPs are hot-swappable (that means we can change the SFP while the switch is running and the switch will recognize the new SFP).

The maximum speed of an SFP is 1 Gbit/s, but the maximum speed of an **SFP+** is 10Gbit/s. It is also known as an **enhanced small form-factor pluggable transceiver**. An SFP+ works with fiber and copper connectors.

For even faster speeds, such as those required in the networks of major Internet Service Providers, the **QSFP** or **Quad Small Form-factor Pluggable transceiver** can be used. The QSFP can provide speeds of up to 4 Gbit/s.

For even faster speeds, now there is the **QSFP+**, which provides speeds of up to 40 Gbit/s. There is also the **QSFP14**, which provides speeds of up to 50 Gbit/s, the **QSFP28**, which provides speeds of up to 100 Gbit/s, and the **QSFP56**, which provides speeds of up to 200 Gbit/s.

Below is an example of a fiber SFP. You will notice that it has space for two fibers. That is because a single stand of fiber typically operates in one direction at a time, whereas an ethernet cable operates in both directions at the same time. Thus, we would need two fiber strands to complete a "circuit".

Some service providers use a **bidirectional** fiber, which allows the signal to travel in both directions at the same time. Each direction transmits a signal in a different wavelength. For example, we might transmit in 1310 nm and receive in 1550 nm. A bidirectional fiber allows a service provider to conserve their fiber resources when they are scarce.

Before SFPs we had **GBIC** (**Gigabit Ethernet and Fibre Channel**) transceivers, but they were much larger. They only operated at rates of up to 1 Gbit/s.

A common termination point for an ethernet cable is a **patch panel**. These panels are commonly available in 24-port and 48-port sizes. The panel fits into a standard network rack. Wall-mounted panels are also available.

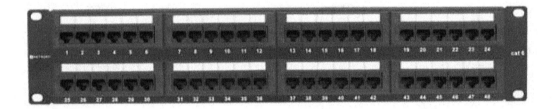

At the back of the panel are spaces to insert each wire. We should peel the STP or UTP cable and stick each of the eight wires into the appropriate slot. We then use a tool called a punch-down tool to terminate the cable.

A panel costs between $50 and $600 depending on the manufacturer, number of ports, and whether it is cat5e, cat6, or cat6A. We can also use modular patch panels and insert jacks directly into them (which I recommend).

The slots in the back of the panel have a specific size. The most common size is "**110**". Other sizes include **66**, **BIX**, and **Krone**. Each size requires a punch-down tool with the correct shaped blade to insert the wire into the slot. The front of the panel looks the same, but the shape of the slots in the back will be different.

In a rack, the panels might look like the photo below

In a telecommunications system, we might use a wall-mounted block known as a 66, 110, or BIX block. Again, the name refers to the shape of the wire inserts.

The telecommunications blocks allow us to cross-connect a single wire at a time. We can connect many different types of copper wire to the block, including cat5e, cat6, or cat3.

Below is a 66 block. The blocks are used to cross connect cables. Wires coming from outside the system (wiring coming from a phone system or wiring coming from outside the building) are normally punched down to the left side of the panel. Building wiring is punched down to the right side. We add jumpers (the metal pieces in the middle of the block) to cross connect one side of the block to the other. Jumpers are also known as **bridging clips**.

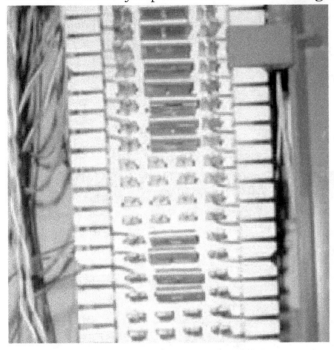

A 110 block is below. 110 blocks don't use bridging clips but we can use a jumper wire to cross connect one side to another.

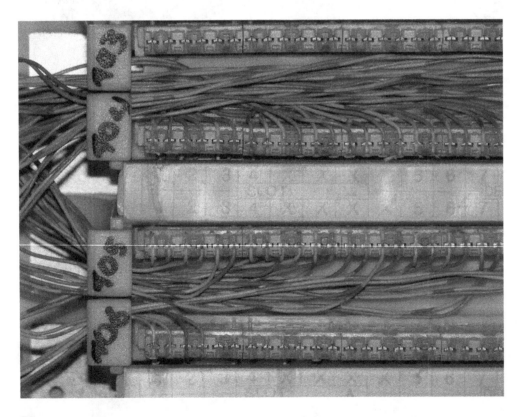

Similar to the 110 block is the BIX block. The BIX and the 110 blocks don't take up much room.

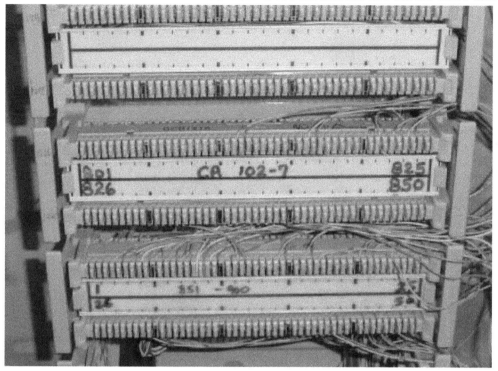

Finally, we have the Krone block. Very few places use the Krone block.

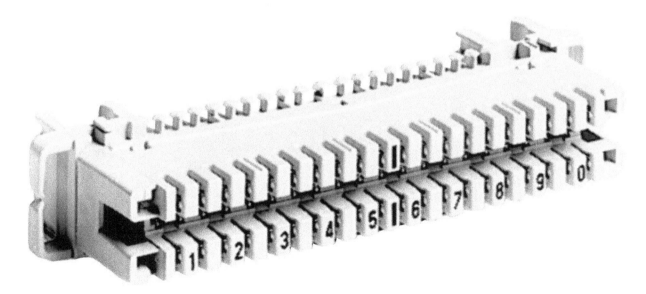

Fiber optic distribution panels can be rack-mounted or wall-mounted. Below is a rack-mounted patch panel. As you will notice, and as I said earlier, we can only terminate a fiber to a male end. The fiber panel below has female couplers at the front. We would run our fiber optic cable into the back of the panel and terminate it inside the panel. Then we can connect each terminated strand to the back of each coupler.

Below is an example of a wall-mount fiber optic patch panel. It also contains female couplers at the front. We can purchase the patch panels and the couplers separately, so that we can mix and match the types of connectors used by the system.

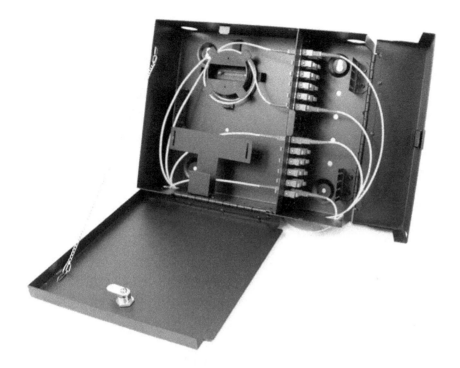

When two devices are connected via an ethernet cable, they will evaluate the wiring between themselves and agree on a speed and duplex setting, in a process known as **autonegotiation**. In a **half-duplex** setting, only one device can transmit at a time; the other device must listen. In a **full-duplex** setting, both devices can transmit and listen at the same time.

There are several standards for speed.

10Base-T was the original copper standard and could transmit at speeds of up to 10 Mbit/s. It could function over cat3 cable. 10Base-T is no longer popular.

100Base-TX came after. It can transmit at a speed of up to 100 Mbit/s over cat5 cable. 100Base-TX is also called **100BaseT** or **Fast Ethernet** and uses two wire pairs – orange and green. One device listens on the orange pair and talks on the green pair, while the other device does the opposite. On a router, you might see ports labelled as FE for Fast Ethernet. The other four wires are not used.

Pin	Pair	Wire	Color
1	2	+/tip	white/orange
2	2	−/ring	orange
3	3	+/tip	white/green
4	1	−/ring	blue
5	1	+/tip	white/blue
6	3	−/ring	green
7	4	+/tip	white/brown
8	4	−/ring	brown

1000BaseT is also known as **Gigabit Ethernet**. It uses all four pairs of an ethernet cable. 1000BaseT is the current standard, and you should not purchase network with components that operate at a lower speed than that.

A 100BaseT connection could be either full duplex or half duplex. A 1000BaseT connection must always be full duplex.

The next standard to develop was **10GBASE-T**, which operates at 10 Gbit/s. 10GBASE-T requires cat6A cable but can operate over cat6 cable for short distances.

When 10GBASE-T came out, wireless access point manufacturers needed something better. As Wi-Fi popularity increased, manufacturers wanted to take advantage of the 10GBASE-T by implementing it in their access points. But building owners did not want to replace existing cat5e or cat6 wiring with cat6A. Thus, **2.5GBASE-T** and **5GBASE-T** were developed. They can provide 2.5 Gbit/s or 5 Gbit/s, respectively over existing cat6 cable.

Finally, **40GBASE-T** was developed, which allows for speeds of 40 Gbit/s over cat8. **25GBASE-T** with a speed of 25 Gbit/s and **50GBASE-T** with a speed of 50 Gbit/s also exist. Both require cat8 cable.

An administrator can manually configure a switch/router/computer ethernet port to a specific speed and duplex setting but must then be careful to ensure that both connected devices/ports have the same settings, or they will not be able to communicate.

The standards that exist in the copper world also exist in the fiber world.

The early standard for fiber was **100Base-FX** and **100Base-SX**, which provided 100 Mbit/s over fiber. The FX standard worked over longer distances but used expensive lasers, while the LX standard worked over shorter distances and used cheaper LEDs.

1000Base-X is the standard for communication over fiber at 1Gbit/s. There are two main standards: **1000BaseLX** uses single-mode fiber and can achieve distances of up to 10km, while **1000BaseSX** uses multi-mode fiber and can achieve distances of up to 220 meters.

10GBaseT or **10 Gigabit Ethernet** is a newer standard that allows devices to communicate at a speed of 10 Gbit/s. It can function over copper wiring or fiber. There are several fiber standards, including 10GBase-S (multi-mode fiber) and 10GBase-L (single-mode fiber).

10GBase-SR (for short range) provides speeds of 10 Gbit/s over multi-mode fiber at distances of up to 26m, while **10GBase-LR** (for long range) provides speeds of 10Gbit/s over single-mode fiber at distances of up to 10km.

A 1000BaseLX SFP costs around $10 while a 10GBase-L SFP may cost up to $2000. Therefore, organizations prefer to use 1000Base-X when they can. 10 Gbit/s ethernet ports are only found on high-end infrastructure.

What if we have many signals to transmit simultaneously over a single fiber strand (or limited fiber strands)? We can combine the signal with a device called a multiplexer.

On one end of the fiber strand, we install a multiplexer, which joins optical signals (each with a different wave length) and sends them down the strand. On the other end of the strand, we install a demultiplexer, which separates the signals. There are three technologies here

- **Coarse Wavelength Division Multiplexing (CWDM).** Coarse refers to a wide separation between the wavelength of each signal. Specifically, the wavelengths are separated by 20 nm. For example, a signal at 1310nm and a signal at 1330nm can be transmitted over the same fiber at the same time.

- **Dense Wavelength Division Multiplexing (DWDM).** DWDM systems transmit signals with a much narrower wavelength separation. DWDM systems must operate very precisely as a small variation in the wavelength or the temperature of the laser can cause substantial loss in the signal. DWDM systems are used in very high bandwidth applications, and require repeaters every 100 km.

- **Bidirectional Wavelength Division Multiplexing (WDM).** Bidirectional WDM allows us to send a signal on a single fiber optic strand in both directions at the same time. This can happen because the signal in one direction has a different wavelength than the signal in the opposite direction.

How can you choose the best type of cable for your project?

- I don't recommend coaxial for anything. The most common application is surveillance cameras, but I strongly recommend that you use ethernet based cameras.

- Install Ethernet cable between your server room and your wall outlets/surveillance cameras/wireless access points. The number of cables to each outlet depends on your needs, but for further guidance look at the BICSI TDMM (Telecommunications Distribution Methods Manual). The full design requirements are beyond the scope of this book.

- In general, use cat6 cable within your building and cat6A to the wireless access points. Remember that a single wall outlet is supporting only one device, but a wireless access point may support up to 50 devices, and thus a cable supporting a higher ethernet speed is warranted. Consider using cat6A for all your cabling if your budget allows.

- When the distance exceeds 100m, install multi-mode fiber. When the distance exceeds 1km, install single-mode fiber. Install a fiber optic cable with at least six strands so that there is adequate capacity for future upgrades. LC connectors are the most common.

- If you have an analog phone system, you may install some cabling between your telecommunications demarcation point and your server room. You can terminate this cabling to a BIX or 110 Block.

- Within a server room you may consider installing cat8 if required by your equipment. It may be better to purchase premanufactured cat8 patch cables and use them as required.

- 1 Gbit/s is the current minimum standard and you should configure your equipment to operate at this speed. Consider your needs and budget. Consider future upgrades, and whether it is better to buy faster equipment now or whether you will have funding to do it later. Connectors that operate at speeds faster than 1Gbit/s are more expensive.

- You may purchase switches that have the capability to operate at up to 40Gbit/s and then purchase the required SFPs at a later date (when the additional bandwidth is required).

1.4 Given a scenario, configure a subnet and use appropriate IP addressing schemes

- *Private vs. Public*
  - *RFC1918*
  - *Network Address Translation (NAT)*
  - *Port Address Translation (PAT)*
- *IPv4 vs IPv6*
  - *Automatic Private IP Addressing (APIPA)*
  - *Extended Unique Identifier (EUI-64)*
  - *Multicast*
  - *Unicast*
  - *Anycast*
  - *Broadcast*
  - *Link Local*
  - *Loopback*
  - *Default Gateway*
- *IPv4 Subnetting*
  - *Classless (Variable Length Subnet Mask)*
  - *Classful*
    - *A*
    - *B*
    - *C*
    - *D*
    - *E*
  - *Classless Inter-Domain Routing (CIDR) Notation*
- *IPv6 Concepts*
  - *Tunneling*
  - *Dual Stack*
  - *Shorthand Notation*
  - *Router Advertisement*
  - *Stateless Address Autoconfiguration (SLAAC)*
- *Virtual IP (VIP)*
- *Subinterfaces*

I briefly mentioned IP addresses at the beginning of this book. Remember that each network device has a MAC address (assigned from the factory) and an IP address (assigned by the network)? We are going to learn where IP addresses come from and who regulates them.

An IP address has four sections, known as octets. For example, 192.168.0.4 is an IP address.

Each octet is a three-digit number separated by a period. The maximum value of an octet is 255 and the minimum value is 0. So, the range of IP addresses is from 0.0.0.0 to 255.255.255.255. How many IP addresses are there? 4,294,967,296. Are there enough IP addresses to go around if you consider that each person probably has a work computer, a home computer, a cell phone, and that there are many other servers and internet of things devices running in the background? Of course not.

A **public IP address** is one that is accessible from anywhere on the internet, and a **private IP address** is one that is only accessible from inside a local network. The devices on your local network (i.e. inside your home or office) probably have private IP addresses.

The router in your home or office probably has a public IP address assigned to the port that connects it with the outside world. The router probably also has a private IP address assigned to the port that connects it to the rest of your internal network.

Who decides what IP address you get? Your internet connection is assigned an IP address by your internet service provider. Your internet service provider is assigned a block of IP addresses by a larger organization (such as a larger ISP if they buy their internet from somebody else). At the top of the food chain is **ARIN (American Registry for Internet Numbers)**.

ARIN assigns blocks of IP addresses to each ISP and to larger organizations. IPv4 addresses are scarce because there are more devices than IP addresses, and because in the early days of the internet, organizations were assigned large blocks of addresses. Nobody thought that the internet would grow to be as big as it is, so ARIN went crazy and gave everybody tons of IP addresses.

The US Department of Defense owns about 5% of the IPv4 addresses (addresses that start in 6, 7, 11, 21, 22, 26, 28, 29, 30, 33, 55, 214, and 215).

A few blocks of IP addresses have been reserved for private IP addresses and some blocks have been reserved for special functions as we will find out later.

The following IP address ranges are reserved for private use per **RFC1918**.
- 10.0.0.0 to 10.255.255.255
- 172.16.0.0 to 172.16.255.255

- 192.168.0.0 to 192.168.0.255

If you have an office or internal network, you can set up an internal addressing scheme by choosing one of the above three ranges. In my example office below, I chose the range 192.168.0.0 to 192.168.0.255. What range will you choose?

- 10.0.0.0 to 10.255.255.255 is the largest network, with a range of 16,581,375 possible addresses. This type of network is known as a **class A** network.

- 172.16.0.0 to 172.16.255.255 is the second largest network, with a range of 65,025 possible addresses. This type of network is known as a **class B** network.

- 192.168.0.0 to 192.168.0.255, is the smallest network, with a range of 256 addresses. This type of network is known as a **class C** network.

If we have a small network, we should choose a small range. Smaller network equipment (such as in a home or small business) might not be able to handle a larger range of IP addresses. As we will see later, we can subdivide a larger range into several smaller range, and assign each one to a different function.

Let's look at our example office. In our example, the ISP assigned us one public address: 44.3.2.1. Most of the IP address space is public. In theory, any device with a public IP can reach any other device with a public IP (unless a firewall blocks it). Thus, other devices on the internet can communicate with our network by contacting 44.3.2.1.

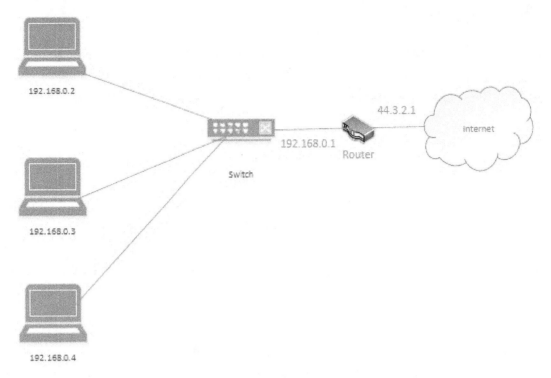

In my example office, there are three computers, with IP addresses of 192.168.0.2, 192.168.0.3, and 192.168.0.4. They connect to the switch. Notice that the router (which sits on the edge of the network) has a private IP address of 192.168.0.1 and a public IP address of 44.3.2.1. This allows the router to pass traffic between the private network and the public network. Devices within the private network can reach the router (and therefore the outside world) by contacting 192.168.0.1.

If our business was so large as to require multiple locations, we could choose the range 10.0.0.0 to 10.255.255.255 and then subdivide it further so that each location receives a block from our range. For example, one location receives the range 10.0.0.0 to 10.0.255.255, and the second location receives the range 10.1.0.0 to 10.1.255.255, etc.. It might look like the drawing below

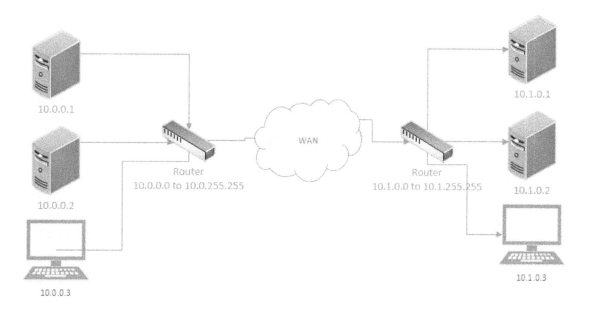

This would require us to implement a Wide Area Network or point-to-point VPN. The WAN allows us to configure the routers so that all the computers in all our offices think that they are on the same physical network.

Each local area network can use the same range of private IP addresses as any other network because a device on one LAN won't talk directly with a device on another LAN. Instead, the pass their messages to their routers, which then deliver the traffic. As long as each router has a unique public IP address, we won't encounter any issues.

So far, when we've been talking about IP addresses, we've actually been referring to **IPv4** (version 4) IP addresses. But the world has been running out of IPv4 addresses, and so a new standard was created. This standard is known as IPv6.

In the IPv6 world, fc00::/7 is the only private range of IP addresses. It is better written as fc00:0000:0000:0000:0000:0000:0000:0000 to fdff:ffff:ffff:ffff:ffff:ffff:ffff:ffff.

How did I get from fc00::/7 to all of that gibberish? We'll find out later. But the point is, the range is massive. There is no need for each private network to have the same address as any other private network.

If we mash two private IPv4 networks together, we will have some conflicts. We will find that two devices have the same IP address, and one of them won't be able to communicate. But if we mash two private IPv6 networks together, we won't have any conflicts because each private IPv6 address is randomly generated. In fact, if mashed all of the private IPv6 networks together, we probably won't have any conflicts.

Loopback and Reserved

Some addresses are reserved. They can't be assigned to anybody.

The addresses that are reserved

- 127.0.0.1 is called the **loopback address** (mapped to the hostname **localhost**). Every network device and computer consider 127.0.0.1 to belong to itself. If I send traffic from my computer to the address 127.0.0.1, it loops back and heads straight back to my computer.

  What's the point? Let's say that my organization maintains two servers – a web server and a database server. The web server connects to the database server over the local network. If I decide to install the web server software and database software on the same physical machine, then I could reprogram the web server to look for the database server at the 127.0.0.1 address.

  What if my server IP address is 192.168.0.1? Why do I need to specify 127.0.0.1? Why can't I just tell the web server to look at 192.168.0.1? I could, but that would create unnecessary traffic along the network for a packet that doesn't need to leave the server. Also, what happens if my server IP address changes frequently? I don't want to reprogram the server every time the IP address changes. Or what if I don't have an active network connection? What if I'm running a sensitive internal application but the application is looking for a network connection? I can specify 127.0.0.1.

  127.0.0.1 is also used to test the internal operation of the network card. If I am troubleshooting a network connection, I might try to send traffic to 127.0.0.1. If it fails, I will know that the network problems are internal to the machine.

- 0.0.0.0 to 0.255.255.255 is reserved for software testing.

- 169.254.0.0 to 169.254.255.255 is reserved for the **link local** IP addresses. This is a random IP address that a device assigns itself when it can't find a DHCP server. That is, if a device joins a network and doesn't have a preprogrammed IP address, and the network doesn't assign it an IP address, it will randomly assign itself an IP address from that range.

- 255.255.255.255 is reserved for broadcasts. That is, when a device wants to send traffic (like an announcement) to all the other devices on its local network, it can send them to that address.

- There are other IP addresses that are reserved but to list them all would take forever.

On the IPv6 side

- ::1 also known as 0000:0000:0000:0000:0000:0000:0000:0001 is the loopback address

- fe80:0000:0000:0000:0000:0000:0000:0000 to febf:ffff:ffff:ffff:ffff:ffff:ffff:ffff is the link local address

- 2002:0000:0000:0000:0000:0000:0000:0000 to 2002:ffff:ffff:ffff:ffff:ffff:ffff:ffff was used by the 6to4 IP address conversion protocol. More on this later.

- ff00:0000:0000:0000:0000:0000:0000:0000 to ffff:ffff:ffff:ffff:ffff:ffff:ffff:ffff is the multicast address range. More on this later.

Default Gateway and Subnet Mask

Recall that we have public IP addresses and private IP addresses. When a device wants to send traffic to another device

- It first must ask itself: is this device on my local network or is it somewhere else?

- If it is local, the computer sends the traffic to the switch, but with the MAC address of the destination device in the header.

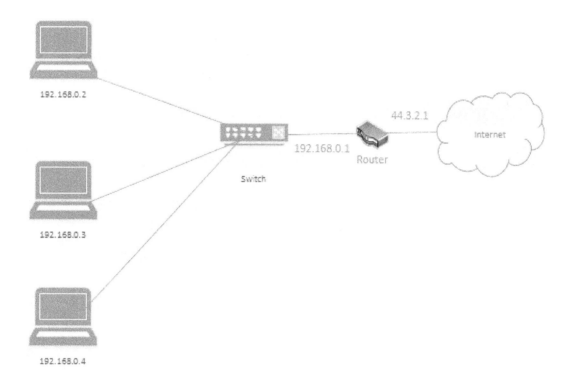

What happens when the destination is not local? Then the device must send the data to a router. But how does it know which router to send it to? And how does it know whether the destination device is local?

Every device has network settings, which include at least three items

- **IP address** – this is the IP address assigned to the device

- **Subnet mask** – this tells the device how big its local network is; the local network is known as a subnet

- **Default gateway** – this is another name for a router. In other words, the default gateway connects the local network with the outside world.

The device uses its IP address and the subnet to figure out the range of IP addresses in its local network. If the destination IP address is not in the local network, then it is sent to the default gateway.

This is going to be the hardest part of the book. Learning the complicated math about subnets.

A subnet mask looks like an IP address. It is 32-bits long (each octet is 8-bits. Remember that computers are electrical. They only think in terms of "on or off". So, a 1 is on, and a 0 is off.

8-bits makes up one byte. A computer with 8-bits can only count to 255 in one operation. If I make a table that is base-two (every entry is double the previous entry), I can combine these eight numbers to make any number from 0 to 255. Below is my table.

128	64	32	16	8	4	2	1

If you look at the 8-bits in a byte, each bit is assigned to one of the numbers in my table. If the bit is a one, or in "on' position, then the number is added to the total, and if the bit is a zero, or in the "off" position, then the bit is ignored.

For example, my byte is 11011001. If we write this byte into the base-two table below, and add up the corresponding values,

128	64	32	16	8	4	2	1
1	1	0	1	1	0	0	1

The value of this byte is 128 + 64 + 16 + 8 + 1 = 217

Thus, we have two ways to write out this number, either as 217 or as 11011001

At its most basic level, when a processor is doing math, it's has an electrical circuit that's turning these different bits on and off.

So what? There is a small microprocessor inside each network card and router that thinks about IP addresses. This allows those devices to make subnet mask and IP address calculations quickly.

255.255.255.252 is an example of a subnet mask.

We could write it out as

11111111.11111111.11111111.11111100 if we wanted to. We call this a **binary number**. How did I get this? I simply went back to my table:

128	64	32	16	8	4	2	1

What numbers to add together to come up with 255? Well, if I start at the left, and work my way to the right, I found that I need all of them.

128	64	32	16	8	4	2	1
1	1	1	1	1	1	1	1

When the computer wants to express the number 255 in binary, it must turn on all of the bits in the byte.

What about 252? To get to 252, the computer must turn on the first six bytes.

128	64	32	16	8	4	2	1
1	1	1	1	1	1	0	0

Now if we write out the binary value of each octet in the subnet mask, we get 11111111.11111111.11111111.11111100.

We could also call it a /30 subnet mask, because it has 30 "1's" in it. Note that you'll never see a subnet mask like 255.255.255.217. In a subnet mask, the 1's always appear on the left and the 0's always appear on the right.

128	64	32	16	8	4	2	1
1	1	0	1	0	1	1	1

In binary, 217 is written as 11010111. Thus the subnet mask 255.255.255.217 would be written as 11111111.11111111.11111111.11010111, which would put some 1's to the right of some 0's, which would be invalid.

Many network engineers like to reference a subnet mask as a "/30" or "/28" or "slash whatever number it is", instead of saying the entire name.

Let's do an example. If my device IP address is 192.168.0.29 and my subnet mask is /28, how big is my network? What IP address does it start on and where does it end? We can figure it out.

- /28 is my subnet.

- We can write it out as 255.255.255.240.
- We can also write it out as 11111111.11111111.11111111.11110000 because we know it contains 28 1's.
- If I told you that the subnet mask was 255.255.255.240 you could figure out how many 1's it was by using my base-two table above (240 = 128 + 64 + 32 + 16).

- 192.168.0.29 is my IP address.
- We can write it out as 11000000.10101000.00000000.00011101
- How did I figure this out?
- First, I write out my base-two table for each octet

128	64	32	16	8	4	2	1

- Then I think about what numbers I need to add together to make each octet. If I use a number in the table, I write a "1" under it, and if I don't, I write a 0.
- I can start on the left side of the table. Follow along with me. I know that 128 is smaller than 192 so that is a 1. If I add 64 to 128, I get 192 so that is also a 1. I am at the correct total so that is where I stop. The rest of the values are 0's.

128	64	32	16	8	4	2	1
1	1	0	0	0	0	0	0

- Now I want to calculate 168. I write out a new table and start on the left. I know that 128 is less than 168 so I write a 1 under the 128. If I add 64 to 128, I get 192 which is too high, so 64 is not part of the equation. I put a 0 under 64. I add 32 to 128 and get 160, which is still less than 168, so I put a 1 under the 32. I know that I need 8 more to get from 160 to 168, so 16 won't work. I put a 0 under the 16. If I add 8 to the 160, I get 168 so I put a 1 under the 8. I don't need to use any of the remaining numbers, so I put 0's under them.

128	64	32	16	8	4	2	1
1	0	1	0	1	0	0	0

- Now I want to calculate 0. It is easy. All of the values in the table must be 0.

128	64	32	16	8	4	2	1
0	0	0	0	0	0	0	0

- Now I want to calculate 29. I write out a new table and start on the left. I know that 128, 64, and 32 are all larger than 29, so I put 0's under them. 16 is smaller than 29, so I put a 1 under it. If I add 8 to 16, I get 24, which is still less than 29, so I put a 1 under the 8. If I add 4 to the 24, I get 28, which is still less than 29, so I put a 1 under the 4. If I add 2 to the 28, I get 30, which is too high, so I put a 0 under the 2. Finally, if I add 1 to the 28, I get 29, which is where I want to be.

128	64	32	16	8	4	2	1
0	0	0	1	1	1	0	1

- Now we have the subnet in binary form and the IP address in binary form
- 11111111.11111111.11111111.11110000 (subnet)
  11000000.10101000.00000000.00011101 (IP address)
- To figure out the first IP address in the subnet, we want to perform a special kind of math called masking. If we write the IP address and subnet on top of each other, then wherever the subnet contains a "0", we change the corresponding digit in the IP address to a 0. Wherever the subnet contains a "1", we keep the corresponding IP address the same.
- In our example, we only need to mask the last four digits of the IP address (1101) because only the last four digits of the subnet mask are 0's.
- The masked IP address is now
  11000000.10101000.00000000.00010000 in binary format.
- We can use the table to convert it back to a decimal format. First, we write out the table.

128	64	32	16	8	4	2	1

- Then we fill in the table and add up the corresponding numbers

128	64	32	16	8	4	2	1
1	1	0	0	0	0	0	0

128	64	32	16	8	4	2	1
1	0	1	0	1	0	0	0

128	64	32	16	8	4	2	1
0	0	0	0	0	0	0	0

128	64	32	16	8	4	2	1
0	0	0	1	0	0	0	0

- The result from the first table: 128+64=192
- The result from the second table: 128+32+8=168
- The result from the third table: 0
- The result from the fourth table: 16

- Thus, the resulting IP address is 192.168.0.16
- Notice that the first three octets didn't change. If an octet in a subnet mask is 255, the corresponding IP address octet won't change. I just did the math as an example.

- 192.168.0.16 is the first IP address in my subnet
- It is also called the **Network ID**
- It is not a "useable" IP address because it defines the subnet
- What is the last address in my subnet?
- There are a few ways to calculate this, but the easiest is to do this is as follows
    - Find out how many "network" bits are remaining from the subnet mask. In this example, my subnet is /28 and the total number of bits is always 32. That leaves me with 4 bits remaining.
    - Use the formula 2^n to calculate the size of the subnet
    - In this case, 2^4 is 16.
    - That means our subnet is 16 IP addresses wide.
    - Since 192.168.0.16 is the first IP, then 192.168.0.31 must be the last IP address
- The last IP address in the subnet is known as the **broadcast IP** and also can't be assigned to a device.
- If a device wants to send a message to all the devices within its network, it sends it to the broadcast address. In this case, it is 192.168.0.31.
- Thus, the range of IP addresses is 192.168.0.17 to 192.168.0.30
- We can calculate the number of useable IP addresses from $2^n - 2 = 14$

- Notice that this is a Class C network.
- The whole range is 192.168.0.0 to 192.168.0.255.
- That is a range of 256 addresses. Our subnet is 16 IP addresses wide.
- Therefore 256 / 16 = 16.
- We can create up to 16 subnets that are each 16 IP addresses wide.

- We could have created subnets that were larger (with fewer IP addresses) or smaller (with more IP addresses).
- If this was a Class B network, it would have a range of 65,536 addresses.
- Therefore 65536 / 16 = 4096.
- We can create up to 4096 subnets that are 16 IP addresses wide, in a Class B network.

- In summary
    - My IP address is 192.168.0.29
    - My subnet mask is 255.255.255.240
    - The subnet name is 192.168.0.16
    - The first IP address is 192.168.0.17
    - The last IP address is 192.168.0.30

o   The broadcast IP address is 192.168.0.31
• What is the IP address of the default gateway? • It could be any IP address between 192.168.0.17 and 192.168.0.30 • An administrator will usually assign the first IP address or the last IP address to the default gateway, but any IP address can be used
• By the way, I can write the IP address 192.168.0.17 as 192.168.000.017. That is, I can include or exclude the leading zeros in each octet to make them three digits wide.

In the IPv6 scheme, there is no such thing as a subnet mask. If there was, the math would be complicated. But we do have subnets. We also have sub-subnets and sub-sub-subnets.

Some things to note about IPv6 addresses

- An IPv6 address is 128 bits wide (unlike an IPv4 which is 32 bits wide).

- Each "octet" in the IPv6 address is 4 characters wide, but each octet is 16 bytes wide (unlike an IPv4 octet which is one byte wide)

- An octet can contain numbers from 0 to 9 and letters from a to f. This is called hexadecimal because each place goes up to 16 with the letters. If I was counting in decimal, I could count 1, 2, 3, 4, 5, 6, 7, 8, 9. When I get to 9, I must move to the next place (10). If I was counting in hexadecimal, I would count 1, 2, 3, 4, 5, 6, 7, 8, 9, a, b, c, d, e f. When I get to f, I must move to the next place (10). My hexadecimal 10 is misleading because it is actually worth 16.

- There are eight octets in an IPv6 address.

- Each octet is separated by a colon

An IPv6 address has two parts. The first part is called the prefix. A /48 prefix is common.

For example,

• An organization is assigned a /48 prefix • The prefix is 2001:0db8:1234: • No other organization will be assigned the same prefix • The organization can use this prefix for both public and private IPs • Since the total length of an address is 128, the organization has 80 bits remaining.
• The organization can subnet the IP address any way they want • 2001:0db8:1234:1000: is the first subnet chosen by the organization

• 2001:0db8:1234:2000: is the second subnet • So on and so forth • 2001:0db8:1234:f000: is the last subnet • Thus, the organization created 16 subnets • Each subnet is 64 bits long, which contains 2^{64} IP addresses • There is no point in creating more complicated subnets
• The organization could break each subnet into sub-subnets • 2001:0db8:1234:1000: is broken into 2001:0db8:1234:1000:1000:, 2001:0db8:1234:1000:2000:, etc
• The organization could break each sub-subnet into sub-sub-subnets • 2001:0db8:1234:1000:1000: is broken into 2001:0db8:1234:1000:1000:1000: • That is 2^{32} IP addresses per subnet, more than anybody will ever use
• There is no subnet mask, just a prefix. • If 2001:0db8:1234:1000:1000:1000: is my prefix, then my first IP address is 2001:0db8:1234:1000:1000:1000:0000:0000, and my last IP address is 2001:0db8:1234:1000:1000:1000:ffff:ffff. • We just fill in the blanks to generate IP addresses that are 128 bits long

Earlier I said that

- 10.0.0.0 to 10.255.255.255 is the largest network, with a range of 16,581,375 possible addresses. This type of network is known as a class A network.

- 172.16.0.0 to 172.16.255.255 is the second largest network, with a range of 65,025 possible addresses. This type of network is known as a class B network.

- 192.168.0.0 to 192.168.0.255, is the smallest network, with a range of 256 addresses. This type of network is known as a class C network.

The network classes applies to both public and private networks, not just the private ranges that I described above.

- A Class A network contains 2^{24} addresses. Networks in the range of 1.0.0.0 to 126.0.0.0.0 are Class A networks. So, a network like 2.0.0.0 to 2.255.255.255 is a Class A network.

- A Class B network contains 2^{16} addresses. Networks in the range of 128.0.0.0 to 191.0.0.0 are Class B networks. So, a network like 130.0.0.0 to 130.0.255.255 is a Class B network.

- A Class C network contains 2^8 addresses. Networks in the range of 192.168.0.0 to 223.0.0.0 are Class C networks. So, a network like 200.0.0.0 to 200.0.0.255 is a Class C network.

We have two more classes of networks

- Networks in the range of 224.0.0.0 to 239.0.0.0 are Class D networks.

- Networks in the range of 240.0.0.0 to 254.0.0.0 are Class E networks.

These networks do not have subnet masks. They are strictly experimental, and most routers will not accept traffic from IP addresses in their ranges. The use of a Class A, B, or C network is called **Classful Subnetting**.

The opposite is **Classless Subnetting**. How does it work?

If my network is 192.168.0.0 to 192.168.0.255, I have 256 IP addresses. I can break it down into one network of 256 addresses, or I can break it down into 2 networks of 128 addresses each, or 4 networks of 64 addresses each, or 8 networks of 32 addresses each, etc.. If my network was a Class A or Class B network, I could break it down into even more subnets and/or have even more IP addresses per subnet.

SUBNET MASK	NUMBER OF IPS PER SUBNET	NUMBER OF SUBNETS
/24	254	1
/25	126	2
/26	62	4
/27	30	8
/28	14	16
/29	6	32
/30	2	64

There is no /31 or /32 subnet because we need at least three IP addresses in a subnet – the network ID, the useable IP, and the broadcast IP. A /31 subnet would be two IP addresses wide and a /32 subnet would be one IP address wide.

We could choose to break down our network into subnets of any size based on our requirements. We might want to create separate logical networks for each class of devices. This allows us to improve security by preventing a device on one subnet from communicating with a device on another subnet. It also makes it easier to manage the network.

We ask ourselves what the largest required subnet is and go from there. This is known as **Fixed Length Subnetting**. Looking at the above table, we have a few choices for how we can break down our network into equally sized subnets.

What if I need subnets of different lengths? Introducing the **Variable Length Subnet Mask**

• What if my range is 192.168.0.0 to 192.168.0.255
• I need
    o A subnet with 100 IP addresses for computers
    o A subnet with 20 IP addresses for servers
    o A subnet with 20 IP addresses for network equipment
    o A subnet with 10 IP addresses for surveillance cameras

• I check the above table and the smallest subnet that can accommodate 100 IP addresses is the /25, with 126 IP addresses per subnet • But the /25 will only provide me with two subnets in the range that I have and I require four.
• With VLSM, I can create four subnets, each with a different size • Create a /25 subnet (192.168.0.0 to 192.168.0.127) for the subnet that requires 100 IP addresses • Create a /26 subnet (192.168.0.128 to 192.168.0.191) for the subnet that requires 20 IP addresses • Create a /27 subnet (192.168.0.192 to 192.168.0.223) for the second subnet that requires 20 IP addresses • Create a /28 subnet (192.168.0.224 to 192.168.0.237) for the subnet that requires 10 IP addresses

• We write the subnets as follows
    o 192.168.0.0/25
    o 192.168.0.128/26
    o 192.168.0.192/27
    o 192.168.0.224/28
• The IP addresses 192.168.0.238 to 192.168.0.255 are still available.

VSLM is part of a system called **Classless Inter-Domain Routing**, or **CIDR**. Writing the IP address with the subnet mask at the end as a slash is known as **Classless Inter-Domain Routing Notation**.

We can also write an IPv6 address in CIDR notation. Instead of writing the full IP address, we would write the IP address and subnet length. For example, we could write 2001:0db8:1234:0000:1111:2222:3333:4444 /48

Since we're on the subject, let's look at some other types of special IP addresses

- **Broadcast**. A broadcast is a message that is sent to all the devices in a single broadcast domain. That is, if my computer wants to send a message to all the other computers in the subnet, it addresses it to the broadcast IP address.

  The broadcast IP address will be the largest IP address in a subnet. For example, if the range of IP addresses is 192.168.0.1 to 192.168.0.255, then the broadcast IP address will be 192.168.0.255.

  On an IP network, this message is called a **broadcast packet**. Remember that a router will not forward a broadcast packet.

  Looking back at the structure of our IP packet, we have a source and destination IP address. The destination will be the broadcast IP.

Length	Protocol	Check Sequence	Source IP	Destination IP	Payload
IP HEADER					PAYLOAD

But the computer must send this packet to the switch that it is connected to, so it must put it inside a frame. A frame with a broadcast packet will be called a broadcast frame. The broadcast MAC address is FF:FF:FF:FF:FF:FF. Any frame addressed to this address will be forwarded to all devices in the **broadcast domain**.

The broadcast domain is all the network devices that will receive a broadcast. That is, all of the devices in a subnet make up a broadcast domain.

When the switch receives this broadcast frame, it will notice that the destination MAC address is FF:FF:FF:FF:FF:FF and send it to all of the connected devices.

Preamble	Delimiter	MAC Destination	MAC Source	Tag	Length	Payload	Check Sequence	Interpacket Gap
FRAME (ETHERNET) HEADER						PAYLOAD	ETHERNET TRAILER	

IPv6 does not use broadcasts, only multicast.

You can think of a broadcast packet like some flyers you see in your mailbox. An advertiser will print a pile of them without any addresses and dump them at the post office. The mail man will stick one flyer in every mailbox on his route. The route is the broadcast domain, and the flyer is the broadcast packet.

- **Multicast**. Both IPv4 and IPv6 use multicast. A multicast message allows a sender to send a message to multiple recipients (but not all the members of a broadcast domain). The sender creates a single multicast packet, but routers and switches replicate that packet and send it to all the required destinations.

  On a network, there can be multiple multicast "groups". Each group has an address. A device that wishes to receive messages addressed to a group sends a "membership report" message to the group's address, indicating its desire to receive the messages.

  Multicast works through the **Internet Group Management Protocol**. The current version is IGMPv3, which allows a device to leave a group that it previously joined (previous versions only allowed a device to join and not leave).

  Who keeps track of the group? The local network router keeps track of the groups and the subscribers. When the local router receives a packet addressed to the group, it sends it to all of the subscribers in the group.

  You can think of a multicast packet like a newsletter. You must subscribe to the newsletter, but every person who subscribes receives a copy. You can unsubscribe if you want.

- **Unicast**. A unicast packet is one that is addressed to a specific recipient. Most communications are unicast. When a device wants to send a packet via unicast, it puts the IP address of the recipient in the destination.

  A unicast packet is like a letter from your friend. It has your address and is sent specifically to you.

- **Anycast**. An anycast packet allows a computer to send a message to one of many recipients. Any anycast group contains more than one recipient. When the router receives a packet addressed to the anycast group, it chooses one recipient from the group and sends the packet to it. The chosen recipient is based on a routing algorithm. The algorithm may choose a recipient that is closest to the sender or use other factors.

  Anycast is used in load balancing. For example, if I have multiple servers that perform the same task, I can assign all of them to the same anycast group. I can direct traffic to the anycast group's address. The router can then decide which server receives each piece of traffic by selecting the closest server.

What happens when we have two networks separated by a router and they have different IP addressing schemes? The IP addresses aren't compatible.

Consider the following example. I have a router with the address 44.3.2.1. That is the address that devices on the internet know it as. Behind the router is my internal network, which has three devices, each with a different address – 192.168.0.1, 192.168.0.2, and 192.168.0.3. Nobody on the internet knows anything about my internal network – they can only see my router.

Remember that addresses that start with 192.168 are known as private IP addresses. They can only be used on internal networks. 44.3.2.1 is an example of a public IP address. But how can a computer on an internal network talk with devices on the internet? And how can devices on the internet talk to a computer on an internal network?

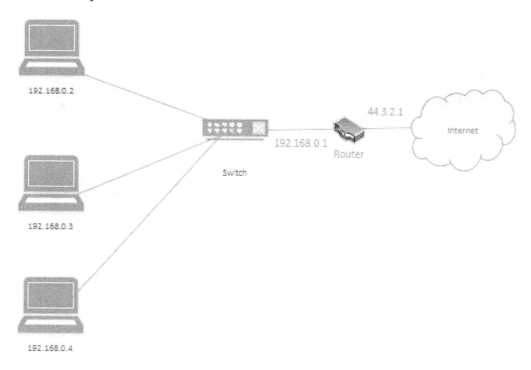

We use a system called **Network Address Translation**, or **NAT**. NAT is a tool used by the router to move traffic between the internet and the local network devices. There are several ways that NAT can work depending on the number of public IP addresses available to the router and depending on the number of devices on the internal network.

Let's say the router has three public IP addresses – 44.3.2.1, 44.3.2.2, and 44.3.2.3 – at least one public IP address for each private IP address. The router has two options for moving traffic between the internet and the internal network

- It can create a **Static NAT**, also known as a **one-to-one translation**. The router says that 44.3.2.1 belongs to the device 192.168.0.2; 44.3.2.2 belongs to the device 192.168.0.3 and 44.3.2.3 belongs to the device 192.168.0.4.

  Let's look at an example. 192.168.0.3 wants to send traffic to google.com (8.8.8.8).
  - The device creates a packet with a source field of 192.168.0.3, and a destination field of 8.8.8.8

Length	Protocol	Check Sequence	192.168.0.3 Source IP	8.8.8.8 Destination IP	Payload
		IP HEADER			**PAYLOAD**

  - The device wraps the packet in an ethernet frame and sends it to the router (the frame's destination MAC address is that of the router)

Preamble	Delimiter	MAC Destination	MAC Source	Tag	Length	Payload	Check Sequence	Interpacket Gap
		FRAME (ETHERNET) HEADER				**PAYLOAD**	**ETHERNET TRAILER**	

  - The router strips the frame header and looks at the packet

  - The router changes the Source IP (192.168.0.3) of the packet to reflect its external address. It knows that it mapped 44.3.2.3 to the internal IP 192.168.0.3, so that is the IP address that it uses.

Length	Protocol	Check Sequence	44.3.2.3 Source IP	8.8.8.8 Destination IP	Payload
		IP HEADER			**PAYLOAD**

  - The router sends the packet to the 8.8.8.8 address. It uses a routing protocol to send this packet, which we will worry about later.

  - The Google server at 8.8.8.8 receives the packet and sees that it came from 44.3.2.3

o The Google server replies to 44.3.2.3 by creating a packet with a Destination IP of 44.3.2.3

Length	Protocol	Check Sequence	8.8.8.8 Source IP	44.3.2.3 Destination IP	Payload
		IP HEADER			**PAYLOAD**

o The router receives this packet and checks the NAT mapping. It knows that 44.3.2.3 is mapped to 192.168.0.3

o It changes the Destination field in the packet to 192.168.0.3 and wraps it in a frame.

o It puts the MAC address of the computer in to field and sends it to the computer through the switch.

Length	Protocol	Check Sequence	44.3.2.3 Source IP	192.168.0.3 Destination IP	Payload
		IP HEADER			**PAYLOAD**

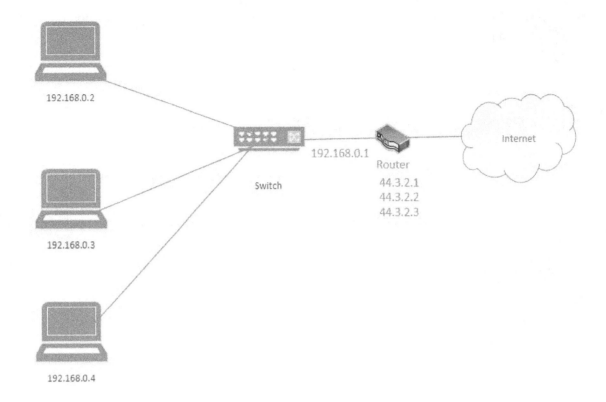

- **One-to-one translation** is great but remember that IPv4 addresses are scarce. What if I have more internal devices than IP addresses (which is usually the case)? I might need to set up a **Dynamic NAT**.

  Dynamic NAT works exactly like the Static NAT with one difference. That is, with a Dynamic NAT, the router maintains a "pool" of external IP addresses. Each time an internal device needs to access the internet, the router assigns it an external address from the pool. The router keeps track of the assignments in a table. It changes the addresses on the packets just like it did with the Static NAT.

  As long as the device is accessing the internet, it continues to be assigned to the external IP address. If a device doesn't access the internet for a while, then the NAT entry is deleted from the table and the IP address returns to the pool.

- But what if I have a massive number of internal devices and they all want to access the internet at the same time? What if I don't have enough IP addresses to go around even with Dynamic NAT? I can use **PAT** or **Port Address Translation**.

  We haven't talked about "ports" yet. But we are going to introduce a new idea. Look at the computers on the left. Each one has one IP address but it might have many different applications that connect to the internet – e-mail, Skype, Teams, Windows Update, web browser, etc.. If it is receiving traffic from multiple sources, how does it know which source should be directed to each application? Introducing ports. A port is a number that is attached to the end of the IP address. In this case, we aren't talking about physical ports, but logical ports.

Things are going to get more complicated. The Google server way in California spends its whole day listening to incoming web traffic. It does so on port 80. That is, it understands that traffic sent to 8.8.8.8:80 is requesting the Google website. It might ignore other traffic, or it might listen for different types of traffic on other ports. For example, it might listen for management traffic on port 300.

Now, let's say that I have 100 browser tabs open at the same time. I am trying to access Google, CNN, YouTube, etc.. If my computer is bombarded with traffic from all these sources at the same time, it will not know which packet goes where. So, what can it do? It adds a port to the end of each request.

For example, it sends a packet to Google.com with the port 55555 as the source. Google.com knows that it should send a reply back to 192.168.0.3:55555.

Length	Protocol	Check Sequence	192.168.0.3:55555 Source IP	8.8.8.8:80 Destination IP	Payload
IP HEADER					PAYLOAD

It sends a packet to CNN.com with the port 55556 as the source. CNN.com knows that it should send a reply back to 192.168.0.3:55556.

Length	Protocol	Check Sequence	192.168.0.3:5556 Source IP	9.9.9.9:80 Destination IP	Payload
IP HEADER					PAYLOAD

It sends a packet to YouTube.com with the port 55557 as the source. Google.com knows that it should send a reply back to 192.168.0.3:55557.

Length	Protocol	Check Sequence	192.168.0.3:55557 Source IP	10.10.10.10:80 Destination IP	Payload
IP HEADER					PAYLOAD

These port numbers were present in the NAT scheme. But the router didn't change the port numbers. It didn't have to because it only changed the IP address (there was a unique address for each internal device). Now there isn't.

A router doesn't really have different software applications. But it can still understand ports. Ports allow the router to expand the number of IP addresses.

Let's look at our example. But now our router has only one external IP address: 44.3.2.1.
- o Our computer wants to access Google.com

- o It creates the following packet and packages it into an Ethernet frame, which it sends to the router

Length	Protocol	Check Sequence	192.168.0.3:55555 Source IP	8.8.8.8:80 Destination IP	Payload
IP HEADER					PAYLOAD

- o Our router sees the source and destination. It creates an internal translation between the source IP/port and the external IP. It chooses an available external port, in this case 1002.
  - ▪ 192.168.0.3:55555 -> 44.3.2.1:1002

- o Now our router knows that any traffic received on 44.3.2.1:1002 should be forwarded to the internal address/port 192.168.0.3:55555
- o The router changes the Source IP/Port in the packet to reflect the external IP/port and forwards it to 8.8.8.8:80

Length	Protocol	Check Sequence	44.3.2.1:1002 Source IP	8.8.8.8:80 Destination IP	Payload
IP HEADER					PAYLOAD

- o Google.com receives the packet and sees that it came from 44.3.2.1:1002.

- o It creates a packet and replies to 44.3.2.1:1002.

Length	Protocol	Check Sequence	8.8.8.8:80 Source IP	44.3.2.1:1002 Destination IP	Payload
IP HEADER					PAYLOAD

- o The router notices that it received a packet on port 44.3.2.1:1002.

- It checks the port mapping table and realizes that this packet belongs to 192.168.0.3:55555

- It changes the destination to 192.168.0.1:80 and forwards the packet. I should say that it wraps the packet inside an ethernet frame (and puts the MAC address of the computer in the destination field).

Length	Protocol	Check Sequence	8.8.8.8:80 Source IP	192.168.0.3:55555 Destination IP	Payload
		IP HEADER			PAYLOAD

- The computer receives the packet and sees that it arrived on port 55555. Based on its records, it knows that it was listening for traffic from Google.com on port 55555, and it knows what to do with the traffic.

- If the computer decides to seek traffic from another website (with another port), the router will learn about the traffic and create a new mapping. For example
    - 192.168.0.3:55556 -> 44.3.2.1:1003
    - 192.168.0.3:55557 -> 44.3.2.1:1004

As we will learn, there are three ways for a device to receive an IP address

- Somebody manually assigns the device a **static IP** address

- The device automatically receives an IP address from the network through a process known as **DHCP**

- The device does not receive an IP address and is not programmed with a static IP address. So, it chooses an IP address at random.

Under IPv4, if a device doesn't have a static IP address and can't reach a DHCP server, it generates a random IP address in the range of 169.254.0.0 to 169.254.255.255. The process for assigning this address is called **link-local address autoconfiguration, auto-IP,** or **Automatic Private IP Addressing (APIPA)**. A router will not pass traffic coming from a link-local address.

Under IPv6, every network interface automatically assigns itself a link-local address in the range of fe80::/10, even when it has a routable (static or DHCP) IP address. Link-local addresses are necessary for some IPv6 protocols to function. This is known as a locally unique address because it is possible for devices in other networks to assign the same address. In other words, it will look like the below IP address (where the xxxx's are unique values).

fe80:0000:0000:0000:xxxx:xxxx:xxxx:xxxx

A link-local IPv4 address is only unique in its own local network, but an IPv6 link-local address is globally unique. Why? A MAC address is considered globally unique (no two devices have the same MAC address). Therefore, if an IPv6 address can be generated from a MAC address, it is also globally unique. The IP address is generated using a process called **Extended Unique Identifier 64 (EUI64)**,

Remember that a MAC address is 48 bits (6 bytes) and follows the format 11:22:33:44:55:66. Like an IP address, a MAC address can be converted into 0's and 1's.

The device calculates the new IP address like this

- Let's say our IPv6 prefix is fe80:0000:0000:0000
- Let's say our MAC address is 11:22:33:44:55:66
- We split the MAC address in half, and add "fffe" in the middle
- Now our MAC address is 11:22:33:ff:fe:44:55:66
- We flip the seventh bit in the MAC address.
- How can we do that?
- Remember that the MAC address now is 16 characters (or 64 bits) wide. Each octet (separated by a colon) is one byte (8 bits) wide.
- Thus the number "11" is one byte.
- I can represent the one byte as a combination of eight 0's and 1's
- 8-bits makes up one byte. A computer with 8-bits can only count to 255 in one operation. If I make a table that is base-two (every entry is double the previous entry), I can combine these eight numbers to make any number from 0 to 255. Below is my table.

128	64	32	16	8	4	2	1

- If you look at the 8-bits in a byte, each bit is assigned to one of the numbers in my table. If the bit is a one, or in "on" position, then the number is added to the total, and if the bit is a zero, or in the "off" position, then the bit is ignored.

- In this example, I want to convert the number 11. 8+2+1 = 11. If I write in my table that

128	64	32	16	8	4	2	1
0	0	0	0	1	0	1	1

- Then the resulting binary number is 00001011
- The seventh bit is "1", so I flip it to "0"
- I rewrite my table to reflect the flip

128	64	32	16	8	4	2	1
0	0	0	0	1	0	0	1

- Now I can recalculate the value as 8+1 = 9
- Thus 11 is replaced by 9 and my new MAC address is 09:22:33:ff:fe:44:55:66
- But wait, there's more!
- We apply this to our IPv6 prefix, and now our globally unique IP address is fe80:0000:0000:0000:0922:33ff:fe44:5566 (I removed some of the colons from the MAC address portion)

An IPv6 address might look like this 2002:0de8:85c3:0010:0300:8b2e:0360:7234.

We can shorten the IP address. If our IP address looked like this: 2002:0de8:0000:0000:0300:8b2e:0360:7234, we could shorten it to 2002:0de8::300:8b2e:0360:7234. See what we did there? We hid the sections with "0000", and replaced them with '::'. In any IPv6 address, we can hide the longest string of 0's, as long as they fill up an entire segment or as long as a segment starts with 0. We can only hide one string per IP address, otherwise it gets confusing.

If my address looked like this: 2002:0de8:0000:0000:0300:8b2e:0000:7234 and I shortened it to 2002:0de8::8b2e::7234, you now have two "::", but you don't know which one had four 0's and which one had eight.

We can also get rid of any 0's that are before a ":". That means 2002:0de8:1824:2383:0300:002e:4e4e:7234 can be shortened to 2002:de8:1824:2383:300:2e:4e4e:7234

Since the IPv6 protocol is still being adopted, not all networks understand it yet. What happens when a router communicating over IPv6 reaches a router that only understands IPv4?

Let's say that you are trying to access google.com. You're in Florida and google.com is in California. Your local router understands IPv6 and Google's router understands IPv6, but the routers in between only understand IPv4.

Your computer and google.com's server create an **IPv4 tunnel** and send your IPv6 data through it. The most common tunneling protocol is called **6to4**. That is, they package an IPv6 packet inside an IPv4 packet. On the outside, it looks like a normal IPv4 packet, so routers that only understand IPv4 can pass it along, but on the inside it is actually an IPv6 packet, so routers that understand IPv6 can read it.

The problem with tunneling is that it reduces the capacity of each packet (we have to include additional header data, leaving less room for meaningful data).

A better approach is for each device to obtain both an IPv4 address and an IPv6 address. This is known as **dual stack**. Most modern ISP's assign both IPv4 and IPv6 addresses to their customers. A device running dual stack will try to connect over IPv6, and if it can't then it will try to connect over IPv4.

Remember that when an IPv6 capable device connects to a network, it generates the link-local address automatically. Well, after generating the link-local address, the device sends a message to it. This message is known as a **Neighbor Solicitation** and the purpose is to ensure that no other device is using the same address. If another device is using the address, it will reply with a **Neighbor Advertisement** message. Otherwise there will be no reply; the device will know that the address is unique and will start using it.

If the address is unique, the device sends a message called a **Router Solicitation** to ff02::2. All IPv6-enabled routers listen on the ff02::2 address (the long version is ff02:0000:0000:0000:0000:0002). Upon receipt, the router replies with a message called a **Router Advertisement**. The advertisement contains several pieces of information including

- Whether the router can be used as a default router (default gateway)

- The IPv6 prefix of the link. The prefix allows the device to generate a globally unique IP address.

- The lifetime of the link prefix. The lifetime tells the device how long it can use the IP prefix before generating a new one. This helps with security.

This process is called **Stateless Address Autoconfiguration (SLAAC)**, because each device can configure its own IP address (a router isn't telling the device what IP address to use). The device will use the process I outlined above (EUI64), but use the prefix provided by the router instead of fe80:0000:0000:0000

A **Virtual IP address** is an address that is not assigned to a specific network interface. Let's say I am running a very high availability application, hosted on servers in Atlanta, New York, and Los Angeles. I don't want any trouble, so even if there is a flood in one city, we continue to operate.

Each server has its own unique IP address (44.1.1.1, 55.1.1.1, and 66.1.1.1). I don't want any disruptions, so I select a single IP address (7.7.7.7) that points to all the servers.

Instead of pointing it to any server, I point it t a router. The magic inside the router allows it to forward traffic from 7.7.7.7 to any of the server IP addresses. We can add and remove servers in different locations across the world without changing the main IP address.

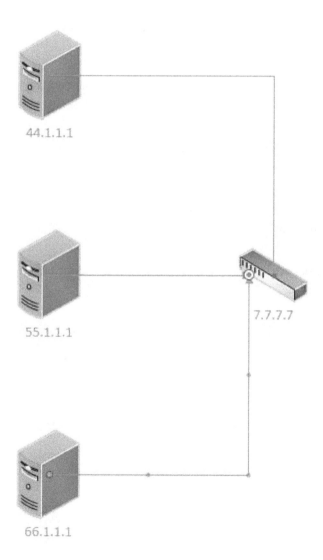

There are many protocols for virtual IP addressing, including **Common Address Redundancy Protocol** and **Proxy ARP**.

We can take this a step further and think about **subinterfaces**. What is the benefit of a subinterface? We might want to assign multiple IP addresses in multiple networks to the same physical interface.

Consider the following example

- I have a local area network with two computers (192.168.0.2, 192.168.0.3) and one surveillance camera (192.168.1.3)

- All the devices are connected to the same switch and are behind the same router/internet connection.
- I don't want the computers to be able to access the camera, but I don't want to build a separate physical network for the camera (since I will need a new switch, router, and internet connection)

- Instead I have created two subnets – 192.168.0.0/24 for the computers and 192.168.1.0/24 for the camera

- The router has only one local interface – but I can create two "logical" subinterfaces on it – I assign one of them 192.168.0.1 and I assign the other 192.168.1.1

- Now the computers can communicate with the router through 192.168.0.1 and the camera can communicate with the router through 192.168.1.1, but they can't talk to each other

- We might call these separate logical networks **VLANs**. When we look in depth at how the switch functions, we will revisit this topic.

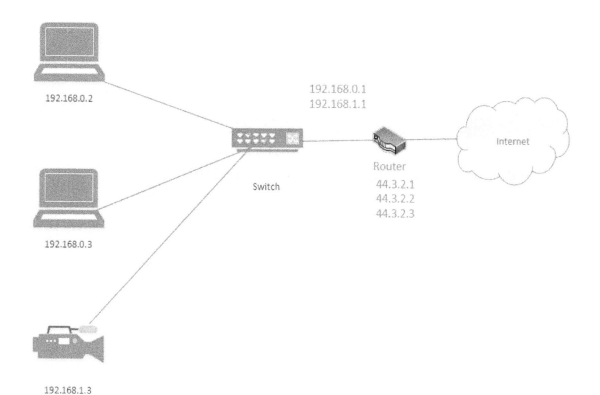

192.168.0.2

192.168.0.3

192.168.1.3

192.168.0.1
192.168.1.1

Switch

Router
44.3.2.1
44.3.2.2
44.3.2.3

Internet

1.5 Explain common ports and protocols, their application, and encrypted alternatives

- *File Transfer Protocol (FTP)*
- *Secure Shell (SSH)*
- *Secure File Transfer Protocol (SFTP)*
- *Telnet*
- *Simple Main Transfer Protocol (SMTP)*
- *Domain Name System (DNS)*
- *Dynamic Host Configuration Protocol (DHCP)*
- *Trivial File Transfer Protocol (TFTP)*
- *Hypertext Transfer Protocol (HTTP)*
- *Post Office Protocol v3 (POP3)*
- *Network Time Protocol (NTP)*
- *Internet Message Access Protocol (IMAP)*
- *Simple Network Management Protocol (SNMP)*
- *Lightweight Directory Access Protocol (LDAP)*
- *Hypertext Transfer Protocol Secure (HTTPS) Secure Sockets Layer (SSL)*
- *HTTPS Transport Layer Security (TLS)*
- *Server Message Block (SMB)*
- *Syslog*
- *SMTP TLS*
- *Lightweight Directory Access Protocol (over SSL) (LDAPS)*
- *IMAP over SSL*
- *POP3 over SSL*
- *Structured Query Language (SQL) Server*
- *SQLnet*
- *MySQL*
- *Remote Desktop Protocol (RDP)*
- *Session Initiation Protocol (SIP)*
- *IP Protocol Types*
  - *Internet Control Message Protocol (ICMP)*
  - *TCP*
  - *UDP*
    - *Generic Routing Encapsulation (GRE)*
    - *Internet Protocol Security (IPSec)*
      - *Authentication Header (AH)*
      - *Encapsulating Security Payload (ESP)*
- *Connectionless vs Connection-Oriented*

We mentioned ports earlier. Remember that a port is a number that is attached to the end of the IP address. In this case, we aren't talking about physical ports, but logical ports.

And I mentioned the example that the Google server way in California spends its whole day listening to incoming web traffic. It does so on port 80. That is, it understands that traffic sent to 8.8.8.8:80 is requesting the Google website. It might ignore other traffic, or it might listen for different types of traffic on other ports. For example, it might listen for management traffic on port 300.

Now, let's say that I have 100 browser tabs open at the same time. I am trying to access Google, CNN, YouTube, etc.. If my computer is bombarded with traffic from all these sources at the same time, it will not know which packet goes where. So, what can it do? It adds a port to the end of each request.

For example, it sends a packet to Google.com with the port 55555 as the source. Google.com knows that it should send a reply back to 192.168.0.3:55555.

Length	Protocol	Check Sequence	192.168.0.3:55555 Source IP	8.8.8.8:80 Destination IP	Payload
IP HEADER					PAYLOAD

It sends a packet to CNN.com with the port 55556 as the source. CNN.com knows that it should send a reply back to 192.168.0.3:55556.

Length	Protocol	Check Sequence	192.168.0.3:5556 Source IP	9.9.9.9:80 Destination IP	Payload
IP HEADER					PAYLOAD

It sends a packet to YouTube.com with the port 55557 as the source. Google.com knows that it should send a reply back to 192.168.0.3:55557.

Length	Protocol	Check Sequence	192.168.0.3:55557 Source IP	10.10.10.10:80 Destination IP	Payload
IP HEADER					PAYLOAD

Many common protocols have ports that are reserved for them. If your computer/server is running a specific application, that application will listen for traffic on a specific port (unless you configure it to use a different, non-standard port). There are 65,535 total ports (range is from 1 to 65,535). Let's look at some of the most common protocols and their associated ports

Port Number/Protocol Name	Use
20 and 21/FTP and FTPS	File Transfer Protocol
	FTP is a protocol for transferring files between two devices
	FTPS adds a security layer to the file transfer. It requires that the server have an SSL certificate installed. The entire session can be encrypted or only specific portions of it.
22/SSH	Secure Shell
	Secure Socket Shell (or Secure Shell) allows a user to connect to a remote computer. SSH authenticates the identity of the remote computer to the user and the user to the remote computer.
	SSH creates a tunnel between the user and the remote computer. The user will require an SSH client such as PuTTY, and the remote computer will require an SSH daemon.
	Each remote computer must be set up to accept SSH logins (typically over port 22). Network firewalls must be configured to allow traffic over port 22. The user's IP address should be whitelisted on the firewall (do not allow SSH connections from any IP address)
22/SFTP	SSH File Transfer
	SFTP is a file transfer protocol within the SSH protocol. Provided that the SSH session is

secured and properly configured, then the SFTP session will be as well.

23/Telnet

Telnet

Telnet provides a text-based terminal to communicate with a network device or server. Telnet is like SSH but does not contain any security.

It is no longer popular due to lack of security. Use SSH instead.

25/SMTP or 587/SMTP over TLS

Simple Mail Transfer Protocol

Used to communicate with an e-mail server (for sending e-mail only)

Can be secure or insecure, depending on whether the client and server agree to encrypt data between them.

SMTP with TLS can be used for encrypted communication.

53/DNS

Domain Name Server

Translates Domain Names/Hostnames to IP addresses (necessary to locate network resource)

Consider that a human can remember text names (such as google.ca or amazon.com), but for a web browser to access a website, it must figure out the corresponding server IP address.

The DNS converts human-readable domain names into machine-readable IP addresses.

By default DNS is not secure, but DNS can be run over the HTTPS protocol.

67/68/DHCP   **Dynamic Host Configuration Protocol**

Allows a device to request a dynamic IP from a DHCP server. Allows a DHCP server to dynamically assign IP addresses to other devices.

When a device first joins a network, it may not need an IP address and must request one.

DHCP does not have a secure alternative, but with proper network security, DHCP messages can be protected.

69/TFTP   **Trivial File Transfer Protocol**

TFTP is like FTP in that it allows a user to transfer files over a network. TFTP has a simple design.

An important use of TFTP is to allow a device to boot over a network. A device with no operating system can load one over the network into memory.

TFTP does not have any security.

80/HTTP or 443/HTTPS   **Hyper Text Transfer Protocol**

Used to transmit web site data (insecure). The secure alternative is HTTPS

HTTPS can use **SSL (Secure Sockets Layer)** to encrypt the data, or the newer **TLS (Transport Layer Security)**. Both methods use port 443.

110/POP or 995/POP over TLS/SSL   **Post Office Protocol**

Allows an e-mail client like Outlook to retrieve messages from a server. With POP, the e-mail server receives messages on behalf of the user. Via POP, the e-mail client asks the server if there are any new messages. If so, the e-mail client downloads messages from the server. The server deletes the messages after they have been downloaded.

POP is no longer common; it has been replaced with IMAP and Exchange, which allow an e-mail client to "sync" with a server.

POP can be encrypted with TLS/SSL and run over port 995.

123/NTP or NTS

Network Time Protocol

NTP allows network-connected devices to sync their clocks, to within a few milliseconds of UTC. NTP can function accurately even when the network has high latency through the clock synchronization algorithm.

NTP can obtain the time from a central server or from a peer.

The secure version is called **Network Time Security (NTS)**.

143/IMAP or 993/IMAP

Internet Message Access Protocol

Allows an e-mail client to communicate with an e-mail server. The client and server "sync" so that both have the same data (e-mails, calendar entries, contacts, etc.).

If an e-mail is deleted in the e-mail client, then it is also deleted on the server.

IMAP may be secure or insecure. The secure version uses TLS and port 993.

161/162/SNMP

Simple Network Management Protocol

Allows a user to collect and manage data about managed network devices, including routers, switches, servers, and printers.

There is no secure version.

389/LDAP or 636/LDAPS

Lightweight Directory Access Protocol

Allows users to access different directories Directories include e-mail directories, users, phone numbers, printers, and services

The secure version is called **Lightweight Directory Access Protocol Secure** and uses port 636.

445/SMB/CIFS

Server Message Block/Common Internet File System

Allows computers on a network to share files and printers

There is no secure version.

514/syslog

Syslog

Syslog allows network devices to generate logging messages and send them to a server. This allows an administrator to remotely view logs from many different devices in a centralized location.

Syslog can be secured with TLS.

548/AFP

Apple Filing Protocol

Allows Apple devices to share files

There is no security

1433/SQL Server

Structured Query Language (SQL) Server

SQL is a database server developed by Microsoft. It can use TLS to encrypt the communication.

1720/H.323

H.323

Allows devices to communicate audio-visual content over a network.

Used in videoconferencing applications.

The communications can be encrypted.

3306/MySQL

MySQL

MySQL is a database server developed by Oracle (similar to SQL). It can use TLS to encrypt the communication.

3389/RDP

Remote Desktop Protocol

Allows a user to remotely connect to a Windows server or computer via a Graphical User Interface

RDP can encrypt the communication if enabled by a user or administrator.

5060/5061/SIP

Session Initiation Protocols

Used for real-time communications involving VoIP and video conferencing. Also used by mobile devices for voice over LTE.

Encryption is possible when there is a direct connection between the sender and the recipient (which is unlikely).

Ports 0 to 1023 are **well known ports** reserved for specific applications. Only those applications should be using those ports. Ports 1024 to 49151 are **registered ports**. An application developer can apply to have his application use one of those ports. Ports 49152 to 65535 are called **dynamic ports** or **ephemeral ports**. An application can borrow one of those ports temporarily if it needs to communicate.

There are four main protocol types. Each protocol can fit into one of the following types.

ICMP   **Internet Control Message Protocol**

ICMP does not carry user traffic, only machine-to-machine communications.

Network equipment use ICMP messages to communicate errors and status with each other.

ICMP messages are used by ping and tracert commands for example.

UDP   **User Datagram Protocol**

UDP is connectionless, unlike TCP. UDP is good for applications that do not check for errors (or that do not have time to check for errors).

Remember that in a communication, the sending device breaks up the data into packets and the receiving device puts the packets back together into something meaningful. If the packets arrive out of order, the receiving device can reorder them. If they arrive damaged, the receiving device can request that they be resent.

If you're downloading a file like an Excel spreadsheet, the sender breaks it up into packets. The receiving computer puts the packets back together. What matters is that the end result makes sense.

If you're on a live video stream or VoIP phone call, the transmission is also broken into packets. Every packet must arrive in the correct order because they are being replayed in real time. If the packets for a video stream or phone call arrived in the wrong order, the call or video wouldn't make any sense.

A poor-quality connection would result in poor video transmission due to errors in the packets but attempting to resend them would be counterproductive.

UDP is

- Transactional (allows a query-response structure, like DNS)
- Simple (useful for protocols that do not need overhead, like DHCP)
- Stateless (allows many clients to receive the same connection, good for protocols like IPTV)
- Lack of retransmissions (no delay caused by retransmissions of missing/incorrect data)
- Multicast (can broadcast information to many clients, like in service discovery protocols)

UDP is like a guy at the top of a hill yelling. He doesn't keep track of who is listening or whether they received the message. And it's possible for multiple people to hear him.

TCP   **Transmission Control Protocol**

TCP is like a one on one conversation where each participant acknowledges every sentence said by the other participant. If one participant misheard something, it asks the other participant to repeat it.

TCP involves a connection between two peers, with a three-way handshake. Each time a peer receives data, it verifies that the data has been received correctly. If not, the recipient requests that the sender retransmit the data.

TCP is more reliable than UTP, but it is not useful for real-time applications because it introduces latency into the connection.

The TCP Model has four layers that follow the OSI Model

- **Link Layer** (Physical and Data Link layers of OSI). TCP doesn't worry about the link layer, because the protocol doesn't deal with the physical link.

- **Internet Layer** (Network layer of OSI). **IP Packets** are created on the Internet Layer.

- **Transport Layer** (Transport layer of OSI). The transport layer moves the packets. On the transport layer, IP Packets are encapsulated inside **segments**.

- **Application Layer** (Session, Presentation, and Application Layers of OSI). The application layer allows programs to talk to the network.

IP   **Internet Protocol**

IP transfers data packets across the internet. IP is considered unreliable because the underlying infrastructure is assumed to be unreliable. Therefore, IP allows a data transmission to adapt to the actual condition of the underlying network.

There are two versions of IP in use: IPv4 and IPv6, as we have already seen.

IP and TCP normally work together, and are known as TCP/IP

GRE　　GRE (Genetic Routing Encapsulation) is a tunnel protocol that is used to encapsulate other protocols.

The way it works is that a normal data packet is encapsulated inside an IP packet. Routers along the route do not look at the internal packet, only the outside. The final destination looks inside the internal packet.

GRE is not secure.

IPSec　　IPSec (Internet Protocol Security) is a protocol that allows two devices to create a tunnel between them across a normal internet connection.

IPSec encapsulated the existing data packet into a larger packet. The interior packet is also encrypted so that routers along the way can't see inside.

Connection-oriented protocols require a connection to be established. That is, two devices agree to communicate with each other.

- A **connection-oriented** protocol is like two people approaching each other at a park and agreeing to have a conversation:

  o *Person One: "Hey can I talk to you?"*
  o *Person Two: "Sure"*
  o *Person One: "Okay, blah, blah, blah"*

- *Person Two: "I acknowledge what you said"*

- The communication is two ways. The two devices must work to establish the connection, acknowledge the connection and agree on how they will communicate throughout the connection

- The two devices will also mutually agree to end the connection once the communication is complete (or a device can unilaterally end the connection if it doesn't hear from the other party after some time).

- The communication involves two parties and only two parties

- The recipient acknowledges receipt of each communication

- TCP is a connection-oriented protocol, and uses a three-way handshake to establish the connection)

  - The first message is called the SYN (hey can I talk to you?)

  - The second message is called the SYN-ACK (yes you can!)

  - The third message is called the ACK (I understood that)

- A **connectionless** protocol is like one person climbing to the top of a hill and yelling at somebody at the bottom of a hill. Nobody agreed to talk to him. He might talk to only one person, or he might talk to many people. The other person might yell back. The other person might not even be there, in which case he will be talking to himself and not know it.
  - The communication is one way

  - The communication may be directed at one recipient or many.

  - Nobody knows if the intended recipient received the message, because the recipient has no way of acknowledging receipt

  - If we're broadcasting a live video stream, we might use a connectionless protocol because it allows anybody to tune in

1.6 Explain the use and purpose of network services

- DHCP
  - Scope
  - Exclusion Ranges
  - Reservation
  - Dynamic Assignment
  - Static Assignment
  - Lease Time
  - Scope Options
  - Available Leases
  - DHCP Relay
  - IP Helper / UDP Forwarding
- DNS
  - Record Types
    - Address (A)
    - Canonical Name (CNAME)
    - Mail Exchange (MX)
    - Authentication, Authorization, Accounting, Auditing (AAAA)
    - Start of Authority (SOA)
    - Pointer (PTR)
    - Text (TXT)
    - Service (SRV)
    - Name Server (NS)
  - Global Hierarchy
    - Root DNS Servers
    - Internal vs External
    - Zone Transfers
    - Authoritative Name Servers
    - Time to Live (TTL)
    - DNS Caching
    - Reverse DNS / Reverse Lookup / Forward Lookup
    - Recursive Lookup / Iterative Lookup
- NTP
  - Stratum
  - Clients
  - Servers

Address Assignments

Remember that there were three ways for a device to have an IP address?

The most common method is **DHCP** or **Dynamic Host Configuration Protocol**. A network administrator sets up a DHCP server (a DHCP server can be a physical computer or can be a function on a router). The administrator allocates a range of IP addresses from his network to be assigned in DHCP. For example, if the network is 192.168.0.0 to 192.168.0.255, the administrator might decide that addresses from 192.168.0.100 to 192.168.0.199 can be used by DHCP. This range is known as the **DHCP Pool**. An **exclusion range** is a range of addresses that should not be assigned via DHCP.

When a device joins a network (and doesn't have a static IP configured), it asks for an IP address over UDP.

- It sends a message on the broadcast address asking to be assigned an IP address. If it was previously connected to the network, it might ask for the same IP address as it had before. The message contains the sender's MAC address and is called **DHCPDISCOVER**. This part of the process is known as **Discovery**.

- Every device on the network ignores the message except for the DHCP server, which replies with an **Offer**, known as **DHCPOFFER**. The offer contains

    o The IP address that the client should acquire

    o The subnet mask

    o The **lease time** – how long the IP address will last before the device must acquire a new one

    o Other details can be assigned to the device, including the DNS server address, gateway address, and NIS address

While the offer is pending, a DHCP server does not offer the IP address to any other device. If there are multiple DHCP servers on the network, they may each make an offer to the same device in response to the one message.

Why would we have multiple DHCP servers on the same network? We can provide different DHCP parameters for different devices. If we have VoIP phones and computers on the same network, the phones could receive DHCP from one server and the computers could receive DHCP from another.

- The client requests the IP address offered by the server by sending a **Request** message, known as **DHCPREQUEST**. All the servers find out which offer the client accepted. The servers whose offers were rejected withdraw their offers.

- The server acknowledges that it has assigned the DHCP address to the client by sending it an **Acknowledgement** message known as **DHCPACK**.

- The client configures its own network interface using the information received from the DHCP server.

A DHCP server can be configured to assign IP addresses using one (or more than one) of three schemes

- **Dynamic Allocation**. The server picks the first available address from the range and assigns it to the device. If I have a large Wi-Fi network such as in an airport, with thousands of different devices connecting to it each day, I would allocate DHCP addresses dynamically. Chances are, my network won't see the same device often.

- **Automatic Allocation**. The server remembers which address it assigned to the device in the past. It tries to assign the device the same IP address each time, if available. If I had an office with users who bring their laptops to work, I would try to allocate the same IP address to each device. I wouldn't make it mandatory because devices are replaced, and new devices are added all the time.

- **Manual Allocation**. The administrator manually programs a relationship between a MAC address and an IP address. If a device with a matching MAC address joins the network, it is automatically assigned the same IP address each time. The network will reserve this IP address and never assign it to any other device.

  I would use this when I have specific devices like printers and surveillance cameras, which are better off accessible at the same address each time, and I'm not able to program a static IP address into each device (or don't want to).

The DHCP protocol is still evolving under IPv6. It's a lot different from IPv4

- A device can configure itself automatically with a tool called **Stateless Address Autoconfiguration**. How does it know what address to give itself? Under IPv6, routers are automatically sending out "advertisements" over the network, telling devices what prefix they follow. A device learns the prefix for the network that it's on and then selects an IP address at random. Remember that the IPv6 address space is massive; the chance that a device chooses the same address as an existing device is small. Nevertheless, a device will check for conflicts. If there is one, the device selects a new address.

- One idea behind IPv6 was that any device could be reached from any device, regardless of whether it was on an internal or external network. Under IPv6, NAT is no longer necessary.

- One problem with IPv6 is that a mobile device can maintain the same IP address across multiple networks. This makes it easy to track. To avoid privacy concerns, mobile devices change their IP addresses often (at least every day).

- Even after a device assigns itself an IPv6 address, it might need some other data from the server, which it can obtain over DHCP.

- In a large network with multiple routers (such as the thousands of residential routers connected to an ISP's network), a router can automatically be assigned a prefix via DHCPv6. This is known as prefix delegation. A router asks for a prefix from the DHCPv6 server. Once assigned, the ISP routers send traffic to the router with the newly assigned prefix.

In the traditional DHCPv6, a device can request an IP address from a DHCPv6 server

- The device sends a **solicit** message asking for an IP address

- The DHCP server replies with an **advertise**, offering an IP address

- The device sends a **request**, requesting the IP address that was offered

- The server confirms that it has assigned the IP address, with a **reply**

We can skip all this DHCP and assign every device a **static** IP address. The static address is manually assigned to the device and doesn't change. We can create a network that uses both static and dynamic addresses.

What if I have a large distributed network but I only have one central DHCP server? I use a tool called a DHCP Relay. The **DHCP Relay** lives in the router. It listens to DHCP messages from the internal network and forwards them to an external DHCP server. It also receives DHCP messages from the external server and forwards them to requesting devices on the internal network. On a Cisco router, this is known as an **IP Helper Address**. It may also be called UDP Forwarding.

We must be careful to assign a static IP address

- That does not conflict with any addresses in the DHCP pool of the network. A DHCP server may assign the same IP address as a statically assigned device, which would result in a conflict.

- That is in the same subnet as the network. If our network is 192.168.0.0 to 192.168.0.255, and we assign the device an IP address of 10.0.0.1, then it won't be able to communicate with any other device.

- That contains all the required parameters including the gateway, subnet mask, and DNS servers. A device that is missing the gateway won't be able to communicate with devices on the outside network. A device that is missing the DNS won't be able to look up hostnames.

Remember that a computer understands addresses in numeric format (like 8.8.8.8) and a human understands text (like google.com). How does the computer know where google.com is (i.e. the IP address of the google.com server)? We use the **DNS (Domain Name Service)** to convert the human-readable address into a computer-readable address.

When I try to visit google.com, my computer calls up the nearest DNS and asks it to provide information about google.com. google.com is known as a **domain name** or a hostname. A DNS will contain a set of records about each domain name. Those records are given to the DNS by the owner of the name. The records for the domain is called a record set. What kind of information can it provide?

- **A or AAAA**. The **A (Address Mapping)** record tells us the IPv4 address of the server that is hosting the domain name. The **AAAA** record tells us the IPv6 address that is hosting the domain name.

- **TXT (SPF, DKIM)**. The **TXT (Text)** record tells us some text. Two common uses of TXT records
  - **SPF** or **Sender Policy Framework**. Think of an e-mail like a letter. It has a "to" address and a "from" address. I could send a fake letter and use a fake "from" address because nobody can verify that the "from" address is correct. An e-mail is the same. A spammer could spoof the "from" address and make it look somebody legitimate sent the e-mail. How can we stop this?

    If the legitimate sender has control over his domain name and server, he can create a Text entry called the SPF and put the IP address of his e-mail server in there. Then when we receive an e-mail from that sender, we can verify that it came from an e-mail server with an IP address matching the record.

When a recipient receives a message, he checks the IP address in the SPF belonging to the legitimate sender. If it matches the actual sender, then he knows that the e-mail is legitimate.

- o **DKIM** or **DomainKeys Identified Mail** is another way to identify an e-mail's legitimate sender. A user of DKIM creates a unique signature via public key cryptography. It's essentially a signature that can't be forged – it has two parts, a private key that only the sender knows, and a public key that recipients can use to verify his identity. The legitimate sender places a copy of the public key in DKIM. He uses the private key to digitally sign every e-mail he sends. When a recipient receives an e-mail, he verifies that the signature in the e-mail matches the public key in the record.

- SRV. The **SRV (Server)** record tells us about the location of servers that operate specific services. The server location includes an IP address or domain name and a port number. The domain name in an SRV record must itself have an A record in its own DNS record set or else it won't be located.

- MX. The **MX (Mail Exchanger)** record tells us the IP address or domain name of the mail server that receives e-mail on behalf of the domain. If my e-mail is hazim@hsmservices.ca and I host my own e-mail, then the record may point to my own server. If my e-mail is hosted by Gmail for example, my MX record may point to gmail.com.

When you send an e-mail, your e-mail program (or SMTP server) will query the MX records for each recipients' address so that it knows where to send the message.

The domain name in an MX record must have its own record in its own record set, or else it won't be located.

- **CNAME** or **Canonical Name** points one domain name to another. The purpose of a CNAME record is to point one name to another. The CNAME record must itself have an A name record.

For example, foo.example.com can point to bar.example.com. bar.example.com must have an A record in its own record set or else it won't be located.

When a computer receives a CNAME reply, it must then look for the corresponding A record.

- **NS** or **Name Server**. The NS record tells us which DNS server is **authoritative** for the domain. The owner of a domain name maintains DNS records for his name on an authoritative name server. The authoritative name server has the most accurate records for that specific name. A name server can be authoritative for one or more domain names.

  Since the internet is distributed, DNS servers operated by other users might copy the records from the authoritative name server and respond to queries from devices close to them. When you access a website, your computer won't necessarily query the authoritative name server for that site. It may query a local nameserver operated by your organization or ISP.

- **PTR** or **Pointer Record**. A Pointer record allows a user to perform a reverse DNS lookup. PTR Records are stored under the IP address of the server, not the domain name.

- **SOA** or **Start of Authority Record**. The SOA gives us information about which DNS is authoritative for the domain. When our domain name server wants an update to the record, it checks the SOA to determine which DNS server to check.

  The SOA contains a serial number. Each time the DNS record is updated, the SOA serial number is increased by one. When a client wants to transfer its DNS record to another server, it checks the serial number first. If the server does not have the current version of the record, then the transfer is authorized. This is known as a **Zone Transfer**.

A **Reverse DNS lookup** is when we have an IP address and want to know which domain name it belongs to. An IP address may belong to multiple domain names. The PTR record is used for the Reverse DNS lookup.

We can obtain the domain name corresponding to an IP address by querying the domain name **in-addr.arpa**. If we want to know the domain name for the IP address 1.2.3.4, we would query the name:

4.3.2.1.in-addr.arpa

Notice that we prepended the IP address in reverse to the front of the in-addr.arpa domain name. This is opposed to the **Forward DNS lookup** that we come to expect.

To provide load balancing and redundancy, each DNS record can contain multiple entries. We can give each entry a different priority. For example, we might have multiple servers to handle our e-mail or website hosting. In case one server is down or can't handle the traffic, then the other servers can run.

An **internal DNS** is one that is operated by an organization for use on its internal network. A network might have devices that are accessible internally such as servers, switches, and printers. Each device is assigned a unique hostname on the network. The internal DNS server provides users with DNS records corresponding to these internal devices. A user may need to access both internal devices and external hosts. Therefore, the user may need to program his computer to query both an internal DNS server and an **external DNS** server. The external DNS provides information about hosts that are available to the public (on the internet). It is possible for an internal DNS to also be an external DNS.

An organization may choose to host its DNS with a third party. Examples of **third-party DNS** include Amazon (AWS) Route 53 and CloudFlare. A third-party DNS is scalable and can provide inquiries to many users at the same time. In addition, a third-party DNS is centrally located so that updates to the DNS propagate across the internet quickly.

The hierarchy of a DNS starts at the **root domain name server**. There are only 13 root servers. The servers provide responses to the "root" domain (i.e. .com, .net, .org). When a computer looks up a domain name, it starts at the right side and looks up the authoritative name server for the root.

Then the computer checks the **authoritative server**, which is maintained by the owner of the domain name. Below the authoritative server are servers operated by national internet service providers. They aggregate DNS records from the different authoritative servers. Below them are servers operated by local ISPs. Below them are servers operated by organizations for local networks.

When we query a DNS server, we might start at the local level. If the local server doesn't have an answer, we check at the next level. If it doesn't have an answer, we continue working our way to the top until we reach the authoritative server.

In a **recursive DNS** search, your computer makes a query with the DNS server. If the DNS server doesn't have an answer, it checks the next higher up server (and up and up) until it finds an answer. It might cache the answer in case other computers request the same DNS record.

In an **iterative DNS** search, your computer makes a request from the DNS server. If the DNS server doesn't have an answer, it gives your computer the IP address of the higher up server. Your computer then makes the query with the higher up server. If it doesn't receive an answer, it continues to make queries up the DNS chain until it reaches the authoritative server.

Each DNS record has a **TTL** or **Time To Live**. This is a number that tells the non-authoritative DNS servers the length of time (in seconds) until a record expires. For example, if a TTL is 3600, then the DNS record expires after one hour. If my local DNS server obtains authoritative DNS records from google.com's DNS, and the TTL is one hour, then it should check with the google DNS again for updated records after one hour. The TTL is set by the authoritative name server. The process of maintaining local DNS records is called **DNS caching**.

If we make the TTL long, then any changes will take a long time to propagate across the entire internet. If we make the TTL short, then changes will propagate quickly, but our DNS server will experience more queries because lower level name servers are requesting updates more frequently.

NTP or **Network Time Protocol** allows network devices to synchronize their clocks. The current version is NTPv4. It is vital that network devices have the same time or else they will not be able to communicate with each other (messages will appear like they are sent or received at the wrong time).

NTP allows network-connected devices to sync their clocks, to within a few milliseconds of UTC (universal time). NTP uses a clock synchronization algorithm, which allows it to function accurately even when the network has high latency. Think about it. If I ask you what time it is, and at exactly 10:30:00AM, you reply that it's 10:30:00AM, but it takes 15 seconds for me to receive your reply, then I will think it is 10:30:00AM when it's really 10:30:15AM.

When a computer asks another computer what time it is, it also accounts for the delay in receiving a response.

NTP can obtain the time from a central server or from a peer.

NTP is hierarchical. A device on a local network can obtain an accurate time from an external server and then update other local devices.

The **stratum** tells us the hierarchy of a device. The stratum level can be from 0 to 15. The highest-level device has a stratum of 0. It will be a directly connected device such as a GPS antenna. A device with a stratum of 0 cannot communicate with another network device. Instead it communicates with a network-connected device that has a stratum of one. Devices that receive their time from a stratum one device have a stratum of two. Devices that receive their time from a stratum two device have a stratum of three, and so on.

An **NTP server** is a device that provides the time to other devices. An **NTP client** is a device that receives the time from an NTP server.

1.7 Explain basic corporate and datacenter network architecture

- *Three-Tiered*
    - *Core*
    - *Distribution/Aggregation Layer*
    - *Access/Edge*
- *Software-Defined Network*
    - *Application Layer*
    - *Control Layer*
    - *Infrastructure Layer*
    - *Management Plane*
- *Spine and Leaf*
    - *Software-Defined Network*
    - *Top-of-Rack Switching*
    - *Backbone*
- *Traffic Flows*
    - *North-South*
    - *East-West*
- *Branch Office vs On-Premises Datacenter vs Colocation*
- *Storage Area Networks*
    - *Connection Types*
        - *Fiber Channel over Ethernet (FCoE)*
        - *Fiber Channel*
        - *Internet Small Computer Systems Interface (iSCSI)*

We are going to look at some more physical network designs. Remember earlier that we had a campus network with three layers? This is a common design in larger networks and consists of three layers.

- **Core** – the core layer is the backbone of the network. It consists of more advanced switches, which may connect to a router. Core switches connect to the aggregation switches.

- **Aggregation** – also known as the Distribution layer. This consists of switches that connect the core with the edge.

- **Edge** – the edge switches are what users connect to. They are also known as access switches.

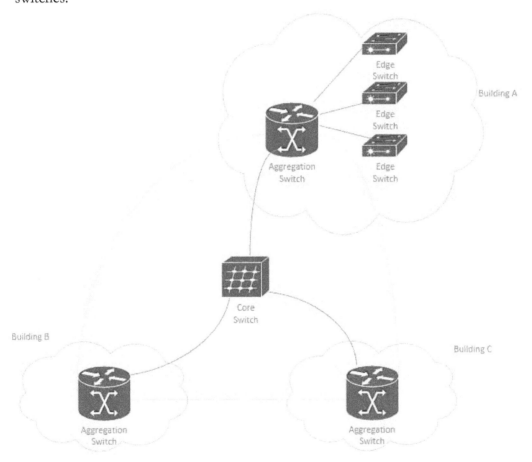

In a physically large network, having a single core switch would not be possible because it would require a data cable to be run from each part of the facility. In a small network, we may only have one or two layers of switches.

There may be redundant links between each set of switches. When we design our network, we should think about the amount of traffic passing through each switch and between the switches. Ideally, most traffic moves between different devices on the same set of access switches.

The second type of network is a **Spine-Leaf**. A spine-leaf network can scale better than a three-tier network. Typically, a Spine-Leaf network contains two layers of switches – the Leaf layer connects directly to user devices, while the Spine connects directly to Leaf switches only. No leaf switch connects to another and no spine switch connects to another. We can enlarge the network by adding more spines and more leaves.

A leaf can connect to multiple spines. If the network is small, the leaf might connect to all the spines. Otherwise, it may only connect to some of the spines. The spine is known as the **backbone**. The path that the traffic takes (which spine a leaf chooses to send fabric to) is chosen at random. This ensures that no spines become overloaded. If a spine fails, the network will continue to function.

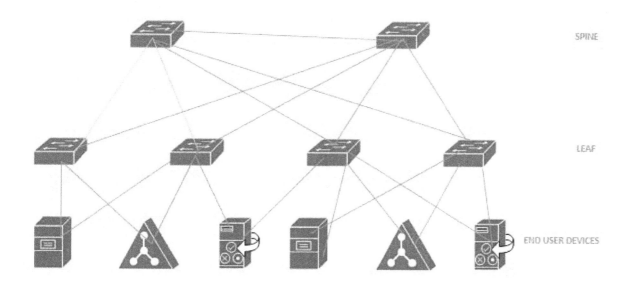

When we have a data center with multiple racks, we might decide to install a switch at the top of each rack. This is known as **top of rack switching**. The switch at the top of the rack is an edge switch and provides access to the devices in the rack. It connects back to an aggregation switch (or to multiple spine switches if we are using the spine-leaf configuration).

In a **software-defined network,** we don't have to worry as much about the physical infrastructure. In other words, in a traditional network, each network device has to be programmed separately, and each network device makes independent decisions about how to forward traffic. In an SDN, control of the network is separate from the physical infrastructure.

We create a set of rules that the software then implements across the entire network.

We can think of the SDN as a set of layers

- **Application Layer** – the application layer contains the rules that manage the network and forward traffic. We create rules in the application layer.

- **Control Layer** – the control layer connects the application layer to the infrastructure layer. The connection between the controller and the application is called the Northbound interface. The connection between the controller and the infrastructure layer is called the Southbound interface.

  The controller takes information from the application layer and translates it into the actual commands that the infrastructure layer will use to forward traffic.

- **Infrastructure Layer** – the infrastructure layer contains the physical devices that are connected. These devices forward traffic based on information given to them by the control layer. The network's actual capacity is limited to what the infrastructure layer can provide. The infrastructure layer may take the form of a Spine-Leaf or Three-Tier, but usually takes the form of a Spine-Leaf.

- **Management Plane** – the management plane contains the configuration information for the network. It is separate from the plane that contains the data being forwarded.

- **Data Plane** – the data plane contains the data that the network is forwarding.

Traffic moving up from the infrastructure layer to the application layer is considered moving "north" while traffic moving from the application layer down to the infrastructure layer is moving "south". Traffic moving between devices is considered moving East-West (i.e. from server to server).

The next topic we will look at is where we should put our data center and/or server infrastructure. There are four options.

- **Branch Office** – If we have an organization with several offices, we can group them into branch offices and head offices. The branch offices are smaller. A branch office is one that might be too small to have dedicated infrastructure. It might have a "branch router" and connect back to the main office via a WAN or a VPN. We might store our main servers in the head office, but users can still access them via the WAN or VPN.

- **On Premise** – We can build a data center in our office. It can be a separate room or separate building. A good data center has multiple internet connections to manage incoming and outgoing connections, battery back up for power, and redundant power supplies. It may also have security and Before we build a data center we must consider

  o Whether we have enough equipment to justify the cost of the construction

  o The cost of cooling the data center.

  o The cost of powering the data center

  o Whether we have dedicated staff to operate the data center

  o Whether we have adequate internet connections to support the data center

  o Whether the function of the infrastructure and the data is too sensitive to outsource to a third party

- **Colocation** – If we can't justify the cost of an on-premise data center, we might outsource it to a colocation. A colocation is where another organization builds a data center and rents out portions of it to other customers. The colocation may charge a flat rate per square foot or per rack unit. The colocation may provide internet connectivity or may require us to provide the connectivity. We are responsible for supplying, installing, and maintaining all of the equipment at the colocation.

- **Cloud** – The cloud is where we outsource our infrastructure to a third party. We don't have to worry about the infrastructure, internet, electricity, or physical devices. We will learn more about the cloud in the next section.

The last topic covers **Storage Area Networks** or SANs. When you buy a computer, it will come with a hard drive, which hopefully will have enough capacity to store your data. When you buy a server, it might come with several hard drives, which will hopefully have enough capacity to store your data. What happens when you have too much data and not enough storage capacity? You can buy more servers, but servers are inefficient for storing large volumes of data. Why? A server has other expensive components such as processors and RAM, which are good for processing data. When the purpose of the server is to just store data, we end up wasting money on the other hardware. Servers also usually have limited network connections that can become overloaded.

The solution? A storage appliance. A storage appliance is like a giant box with a large data storage capacity. In reality, it is a special-purpose server with many hard drives. Its only purpose is to store data. When connected to a network, the storage appliance will allow multiple users to store their data on it. We can create multiple "virtual" drives on the storage appliance, each of which can span multiple physical drives. A user or server can connect to a virtual drive on the network almost in the same process as if it were physically connected to his computer.

A popular storage appliance is the NetApp. It's basically a box of hard drives. It's more complicated than that, but entire books have been written on storage appliances.

A Storage Area Network uses some of the same principles as an ethernet network. A server might connect to both a normal ethernet network (for communicating with users) and a storage area network (for communicating with the storage appliances).

Some concepts

- A **Host Bus Adapter** or **HBA** is like a network interface card. It connects the server to the storage area network. The HBA operates on the first layer, known as the **Host Layer**.

- A **SAN Switch** is like an ethernet switch, but it forwards traffic between devices on the storage are network

- We call the SAN network devices (switches, routers, and cables) the **fabric**

- Each device in the SAN has a hardcoded World-Wide Name (WWN) which is like a MAC address in the ethernet world. The switch uses the WWN to route traffic between devices. The switch operates on the second layer, known as the **Fabric Layer**.

- Switches and HBAs don't understand what files are. They only see data moving as "blocks", or groups of 0's and 1's.

- SAN networks can operate over copper or fiber links

- The third layer is known as the **Storage Layer**.

- Each storage appliance is assigned a unique LUN or **Logical Unit Number**. A storage appliance is a box of hard disk drives. We can subdivide a storage appliance into multiple partitions and assign each partition a unique LUN.

- Each server (or device that can read from or write to a storage appliance) is assigned a LUN.

- We can use the LUN to restrict access from specific servers to specific storage locations. The storage appliance maintains an access control list, which determines (on a LUN by LUN basis) which devices can access each of the storage appliance's LUNs.

There are many network protocols that can be used for communicating over a SAN

- FCoE or Fiber Channel over Ethernet

- Fiber Channel Protocol

- iSCSI

- SCSI RDMA Protocol

The SAN does not provide "file level" storage, only "block level" storage. That is, a server can't call up the storage appliance and say something like "give me the file called DraftProposal.docx", because the storage appliance doesn't know what files are.

Instead, SAN says to the server, "here is a bunch of storage space, do what you want with it". The server says, "here is a bunch of data in the form of 0's and 1's, put them there, there, and there". The server must be able to manage the file system. When a user asks the server for the file DraftProposal.docx, the server asks itself "where did I put DraftProposal.docx…oh yeah…I put there, there, and there?". The server treats the storage appliance like its own hard drive. It may create a file allocation table on the storage appliance to help itself find files.

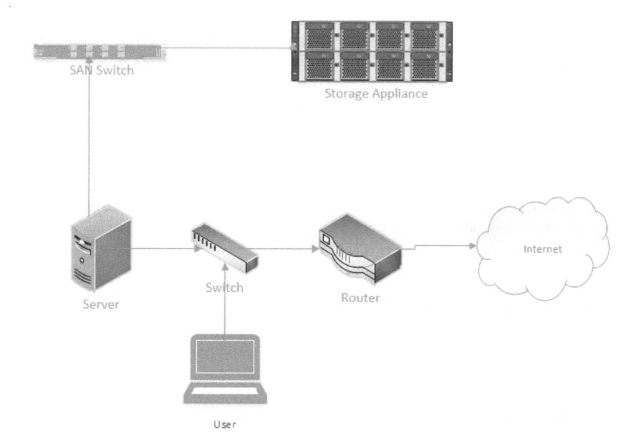

In a less-complicated environment, we could use a NAS or Network Attached Storage device. Like a storage appliance, a NAS is a box of hard disk drives. But unlike a storage appliance, a NAS connects to the ethernet and provides file level storage. A NAS is more like a server that can store data (and does nothing else).

Some protocols that can be used with a NAS

- Apple File System

- Network File System

- FTP

- HTTP

- SFTP

- Server Message Block

Let's dig deeper into the storage appliance's connections.

If we didn't want to build out a separate storage area network, we could use **FCoE** or **Fiber Channel over Ethernet** to transmit all our storage data on our existing ethernet network.

FCoE uses 10 Gbit Ethernet to communicate. Just like ethernet, fiber channel uses frames to communicate. When transmitted over FCoE, each fiber channel frame is encapsulated (packaged) inside an ethernet frame, transmitted to the recipient, and then deencapsulated by the recipient.

Each device connected to an ethernet network must have its fiber channel name mapped to a unique MAC address, so that the ethernet network knows where to deliver the data. This can be completed by a **converged network adapter** or **CNA**. A CNA is a device that contains a host bus adapter and an ethernet adapter.

A **Fiber Channel** network communicates between 1 Gbit/s and 128 Gbit/s via the Fiber Channel Protocol. We can create the following types of connections

- **Point-to-Point**: two devices communicate with each other through a direct cable connection

- **Arbitrated Loop**: devices are connected in a loop. The failure of a single device or link will cause all devices in the loop to stop communicating. This connection type is no longer used.

- **Switched Fabric**: devices are connected to a SAN switch. The fabric works like an ethernet network and can scale to tens of thousands of devices.

There are five layers in fiber channel

- The Physical Layer (Layer 0), which includes the physical connections

- The Coding Layer (Layer 1), which includes the transmission/creation of signals

- The Protocol Layer, known as the fabric (Layer 2), which transmits the data frames

- The Common Services Layer (Layer 3), which is not currently used but can be used for RAID or encryption if the protocol is further developed

- The Protocol Mapping Layer (Layer 4), which is used by protocols such as NVMe and SCSI

We use SFPs, SFP+s, and QSFPs with fiber optic cables to connect the various devices in a Fiber Channel network.

iSCSI or **Internet Small Computer Systems Interface** is another network protocol that allows storage devices and servers to communicate. iSCSI operates over the existing ethernet network without the need for special cabling or adapters. We typically use iSCSI for two purposes

- Centralize our data storage to one or several storage appliances

- Mirror an entire data storage appliance to an appliance in another location to protect in the event of a disaster

The different iSCSI devices

- **Initiator**. An initiator is a client device such as a computer or server. A software application or driver sends commands over the device's ethernet adapter in the iSCSI format. For faster communications, a hardware iSCSI host bus adapter can be used.

- **Target**. A target is a storage device such as a server or storage appliance. A device can be both an initiator and a target.

- Like Fiber Channel, each device is given a LUN or Logical Unit Number.

Some features of iSCSI

- **Network Booting**. A device can boot from a network operating system and then access an iSCSI target to store and retrieve its data. When the computer boots, instead of looking at its hard disk for the operating system, it contacts a DHCP server that contains a boot image of an operating system. The DHCP server uses the device's MAC address to forward it to the correct iSCSI device. The iSCSI drive is then mounted to the computer as a local drive.

- iSCSI uses ports 860 and 3260

Security Problems

- iSCSI devices authenticate via CHAP by default but can use other protocols. CHAP is not secure. We will learn more about CHAP later.

- iSCSI devices can be connected over a VLAN so that they are logically isolated from unauthorized users or devices. If we automatically trust all the devices on the VLAN, then a compromised device can gain access to the entire system.

- iSCSI devices can be connected over a separate physical network. If we trust all devices on the physical network, then a compromised device can gain access to the entire system.

- An eavesdropper can spy on the data being transferred over the iSCSI network if the data is not encrypted (and it frequently isn't).

InfiniBand is another storage area network connection format. InfiniBand is typically used by supercomputers that need a very high level of data transfer and a low latency. It can support transfer rates of up to 3000 Gbit/s. It uses QSFP connectors and copper or fiber cables.

We can also transfer Ethernet over an InfiniBand network.

1.8 Summarize Cloud Concepts and Connectivity Options

- *Deployment Models*
  - *Public*
  - *Private*
  - *Hybrid*
  - *Community*
- *Service Models*
  - *Software as a Service (SaaS)*
  - *Infrastructure as a Service (IaaS)*
  - *Platform as a Service (PaaS)*
  - *Desktop as a Service (DaaS)*
- *Infrastructure as Code*
  - *Automation/Orchestration*
- *Connectivity Options*
  - *Virtual Private Network (VPN)*
  - *Private-Direct Connection to Cloud Provider*
- *Multitenancy*
- *Elasticity*
- *Scalability*
- *Security Implications*

Types of Service

What is the cloud? It's a concept where we outsource our computing resources to a third party and then connect to it remotely. Somebody else manages our infrastructure and we don't have to worry about it (in theory). How do we pay for the cloud? How do we receive services? There are a few general models.

SaaS or **Software as a Service** is a concept where we pay for the right to use a software application. Somebody else takes care of writing the software, hosting the software, and backing up the data. Our only responsibility is to use the software. The software might be entirely web based or include components that are installed on our computers/phones. We don't have to worry about the physical hardware. Examples of SaaS include Salesforce, Microsoft Exchange Online, and Office 365. SaaS is typically billed on a per user per month basis.

IaaS or **Infrastructure as a Service** is a concept where we pay for the right to use different hardware components. For example, we can rent different server types from Amazon Web Services' EC2, or we could rent DNS services from Route 53. IaaS is usually charged on a per device per hour (or per month) basis. For example, a server might cost $0.35 per hour. If I buy an EC2 server it may come with a license for an operating system, such as Windows Server 2019 (for a higher hourly rate), or I could buy it "bare metal" and install my own operating system.

BYOL (**Bring Your Own License**) is a concept where we can transfer our operating system licenses to the cloud infrastructure. This avoids us having to pay a monthly rental cost for operating system licenses that we already own. A Windows Server license could cost upwards of thousands of dollars per server.

The cloud allows us to mix and match different hardware components so that we can build the type of infrastructure that we require, but we usually have to choose from the hardware combinations that the cloud service provider has. IaaS allows us to pay for only what we use. If we use a server for five hours, we pay for five hours (unless the service provider has minimum charges).

Increasingly, vendors of proprietary network equipment such as Cisco and Bomgar sell virtual images of their equipment that can be loaded into the cloud. Thus, you can build an entire virtual LAN in the cloud complete with servers, routers, firewalls, and load balancers, and pay for what you use, without having to touch any physical infrastructure.

PaaS or **Platform as a Service** is a hybrid between the SaaS and IaaS. In PaaS, we don't have to worry about the hardware. We simply upload the applications we want, and the cloud provisions the necessary hardware to run them. We are still responsible for configuring the applications and backing up their data. An example is Amazon Hadoop. PaaS is typically billed on a per hour per resource basis. For example, we could be billed for each GB of data we store each month, or we could be billed for processing capacity we use. We can reduce our costs by using or writing more efficient applications.

DaaS or **Desktop as a Service** is a new offering where an office's computing infrastructure is stored in the cloud. It is also known as Desktop Virtualization. You can think of it like having a monitor, mouse, and keyboard at your desk but no computer. Your actual computer is in the cloud. In reality, you have a computer or thin client (a computer with no operating system). But your files, software applications, and desktop are located on a cloud server. You remotely connect to the cloud server via RDP, Citrix, or another type of application.

The main benefits of DaaS

- Centralized hardware – our computing infrastructure is stored in the cloud. One server might host desktops for twenty to fifty people. This reduces the need for computer resources.

- Standardized hardware – since each user needs only a thin client or basic computer, monitor, mouse and keyboard, we can use cheaper standardized hardware. We don't need to stock multiple types of devices or spend money on expensive desktops.

- Security – the devices that users use to connect to the remote desktop won't store any data so we don't have to worry about data leaks if they getting lost or stolen.

- Flexibility – you can log in to your desktop from multiple computers and not lose any data or program sessions. You will resume work exactly where you left off.

- Disaster recovery – we can move our workforce to another location and quickly have them back to work. Users can also work from home. The computing infrastructure is centralized, and cloud technology allows us to replicate it to multiple zones.

The main disadvantages

- Standardized hardware – users are forced to use a standard type of computer hardware

- Internet access – users are unable to use the DaaS when on the road or when access to the internet is interrupted. When the latency is too high (poor internet connection quality) the user experience will be affected.

The cloud is defined by three concepts

- **Multitenancy** – multiple users and customers have access to the same physical infrastructure or software. When you rent a server from AWS, you are renting a portion the physical infrastructure in the AWS data center. You might be renting a virtual server that is hosted on a physical server, and that physical server might have several other virtual servers belonging to other clients.

- **Scalability** – we can increase the workload without affecting performance of the application. We can do this by ensuring that we have enough capacity in our hardware (virtual hardware) for our application to grow. Scalability relates to the software layer in that the software layer can grow without issues either using the existing hardware or with additional hardware. A scalable system guarantees that the software will continue to function at a peak load (there is enough hardware available).

- **Elasticity** – elasticity ensures that we fit the amount of resources to the demand posed by the software. Elasticity grows or shrinks the underlying hardware in response to demand from the application.

Elasticity is more cost effective than scalability because we only pay for what we use, whereas scalability requires us to pay for the maximum amount of resources that we will eventually require. Elasticity can be difficult to implement if we are not able to predict the amount of resources that will be required or if we are unable to add resources in real time.

For example, if our application requires 100 servers during regular operation and 200 servers at peak capacity, we can always ensure scalability by having 200 servers. If we need 101 servers, then we already have capacity. If we need 102 servers, then we have capacity. As the needs of the application grows, the underlying hardware is already available to keep it operating. The problem is that we are paying for 200 servers even when we are only using 100 of them.

With elasticity, we keep 100 servers until we need 101 servers. Then we add another server. When we need 102 servers, we add another server, and so on. The problem is that the time between when we realize that we need 101 servers and the time that we buy another server is time that the application will perform poorly.

The best way to implement elasticity is to maintain a buffer zone. We should think about how rapidly the needs of the application will change and build a buffer zone based on that time. For example, if we have a buffer of two servers, then when we need 100 servers, we rent 102 servers. When we need 101 servers, we add another server and now we have 103 servers, and so on. When the application demand drops, and we only need 100 servers, we shut down one server, and have only 102 servers.

Cloud Delivery Models

There are different cloud models.

A **public cloud** is available to the public. The hardware resources inside a public cloud are shared amongst all customers, which improves efficiency and reduces cost. Multiple customers may be provided access to the same physical server without realizing it (cloud software should prevent data leaks)

A **private cloud** is built by one organization for its internal use. A large organization can use a private cloud to share resources amongst different departments. For example, a large city can merge the computing resources of its engineering, fire, police, and road repair departments. Instead of having each department purchase and maintain its own hardware, all the departments pool their resources, resulting in reduced costs. Each department can rent a portion of the cloud and be charged accordingly.

A **hybrid cloud** is a mix of a public cloud and a private cloud. A company may decide that some applications are t*oo sensitive to host on a public cloud, or that some applications will not run properly when they are off site but would like to take advantage of the public cloud. Applications/infrastructure that can run on the public cloud are placed there, and remaining applications/infrastructure are placed on a private cloud.

Infrastructure as Code (IaC) is a concept where we can deploy servers and other infrastructure through software code instead of manually setting them up. The cloud computing provider physically installs hardware including large servers and storage appliances. Then they make available virtual "instances" of server types. We can then write code to deploy the specific instances that we need.

IaC has some advantages

- We can deploy infrastructure quickly and automatically

- We can deploy infrastructure in a standardized manner – that means that there is less room for human error

- If we are building an application (such as a website) that must scale up and down frequently, we can write code to deploy more infrastructure when we need it and shut them down. This allows us to pay for only the infrastructure that we need at the time that we need it.

Connectivity Methods / Relationship Between Local and Cloud Resources

How do we connect to the cloud? Devices in the cloud might have their own public IP addresses. An internet connection is the easiest way. We could connect to a cloud server via Remote Desktop Protocol, or we could connect to a database via SSH. Other types of applications may have web-based interfaces.

What if my cloud resources are vital to the organization or what if I need to move large amounts of data? I could create a direct connection between the cloud and the local network via a WAN or VPN. The cloud service provider would need to set up a WAN or VPN connector on their own network so that the two networks can communicate. With a WAN or VPN, devices in the cloud behave like they are on the local network. This is the best approach for a corporate cloud.

If you need to move lots of data into the cloud, you can physically ship your storage appliances (or hard drives) to the cloud where they can be copied. AWS (Amazon Web Services) offers a semi-trailer called the Snowmobile that is full of storage appliances. They drive it to your office. You connect it to your network and fill it with data. Then AWS takes the semi-trailer back to their data center and unloads the data into your account. The Snowmobile can store up to 100PB of data.

Security Implications/Considerations

How can we protect our cloud information? Keep in mind that the cloud is under the physical control of a third party and that they might be able to access it, and that we are sharing the same physical hardware with other users. Consider the following

- Use multi-factor authentication when connecting to the cloud

- Set up firewalls to protect the cloud infrastructure and deny all traffic except for what is necessary

- Internal devices such as database servers should only connect to other cloud devices and not the internet

- Install required security updates regularly

- Use dedicated hardware (hardware not shared with other users) when available and cost-effective. This reduces the risk that another user can see your data if there is a security hole in the underlying hypervisor.

- Encrypt all data in use and at rest, and store decryption keys externally where possible

- Ensure that you have the legal right to store customer data in the cloud. It may be illegal to transfer customer's personal information to a cloud if it is in a different country than your own.

- Ensure that the cloud storage provider is audited and perform inspections of their facility if possible.

Part C: N10-008 2.0 Network Implementations

2.1 Compare and contrast various devices, their features, and their appropriate placement on the network

- *Networking Devices*
  - *Layer 2 Switch*
  - *Layer 3 Capable Switch*
  - *Router*
  - *Hub*
  - *Access Point*
  - *Bridge*
  - *Wireless LAN Controller*
  - *Load Balancer*
  - *Proxy Server*
  - *Cable Modem*
  - *DSL Modem*
  - *Repeater*
  - *Voice Gateway*
  - *Media Converter*
  - *Intrusion Prevention System (IPS) / Intrusion Detection System (IDS)*
  - *Firewall*
  - *VPN Headend*
- *Networked Devices*
  - *Voice over Internet Protocol (VoIP) Phone*
  - *Printer*
  - *Physical Access Control Devices*
  - *Cameras*
  - *Heating, Ventilation, and Air Conditioning (HVAC) Sensors*
  - *Internet of Things (IoT)*
    - *Refrigerator*
    - *Smart Speakers*
    - *Smart Thermostats*
    - *Smart Doorbells*
  - *Industrial Control Systems / Supervisory Control and Data Acquisition (SCADA)*

Now that we know a bit about how devices communicate and a bit about the wiring, let's think about all the different devices we need to set up a network. The first device is a **firewall**.

A firewall monitors and filters traffic on a network.

A firewall sits between the internet (WAN) and the local network (LAN). A firewall could also sit between different segments of a LAN. For example, a firewall could sit between a group of servers and the remainder of the network.

A firewall could be hardware-based or software-based. A firewall could be a component of a larger network device such as a router. In a large organization where a great deal of traffic passes through the network, a large, hardware-based firewall must be installed. Firewalls are rated based on the volume of traffic that they can handle. Of course, more complicated configurations can reduce the amount of traffic that a firewall can handle. If the firewall has to evaluate ten rules per packet, it will operate faster than if it has to evaluate one-hundred rules per packet.

Common firewall brands include

- Sonicwall

- Cisco ASA (Adaptive Security Appliance)

- Fortigate

- Cisco Meraki MX

Configuration of a firewall may be

- Through a console (requiring special commands)

- Through a web-based GUI or software-based GUI

- Automatically through the cloud, which is useful for organizations that deploy dozens, hundreds, or thousands of devices

An organization may select a firewall brand based on their existing network infrastructure. For example, if the customer uses Cisco switches and routers in their network, they may choose to install Cisco ASA firewalls as well.

There are four components to a firewall configuration

- **ACL** or **Access Control List**. The Access Control List is a set of rules for what traffic is permitted to pass and what traffic is not permitted. There are many types of rules, based on

  - Source IP address. Where is the traffic coming from? The source IP address could be on the LAN or on the WAN. It could be a specific IP address or a range of addresses.

  - Destination IP address. Where is the traffic going? The destination IP address could be on the LAN or on the WAN. It could be a specific IP address or a range of addresses.

  - Source Port Number. What is the port number of the source traffic? The source port could be on the LAN or on the WAN. It could be a specific port or a range of ports.

  - Destination Port Number. What is the port number of the destination traffic? The destination port could be on the LAN or on the WAN. It could be a specific port or a range of ports.

  - Username. Access Control Lists can be user-based. Permissions can be granted or denied to specific users based on their needs in the organization. For example, guests can be permitted to access only the internet and not resources such as remote desktop or SQL servers.

  - Rules can be specific or could combine a combination of parameters

    - For example, a rule could say 'Allow traffic from 10.1.1.1, port 5 to the range of IPs 192.168.3.0 to 192.168.3.255'. All traffic received from 10.1.1.1 port 5 will be permitted to access destinations in the range of 192.168.3.0 to 192.168.3.255. Traffic from other source IP addresses and/or ports will be rejected. Traffic from 10.1.1.1 to destinations outside of 192.168.3.0 and 192.168.3.255 will be rejected.

    - **Always Allow**. An Always Allow rule allows all traffic matching a rule. For example, "always allow traffic from the source IP 10.1.1.1". All traffic from 10.1.1.1 will be permitted regardless of the port number or destination.

    - **Always Deny**. An Always Deny rule denies all traffic matching a rule. For example, "always deny traffic from the source IP 10.1.1.1". All traffic from 10.1.1.1 will be denied regardless of the port number or destination.

o Order of Operations

  ▪ A firewall could have dozens or thousands of rules. The rules are ranked in order of priority.

  ▪ When the firewall receives a piece of traffic, it starts checking the rules in order until it finds one that matches the traffic's source and destination. It then applies that rule to the traffic.

  ▪ The firewall will only apply one rule to a piece of traffic. Once that rule is applied, the firewall stops checking additional rules.

  ▪ It is important to put the rules in logical order so that traffic is not accidentally accepted or rejected. When a firewall receives a piece of traffic that does not match any rules, it will either allow or reject the traffic based on its configuration.

  ▪ Many firewalls are preconfigured with two default rules

      • Always allow traffic with a source inside the network (LAN)

      • Always reject traffic with a source outside the network (WAN)

  ▪ The two default rules should be put at the bottom of the list.

      • The first rule (allowing all traffic from inside the LAN) is dangerous because users cannot be trusted to access only safe resources on the internet. It should be modified (broken down) into two rules.

          o Always allow traffic with a

              ▪ Source inside the network (LAN)

              ▪ Destination outside the network (WAN)

              ▪ Limited to specific ports outside the network (port 80, port 443, port 3306, etc.). The specific ports should be based on resources that users need to access.

o Always deny traffic

- Source inside the network (LAN)

- Destination outside the network (WAN)

- This rule applies second; any traffic not matching the previous rule will be denied

- Application-Based vs Network-Based

  o An application-based firewall will analyse traffic on a deeper level than a network-based firewall

  o The network-based firewall looks at traffic source and destination IP addresses, but the application-based firewall also looks at its contents

  o The application-based firewall looks at the content of each packet before applying a rule.

  o An analogy is a person who is screening mail. A network-based firewall would look at the to and from addresses on the envelope before deciding whether to forward the mail. An application-based firewall would open each envelope and look at the contents before deciding whether to forward the mail.

  o Application-based firewalls can slow down traffic because they are analyzing the contents of each packet, which takes longer.

- Stateful vs Stateless

  o Consider that almost all traffic on the internet is two-way traffic. When a user downloads a file from the internet, that file download is two-way. The downloader's computer first makes a request to the server hosting the file (the sender). The sender's computer breaks the file into packets and sends them one at a time. Each time the downloader's computer receives a packet, it acknowledges receipt by sending a message. This is known as a connection (from TCP/IP).

  o One party is responsible for originating each connection. In this case, the person who downloaded the file originated the connection (the person who is inside the network).

o A stateless firewall applies rules based only on the source and destination IP addresses and ports of the packets, but a stateful firewall will identify which party originated the connection (whether that party was inside the network or outside), and then block or allow it based on the source. A packet that is normally permitted or denied by an ACL may be denied or permitted by a stateful firewall.

o A stateful firewall requires additional hardware to process the decision making.

- Implicit Deny

  o As mentioned previously, a firewall lists its rules in order and applies the first rule that matches the traffic

  o If the traffic does not match any rule, the firewall should deny it

  o This is known as "**implicit deny**"

  o The last rule in the list should be to deny all traffic

Cloud-Based Firewalls

Newer firewalls such as Fortigates and Cisco Meraki MX Series routers connect to the cloud. The cloud allows them to

- Automatically receive firmware updates

- Automatically download and update their configuration (and allow an administrator to configure multiple devices at the same time)

- Share threat intelligence data, even across organizations. For example, if a firewall detects a threat, it can upload the data to the cloud, where it is shared by many firewalls across the organization.

NGFW/Layer 7 Firewall

A NGFW or Next Generation Firewall, also known as a Layer 7 Firewall, is part of the third generation of firewalls. It can perform deep packet inspection and can be combined with a RADIUS server, quality of service management, and website filter.

Why do we need a NGFW? Security threats are becoming more complicated. The traditional firewall rules block traffic to/from specific addresses and ports. That's not good enough anymore, because bad traffic can come in disguised as good traffic. Legitimate, trusted devices can become infected and used to launch attacks. The NGFW can look inside the traffic – not just at its source or destination – to decide whether it is legitimate.

An NGFW can also verify the identity of the user sending or receiving the traffic.

Router

A **router** connects two or more networks together. A router receives packets of data (from inside and outside the network) and then decides where to forward the packets to.

A router will contain a routing table (a set of static routes), which tell it where to send data based on the subnet of its destination address. In a simple setup, a router may only have one destination to send data to.

The most common type of router security is an ACL or Access Control List. An ACL is a list of source subnets (networks) and their permitted destinations. Like a set of firewall rules, an ACL check each data packet against the ACL and apply the first rule that matches.

A rule can be "always allow" or "always deny". For example

- Always deny traffic from addresses in the range of 252.252.252.0 to 252.252.252.255

- Always allow traffic from 192.168.2.1

A rule can apply to one or more router interfaces and to one or both directions. Each router manufacturer may have a different scheme for configuring a router ACL, but the concept is the same.

Router antispoofing is a process to prevent fake routers from joining the network. Remember that a rogue user could connect his own router to the network and attempt to route the traffic somewhere else.

More advanced routers such as Cisco ISRs can also perform some of the following functions

- DHCP server

- DNS Server

- VoIP controller

- Wireless controller

Consider an unfortunately common situation where a rogue or clumsy user connects a router to a network that already has a router. Devices on the network are already configured to communicate with the existing router and will likely ignore the new one, so not much data will flow to it. But if a rogue router is also acting as a DHCP server, then when the DHCP lease expires on any network clients, they may contact the new router for a new IP address. The rogue router will also provide a different default gateway (its own) and begin to intercept traffic.

How to prevent rogue routers? Enforce MAC filtering and other security measures on network switches as discussed further in this section.

Does the router sit behind the firewall or does the firewall sit behind the router? Which of the below scenarios is correct? Either can be correct and network administrators have been debating this issue.

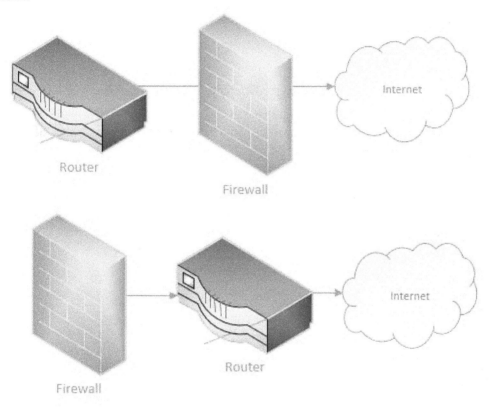

If the firewall sits between the internet and the router, it can protect the router from attacks. But if the router sits at the edge of the network, it can better communicate with external devices. Sometimes you don't even need a separate physical router because a single device can handle all the functions – firewall, DHCP, DNS, etc.

The basic configuration of the router

- Set up a username/password, other credentials to monitor and access the router

- Identify the type of internet connection that you have, and whether the IP address is DHCP or static. Assign the correct static IP address to each WAN port if necessary

- On the LAN side, set up the scope of the LAN. What class of network will you use? Set up DHCP.

- Add routes or let the router automatically create routes.

- Create security rules

- Set up other features such as a firewall if applicable

Some Cisco routers are known as Integrated Service Routers (ISR). If we look at the left side of this ISR, we can see several standard ethernet ports and a few SFP ports. These ports allow us to connect WAN connections (ethernet or fiber if we use an SFP). We can also connect USB-based cellular modems using the USB ports.

On the right side of the router, and on the bottom are panels that can be removed. We can add different modules to this router that give it additional features (such as switching, connections to more advanced internet connections, and VoIP services).

Some of the modules we can add

- An FXO card that allows us to connect analog phone lines to the router

- An FXS card that allows us to connect devices such as fax machines and other devices that require analog phone lines

- An EHWIC card that allows us to connect a T1 internet connection to the router

- A switch module that allows us to connect up to 24 ethernet-based devices directly to the router. This turns the router into a router and a switch

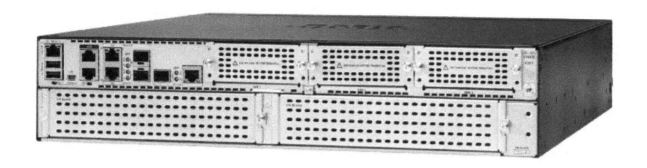

Switch

A **switch** connects multiple devices on the internal network. We install the switches after the router.

In a larger network, switches can be distributed in a hierarchy such as a three-tier or a leaf topology.

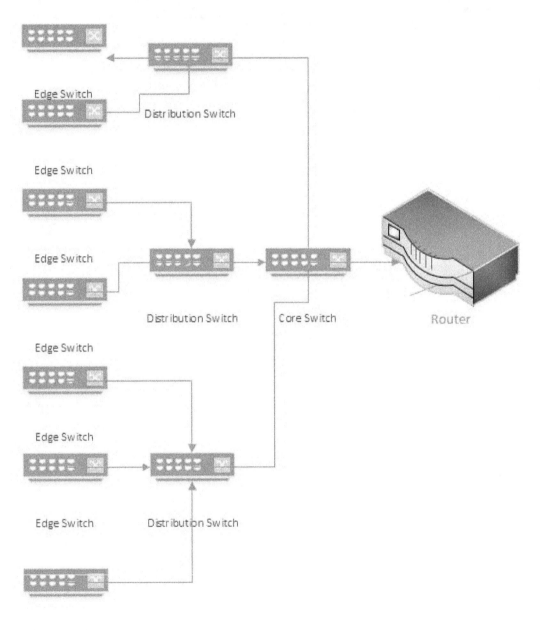

It is recommended for any switch that the following security measures are taken during initial configuration

- Create a separate, unused VLAN and shut it down

- Move all unused ports to the unused VLAN

- Shut down all unused ports

- On a physical security level, unused patch panel ports should not be physically patched in to the switch. An exposed data jack can permit a user to connect a device which should not otherwise be connected.

Switches also employ MAC address filtering, which is rarely enabled by administrators in practice (but should be)

- The switch knows the MAC address of every device on every port. This data goes to a MAC address table.

- Once a network is set up, and devices are connected to a network switch, an administrator will have a list of device MAC addresses on the network.

- The administrator can configure the switch to block devices with MAC addresses different from the ones on the list.

- A switch port can be configured to

  o Allow traffic from a single MAC address. In an ideal scenario, each switch port should see incoming traffic from only one MAC address. For example, if a printer is connected to switch port number four, only traffic from the printer should appear on switch port 4.

  o Allow traffic from a limited number of MAC addresses (for example, traffic from up to ten unique MAC addresses is permitted). For example, a user may have only one data jack in their office but must connect multiple devices such as printers and computers. The user would install a small switch in their office. The larger switch would see the MAC address of the small switch and the MAC address of the devices that are connected to the smaller switch. If the switch sees traffic from say eleven MAC addresses on the same port, the switch closes the port.

  o Allow traffic from an unlimited number of MAC addresses. Sometimes users connect and disconnect devices randomly and administrators do not want to be forced to shut down and reopen ports all the time because it can be a drain on their resources and cause disruption to their networks. Therefore, some administrators do not enforce the MAC address rule at all.

- When a switch detects a violation of the MAC address rule, it can

  o Place a warning in the log

  o Shut down the port, in which case no devices will be permitted to connect to that specific port

Typical switches are "layer two" in the OSI model; that is, they can only forward data frames on the same subnet. Data outside the subnet must be forwarded to a router, even if multiple subnets are connected to the same switch. A **layer three switch** acts as a router in that it can forward traffic between different VLANs. Layer three switches have additional security settings, including Access Control Lists.

Switches also provide the following security features

- **Spanning Tree Protocol** which prevents loops between two switches. If a switch detects a loop, it shuts down one of the ports.

- **Flood Guard**. A flood occurs when a switch receives a large amount of traffic on a single port. Like many other electronic devices, a switch has a buffer. The buffer stores received data that the switch is waiting to process. A hacker could attempt to bypass a switch's security measures by sending a large amount of traffic and overflow the buffer.

  o Newer switches have security settings in place that can drop additional traffic or shut down the ports when flooded.

I might connect my network like the following diagram (this is common in some corporate networks)

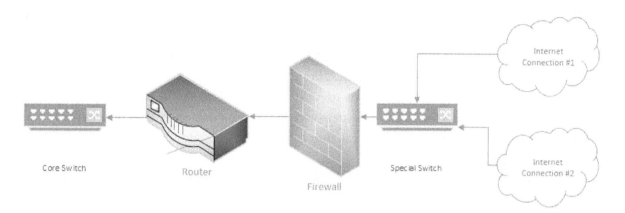

What's up with the "special switch" that sits between the internet connections and the firewall? If I bought multiple internet connections for redundancy, but I only have one WAN port on my router or firewall, then I can connect the internet connections to a switch. The router/firewall and internet connections sit in the same subnet on the special switch. If we need to failover from one internet connection to another, we can do so through the switch.

Sometimes an ISP will provide a switch as part of their customer premises equipment. Instead of connecting to the ISP's router or modem, you to connect to the ISPs switch. An ISP uses a switch for traffic shaping, monitoring the quality of the internet connection, delivering an ethernet WAN connection.

Hub

A **hub** is like a switch except that it doesn't remember the MAC address of any device that is connected to it. When a hub receives a frame, it floods it out of all its other ports. It doesn't think about who needs to receive it (or which ports to send it out of). This results in frequent collisions because other devices connected to the hub may be trying to send data to it. The data that the user devices send may collide with the data that the hub is sending.

Hubs can be found in older networks, but they have been largely replaced by switches. A hub performs most of the same basic functions as a switch, in other words, moving traffic between internal network devices. A hub doesn't understand subnets either.

Multilayer Switch

Remember that a switch works on Layer 2 to route frames between devices on the same subnet. A device isn't supposed to be able to send traffic to a device on another subnet. What if I have multiple subnets but I don't want to set up multiple physical switches (one for each subnet)? I can create what is called a VLAN (Virtual Local Area Network).

We can assign each port on the switch a VLAN. If devices are connected to the correct port, then the switch can then enforce the VLAN rule. In order for a device on one VLAN to talk to a device on another VLAN, it must send the traffic to the router.

A **Multilayer Switch**, also known as a **Layer 3 Switch**, can route traffic between different VLANs without the use of a router. A switch may also be able to operate on Layer 4; the transport layer. It can decide based on the

- MAC Address (in a frame)

- Protocol (in a frame)

- IP address (in a packet)

- Protocol (in a packet)

- Port number (on layer 4)

The benefit of installing a Layer 3 switch is that packets travelling from one VLAN to another do not have to travel to a router. If we used a Layer 2 switch and a router, this setup is known as a **Router on a Stick**, or **ROAS**, because the router is physically connected to a switch over one cable (on a trunk port – a trunk port is a port that has access to all of the VLANs). A data packet travelling from VLAN 1 to VLAN 2 for example, travels from the top device to the switch, to the router, back to the switch and then out to the middle device.

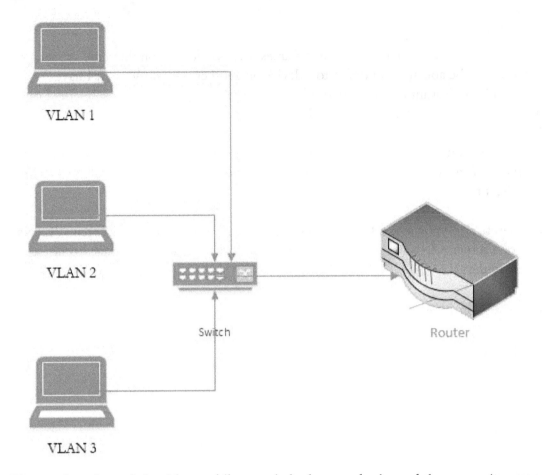

VLAN 1

VLAN 2

Switch

Router

VLAN 3

If we replace the switch with a multilayer switch, then we don't need the router (except to communicate with external networks). A layer 3 switch decreases latency because packets travel a shorter distance.

A **Layer 4 switch** takes a deeper look at the traffic before forwarding it. It can check the port number (the virtual port numbers we talked about at the beginning of the book), not the physical port number. Thus, we can configure a switch to route traffic based on its type (HTTP, FTP, etc.) and prioritize traffic based on its content, not just its destination/source.

A switch can make routing decisions based on the Layer 5, 6, or 7 content of a packet. These switches are called **content switches**. Common applications of a Layer 7 switch are load balancing and content delivery.

Bridge

A network **bridge** is a device that connects two networks to act like one network. A bridge is different from a router, which connects two separate networks.

Consider a network with two devices, having MAC addresses, connected to the bridge on port 1
AAAA.AAAA.AAAA
BBBB.BBBB.BBBB

And another network with two devices, having MAC addresses, connected to the bridge on port 2
CCCC.CCCC.CCCC
DDDD.DDDD.DDDD

The bridge connects the two networks together. A network bridge works like a network switch in that it records MAC addresses of packets arriving on each port. For example, if device AAAA.AAAA.AAAA sends a network packet to device DDDD.DDDD.DDDD, the network bridge learns that device AAAA.AAAA.AAAA is on Port 1.

The bridge does not know the location of the other three devices, so it floods the both ports with the packet intended for DDDD.DDDD.DDDD. When DDDD.DDDD.DDDD responds, the bridge learns that it is located on port 2. Eventually, enough traffic passes, and the bridge learns the location of all of the devices. This is a simplified example as a network may contain hundreds or thousands of devices.

The bridge will eventually learn that AAAA.AAAA.AAAA and BBBB.BBBB.BBBB are on the same segment, and will not forward traffic from AAAA.AAAA.AAAA to BBBB.BBBB.BBBB. In reality, the traffic from AAAA.AAAA.AAAA to BBBB.BBBB.BBBB will not reach the bridge because a properly functioning network switch installed before the bridge will direct the traffic to BBBB.BBBB.BBBB appropriately. A switch on the same network segment as the bridge will have the same MAC address information as the bridge.

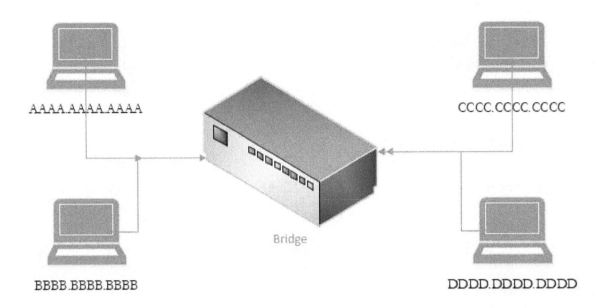

AAAA.AAAA.AAAA

CCCC.CCCC.CCCC

Bridge

BBBB.BBBB.BBBB

DDDD.DDDD.DDDD

Bridges are not common as their functions are typically handled by switches or routers. A bridge can connect more than two network segments at the same time.

An example of a bridge is a point-to-point antenna such as Ubiquiti AirFiber, which allows a bridge to be established between two separate buildings without any wiring. It uses a radio signal.
For example, consider a car dealership having a central show room with network equipment. The dealership has installed IP surveillance cameras on the light poles surrounding the parking lot. The dealership was able to power the cameras through the electrical connection on the poles, but the cost of running data cable to each pole from the central show room was too high. The cameras must be on the same network as the central show room. The solution is to bridge these cameras with the central show room through point-to-point antennas.

Modem

A **modem** sits at the edge of a network. Typically, a modem is supplied and configured by an internet service provider. The modem is configured to connect to the ISPs network. It may require a username, password, or other parameters.

Some types of modems

- Dial up Modem, which operates over a phone line. The maximum speed is 56 Kbps

- DSL modem, which operates over a phone line, but provides speeds of up to 1.5 Mbps

- Cable modem, which operates over a coaxial cable, and provides speeds of up to 10 Mbps

- Fiber optic cable modem, which operates over a fiber optic cable, and provides speeds of up to 1 Gbps

- Cellular modem, which connects to a cellular network. The speed could vary with the cellular network, but could be up to 100 Mbps

Wireless Access Point

Wireless Access Points are dispersed throughout the network and connect to a switch or multiple switches (preferably a PoE switch).

An access point sends and receives traffic over one or more "WLANs" or Wireless LANs. Each wireless LAN can be mapped to a subnet (VLAN). Each wireless network WLAN is associated with one or more SSIDs (multiple SSIDs can be associated with a single WLAN). The access point broadcasts SSIDs, which client devices can detect and connect to. An SSID can also be hidden. If an SSID is hidden, a client will be required to know its name to connect to it. In theory, hidden SSIDs can prevent hackers from connecting to the network, but SSIDs can be easily cracked.

An SSID can be configured as

- An open network, where any device can connect. This is a common setting for guest Wi-Fi.

- An encrypted network, requiring a user to enter a passphrase. There are several forms of encryption, discussed later.

- An encrypted network, authenticating through a username/password and RADIUS server/Active Directory server, or authenticating with a certificate.

An access point can be set up to

- Block connections from devices with specific MAC addresses. This is known as a blacklist.

- Allow connections only from devices with specific MAC addresses. This is known as a whitelist. We can create an open network, but only allow connections from devices with specific MAC addresses. In theory, this will work to prevent intruders without having to configure devices or provide passwords. A hacker can use a packet sniffer to intercept wireless data and then spoof the MAC address of a rogue device to match an authorized one.

   Remember that every MAC address is unique and that it comes from the factory? Well, a hacker can change his! If a hacker knows the MAC address of a device that is authorized to connect he can change his and attempt to connect.

The signal strength of an access point should at least -70 dBm everywhere that Wi-Fi is required. A weaker signal will result in frequently dropped connections.

The two main Wi-Fi frequencies are 2.4 GHz and 5 GHz. Each of these bands is subdivided into channels. The 2.4 GHz band has 11 channels, and the 5 GHz band has 54 channels.

An access point will typically broadcast on both frequencies at the same time, but only one channel per frequency at a time. The channel

- May be preconfigured by the administrator and set permanently. The access point operates only on that specific channel.

- May be set so that the access point can choose a channel and change it when necessary.

- Two nearby access points should never broadcast on the same channel at the same time. If they do, signal interference will result, and no clients will be able to connect. Consider a network in an office building, with many access points. Signals from neighboring access points will interfere and cancel each other's signals. Signals from access points on floors above and below will also interfere. Signals from rogue devices and mobile hotspots may also interfere. An access point may receive interference from dozens of devices at the same time and must therefore be able to select a specific channel that is free of interference.

Each access point comes with a built-in antenna. You can connect an external antenna to some access points. There are many shapes and sizes of antennas and the best antenna depends on the desired coverage area and signal strength increase required.

Special software such as AirMagnet Survey Pro or ekahau can be used to plan out wireless networks and optimize the placement of each access point. The signal strength of an access point can be affected (reduced by metal shelves, concrete walls, and other construction materials). The quantity of access points may need to be increased in densely occupied areas such as conference rooms and lecture theaters.

Access points can be fat or thin. A **fat access point** contains software to process the traffic whereas a **thin access point** sends data back to the controller.

Access points can be **controller-based** or **standalone**. When access points are standalone, each access point must be configured separately and operates independently. When there are multiple access points, a wireless controller is optimal. A controller

- Automatically configures access points based on a template; a controller can automatically detect and configure new access points

- Will optimize broadcast channel and power for each access point based on its traffic and signal-to-noise ratio

Cloud-based controllers and access points such as Cisco Meraki are available.

How do Wi-Fi networks detect collisions when they're broadcasting data everywhere at the same time? In other words, if my laptop is sending data to the access point and the access point is sending data back to the laptop at the same time, the two signals will collide and cancel each other out. We use a system called the **Distributed Coordination Function** or DCF. If a wireless network device or access point tries to send a signal and determines that the recipient is busy, then it waits for some time before resending. Each device waits a random time to ensure that their signals do not collide a second time.

Media Converter

A **Media Converter** changes one form of media to another. Some media conversions include

- Convert between a fiber optic signal and a copper ethernet signal. An ISP may need to transport a data signal long distances (where only fiber can carry it), but the network equipment at the customer site only supports copper. The media converter sits between the modem and the outside world, or between the modem and the customer's equipment. An example of a media converter is below.

- Convert a **POTS** (**Plain Old Telephone System**) line into a digital signal and vice versa for a VoIP system. A device that does this is known as a **Voice Gateway**. **Voice Gateways** can include the Cisco Voice Gateway and Cisco ISR Routers with FXO cards. A voice gateway might be called an analog voice gateway.

Wireless Range Extender

A **wireless range extender** is also known as a **repeater**. When placed at the edge of a wireless network, the range can be increased. Essentially, it repeats the signal that it "hears" from the nearest access point. It acts as a relay between the nearest access point and a device that is further away.

Consider the following scenario. On the left, I have an access point connected to a switch. Its range is shown by the circle around it. On the right, I have a user who wishes to connect, but is out of range. I don't have the network infrastructure to install a second access point closer to the user.

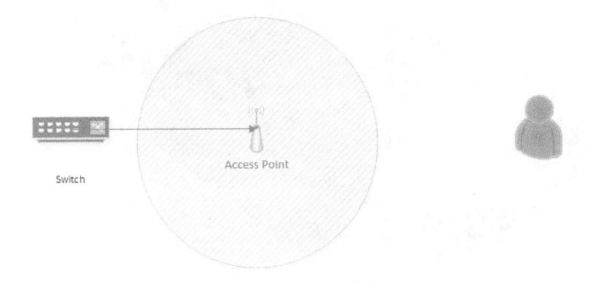

If I install a repeater, I now can extend the range of the access point to the user.

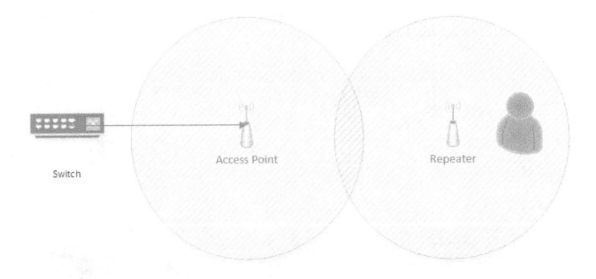

Wireless Controller

A **wireless controller** is a device that manages access points. The wireless controller may directly connect to each access point, or it may connect to a switch that is on the same subnet as the access points. We can place the controller anywhere on the network that makes sense, as long is the access points can logically reach it. It is typically installed in the MDF.

The controller uses the **Control and Provisioning of Wireless Access Points Protocol**, or **CAPWAP**. Cisco devices use the **Lightweight Access Point Protocol** or **LWAPP**.

The controller

- Monitors the status of each access point

- Updates the configuration of each access point

- Sends configuration to each new access point

- Updates the firmware of each access point

A controller might be cloud-based, such as Cisco Meraki.

A controller may be licensed for a specific number of access points. We should purchase a controller that can support the number of access points in use on our network.

Load Balancer

A **load balancer** distributes traffic among multiple resources. For example, consider that the Google.com website has only one URL (www.google.com), which would ordinarily point to one IP address. That IP address would ordinarily point to one web server. But one single web server would be overloaded by the traffic; in fact, the Google.com website has millions of web servers. The solution is to install a load balancer in front of those servers. The load balancer can distribute the incoming traffic among all the web servers.

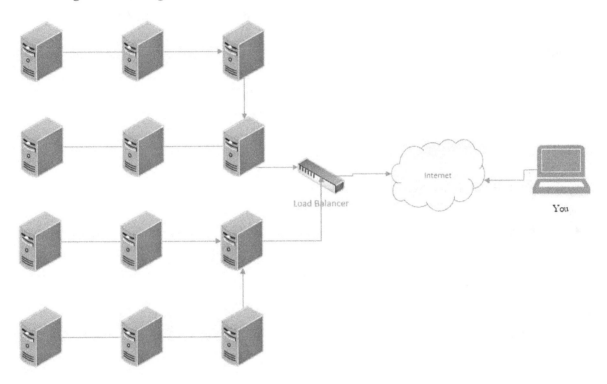

DNS load balancing is when a domain name's DNS records point to multiple web servers. For example, Google.com's DNS records could point to both 11.11.11.11 and 12.12.12.12, each of which is assigned to a separate server. This would balance the traffic among two servers (which is not enough for Google). Attempting to balance millions of servers on one DNS record would not work because the customer would not have enough public IP addresses to cover all the servers in use, and the DNS record would be massive.

A load balancer uses a **scheduling algorithm** to determine how to distribute traffic among the servers connected to it. Consider a scenario where there is one load balancer and three servers, Server A, Server B, and Server C. There are several types of load balancing algorithms

- **First Come First Served** – each request is handled in the order that it arrives; when the servers are busy then additional requests are put on hold. The load balancer sends the first request to Server A, the second request to Server B, and the third request to Server C. The load balancer does not send additional requests to the servers until a server indicates that it has spare capacity (i.e. that it has completed the current request).

- **Round-Robin** – each request is handled in the order that it arrives. The load balancer sends the first request to Server A, the second request to Server B, and the third request to Server C. The fourth request is sent to Server A, the fifth request is sent to Server B, and so on. The round-robin algorithm assumes that all the servers have the same capacity, and that all requests are of the same size. If some requests take a server longer to process, they could overload the servers. If one server is more powerful then the rest, it could remain idle for extended periods of time (since all servers receive the same number of requests).

- **Weighed Round-Robin** – like round robin, but each server is given a specific weight based on its capacity. For example, if server A is twice as powerful as Server B or Server C, it can be given a weight of two, while Servers B and C are each given a weight of one. Server A would then receive twice as many requests as Server B and Server C.

A **sticky session** allows a load balancer to remember each client (based on their HTTP session). When a returning client is recognized, the load balancer sends that client back to the same server that they were previously connected to, regardless of the server load. This allows the server to maintain the client's data locally (and not in a central database). This is also known as **affinity**. Load balancers typically work in pairs or groups. This prevents the load balancer from becoming a single point of failure.

In a logical network topology, the load balancer is shown to be connected between the internet and the servers that it is balancing. In the physical reality, the load balancer can be connected anywhere on the network. If a load balancer has 1000 servers connected behind it, it wouldn't have 1000 physical connections to those servers, but instead would route traffic to them over the local network. Regardless of the load balancer's location, it must have a good network connection, typically 1 Gbps or 10 Gbps.

The group of servers connected to the load balancer can be **active-passive** or **active-active**. In an active-active configuration, the load balancer distributes the work among all the connected servers. In an active-passive configuration, some servers remain active (receive work) and some remain passive (do not receive work). In the event of a failure of one of the active servers, a passive server is activated and begins to receive work.

An active-active configuration is better because it can quickly respond to surges in traffic and allows the system to fully utilize all its resources.

In a Virtual IP scenario, the load balancer does not exist. Instead, all the servers work together to share the workload. Consider that we have three servers:

Server A has a private IP of 10.0.0.1
Server B has a private IP of 10.0.0.2
Server C has a private IP of 10.0.0.3
The public IP address is 11.11.11.11

Servers A, B, and C communicate with each other over their private IPs 10.0.0.1, 10.0.0.2, and 10.0.0.3. The servers all set 11.11.11.11 as their public IP, and then elect one server to respond to requests. For example, Server A, B, and C choose to have Server B respond to all requests on 11.11.11.11. If Server B is overloaded, it may communicate this fact with Server A and C (over their private IPs), which designate Server A to temporarily respond to requests on 11.11.11.11.

The servers continually ping each other to ensure that all the servers are functional. This form of communication is known as a **heartbeat**. If Server B were to stop responding within a specific period, Server A and Server C would choose to designate Server A to respond to new requests. The algorithm used to determine which server would respond will vary from scenario to scenario.

IDS/IPS

An **IPS** (also known as a **NIPS**) is a **Network-Based Intrusion Prevention System**, and an **IDS** (also known as a **NIDS**) is a **Network-Based Intrusion Detection System**.

A NIDS can only detect unauthorized access, but a NIPS can detect and react to the unauthorized access.

Why bother with a NIDS if it doesn't stop bad traffic? Every device has "false positives". A false positive is when the NIDS/NIPS falsely marks legitimate traffic as illegitimate. A NIPS can also slow down a network, if it can't screen traffic as fast as it is passing through.

A NIDS can flag what is bad but let it through. A network administrator can investigate the traffic later and if it is bad, he can update the firewall based on what he found.

A NIPS can block all the traffic that it thinks is bad. If users complain, the network administrator can investigate later.

As a network administrator, you may think a NIPS is better. But a large organization may not be able to afford a drop-in productivity associated with blocked traffic. It may choose to take the risk of letting everything through (even the bad stuff), and letting an administrator follow up later.

Its like the border. We can't search every box, every truck, and every person. So, we look for suspicious activity and search those people extra. Some of the bad stuff gets through, but the border keeps operating smoothly.

NIPS and NIDS have the following characteristics:

- **Signature-Based**: Similar to an antivirus program, a NIPS can detect an intrusion based on its "signature" or specific characteristics. For example, an intrusion enters through a specific port or from a specific source IP address. A signature-based NIPS/NIDS will not detect attacks that are zero-day or attacks that don't match the signature.

- **Heuristic/Behavioral**: Like an antivirus program, a NIPS can detect an intrusion based on the way it behaves, more like artificial intelligence. A heuristic-based NIPS can detect zero-day attacks but has a higher rate of false positives.

- **Anomaly**. An anomaly-based NIPS/NIDS compares new traffic against a baseline. The NIPS/NIDS calibrates itself to understand normal network behavior, and then compares new traffic against that calibration. Traffic that does not match is denied.

- **Inline vs Passive**. An inline sensor sits between the internet and the internal network. All traffic passes through the sensor, which decides if it should be permitted or denied. An inline sensor can turn off the flow of bad traffic. If the inline sensor is overloaded, it can reduce the speed or capacity of the network. A passive sensor sits on the network but receives a copy of the traffic. A passive sensor cannot turn off the flow of bad traffic.

- **In-Band** vs **Out-of-Band**. An in-band sensor is a complete system that monitors traffic and decides whether to allow or prevent it. An out-of-band sensor monitors traffic and sends results to another system that decides whether to block it.

- **Rules**. Rules are decision making processes that the NIPS/NIDS uses to determine whether the traffic should be permitted or denied. NIPS/NIDS can be preloaded with rules, and an administrator can add additional rules as needed. A NIPS/NIDS with heuristic behavior can automatically create additional rules based on its findings.

- Analytics

  o **False Positive**. A false positive is when a NIPS or NIDS alerts to an intrusion attempt that is a source of legitimate network activity.

  o **False Negative**. A false negative is when the NIPS or NIDS allows traffic through that is an intrusion attempt.

  o There must be a balance between false positives and false negatives. Increasing the sensitivity of the NIPS/NIDS will create more false positives. False positives that block legitimate traffic can disrupt the operations of the organization and frustrate users. They require additional administrator attention to correct the false positives. False negatives are dangerous because they allow intrusion attempts. There is no way to identify a false negative until after it has occurred, and many false negatives go undetected. Lowering the sensitivity of the NIPS/NIDS increases the number of false negatives. A NIPS/NIDS with artificial intelligence can learn from its mistakes.

Proxy Server

A **proxy** or **proxy server** is a device that masks the true source of an internet connection. There are several types of proxies

An **anonymous (forward) proxy** hides the source of the internet connection. For example, if a user visits Google through an anonymous proxy, Google's servers will see the IP address of the proxy as originating the connection, and not that of the user's PC. A popular website (such as Google) may see thousands or millions of requests from the same proxy and may choose to block them to avoid the risk of abuse or SPAM.

A **transparent (forward) proxy** does not hide the source of the internet connection. For example, if a user visits Google through transparent proxy, Google's servers will see the IP address of the proxy as originating the connection but will also see the IP address of the user's PC. A transparent proxy can be used to cache a website. By caching a website, a transparent proxy reduces traffic on a network.

A **reverse proxy** sits in front of a set of web servers. Consider that a website may have a single IP address, but multiple (even millions) of web servers. The reverse proxy filters incoming requests and forwards them to the appropriate server. A reverse proxy can

- Provide load balancing

- Encrypt data between the proxy and the user's PC

- Compress web content

- Cache static web content

A proxy can be used to

- Cache web content

- Filter/restrict users from accessing inappropriate web content

- Block malware and viruses

- Allow users to access web content that is blocked in their geographic location

- Eavesdrop on all content transmitted over the internet connection

In a large network, a proxy should be configured to prevent access to malicious websites and enforce the organization's acceptable use policy.

VPN Concentrator

A **VPN** is a **Virtual Private Network**. It allows a remote user (working from home, a hotel, a hotspot, etc.) to connect to a corporate network through a tunnel. Essentially, the traffic from the user's computer is packaged and sent through a tunnel to the corporate network. If the user attempts to access a website while connected to the VPN, that request is first sent to the corporate network, which forwards the request to the website. The corporate network also takes the traffic that it received from the website and sends it back to the user through the VPN. Therefore, traffic received from the user appears to be coming from the corporate network, regardless of the user's location.

A VPN "tricks" the user's computer into thinking that it is on the corporate network so that the user can access resources such as internal applications, shared drives, and printers.

A **VPN concentrator** is a device that collects and manages VPN connections from multiple users and passes their traffic to the LAN. It could be hardware-based or software-based. The VPN concentrator functionality can be incorporated into another network device such as a router.

VPN functionality is incorporated into devices such as

- Cisco Routers

- Cisco ASAs

- Fortigates

- Sonicwalls

- Cisco Meraki Routers

Remote users can use software to establish VPNs (such as Windows VPN or Cisco AnyConnect) or can install hardware-based VPN appliances such as a Meraki Z3.

Features of the VPN concentrator include

- **Remote Access** vs. **Site-to-Site**. A Remote Access VPN allows users to connect back to a corporate network, typically through their computer. A Site-to-Site VPN allows two offices to connect to each other and pretend like they are part of the same physical network. A Site-to-Site VPN typically applies to the site's router and not to individual devices on the network.

- The performance on a VPN is affected by the quality of the user's internet connection, by the quality of the corporate network's internet connection, by the number of active users, and by the type of resources being accessed.

- When there are multiple sites that need to be connected, a site-to-site VPN should be replaced by a WAN

- **IPSec**. IPSec is a set of protocols that allow hosts to exchange packets securely. IPSec has several modes of operation, including

  - **Tunnel Mode**. The Tunnel Mode encrypts the source, destination, and contents of every packet. Essentially, it establishes a secure tunnel between two network devices where data can travel securely. The devices that are establishing the tunnel are not necessarily the devices that are creating the traffic. For example, a router could be sending traffic on behalf of a server inside the network. An outsider will not be able to examine the source, destination, or contents of any traffic.

  - **Transport Mode**. The Transport Mode only encrypts the contents of the packet. It does not encrypt the source or destination. An outsider will be able to examine the source and destination. Transport Mode is established by the two network devices who are communicating, and not by the routers on the edges of the network.

  - **SA**. An SA, or Security Association is an algorithm and key that are used to encrypt traffic in an IPSec tunnel. Each direction of communication requires a separate SA. Therefore, most IPSec tunnels will require two SAs.

  - There are four methods of connecting a tunnel. Consider that two computers (each inside a separate network and behind a router) would like to communicate securely across the internet. How can an IPSec tunnel be established?

    - **Machine-to-Machine**. Two computers (or smartphones) establish a tunnel and communicate. This is not practical because each computer will expend a substantial amount of computing power encrypting and decrypting the IPSec traffic.

    - **Router-to-Router**. It is assumed that the connection between the computer and the router (on the internal network) is secure. The routers establish an IPSec tunnel. The computers no longer encrypt traffic between themselves and the routers. The routers encrypt all traffic between themselves.

- **Machine-to-Machine and Router-to-Router**. This combines the previous two scenarios. Each machine establishes an IPSec tunnel with the router on its network, and the routers establish an IPSec tunnel between themselves.

- **Remote User**. A remote user connects to a router through an IPSec tunnel, and then establishes a secondary IPSec tunnel to connect to a device deeper in the network.

- **Tunnel Mode Encryption**. The tunnel mode is the method for encrypting the traffic. Consider that two routers have created an IPSec tunnel and that behind each router is a computer that wants to communicate. What is the order of operations?

  - The computer generates some data and places it in a packet.

  - The computer puts the address of the remote computer in the header of the packet (or the address of the network that it is sending it to, when the network employs NAT – more on this later).

  - The computer sends the packet to the router (through the switch)

  - The router encrypts this packet, including the headers

  - The router encapsulates this packet inside a larger packet and adds the recipient's router address to the header

  - The router sends the packet to the destination router

  - The destination router removes the outer header, decrypts the packet, and forwards it to the computer inside its network

  - Neither computer is aware of the existence of the IPSec tunnel

- Tunnel encryption works through the following security protocols

- AH. **Authentication Header**. When AH is used, the original IP header (created by the computer that generated the data) is visible to outsiders, but the contents are protected. AH protects the integrity of the data. That is, the recipient can be sure that the sender listed on the packet is in fact the true sender.

- ESP. **Encapsulating Security Payload**. ESP encrypts the contents of the data, but it does not guarantee integrity.

- It is recommended to use both AH and ESP, thereby providing privacy and integrity.

- IPSec algorithms

  - IPSec is a framework for exchanging data, but the contents of the framework vary from vendor to vendor and network to network. Just like there can be many different models of vehicles on a road, all following the same traffic rules, there can be many different types of algorithms to exchange data within a tunnel.

  - Many different encryption algorithms can be used. This flexibility allows an algorithm to be replaced when it is discovered to be weak.

  - Methods include

    - Diffie-Hellman key exchange with public key signing

    - MD5 and SHA-1 hashing algorithms to ensure data integrity

- IPv4 vs IPv6. IPSec is integrated into all IPv6 packets by default, but not IPv4 packets. When IPv4 was designed, security was not a primary consideration. As the internet grew, the design of IPv6 required security to be integrated into all communications. A device can use IPv6 and not activate the IPSec feature however.

- Split Tunnel vs. Full Tunnel

  - In a **Full Tunnel VPN**, all traffic is routed through the VPN, but in a **Split Tunnel VPN**, only specific traffic is routed through the VPN.

- The advantage of a split tunnel is that it reduces bottlenecks. Consider a corporate user working from home. The user needs to access network resources such as a shared drive and corporate finance applications. This traffic must go over the VPN. The user is also watching YouTube videos in the background. There is no reason to route YouTube videos over the corporate network (requiring encryption on both sides). YouTube traffic can travel over the user's home internet connection.

- TLS. In addition to providing internet security, Transport Layer Security is an alternative to IPSec VPN. A TLS VPN is useful when the network uses NAT.

- **Always-On VPN**. An Always-On VPN is just like it sounds. It is a VPN that is always on. Typically, an Always-On VPN is part of a hardware appliance, but it could also be software-based. When the VPN detects an active internet connection, it automatically attempts to re-establish the VPN.

  For security purposes, an Always-On VPN can block traffic from travelling over the internet when the VPN is not running. This would prevent a user from inadvertently disclosing his true location to websites that shouldn't know it.

AAA/RADIUS Server

AAA or **Authentication, Authorization and Accounting** is a concept of verifying the identity of a user, providing him with access to specific resources, and keeping track of each access attempt. **RADIUS** stands for **Remote Authentication Dial-In User Service** and is a form of AAA.

When a user attempts to access a device, that device asks the AAA or RADIUS server for permission to allow the user. The server determines whether to allow or deny access to the user and responds to the device. The server also determines how much access the user is entitled to.

An AAA/RADIUS server can be installed locally or remotely. We will look at RADIUS in more detail later.

UTM Appliance

UTM stands for **Unified Threat Management**. It is the term given to most modern enterprise firewalls, which can include antivirus, antimalware, SPAM filtering, and intrusion detection tools all in one box. A threat from a single malicious actor can enter the organization through multiple routes. For example, a hacker could enter an organization's network through an unsecured firewall, log in to a server that has weak credentials, and install a piece of malware that allows him to copy the corporation's sensitive data.

UTM devices can detect patterns in network traffic and user activity. They can send this data to the cloud where it can be further analysed to determine whether it is a threat.

A UTM must be connected to the internet to be effective. Like any other threat management application, a UTM must be properly configured.

VoIP PBX

A **PBX** or **Private Branch Exchange** is a device that manages a phone system. There are several models

- Cisco Unified Communications Manager

- Avaya IP Office 500 V2

The PBX does the following

- Provides DHCP to each phone

- Configures each phone

- Routes phone calls between phones on the same network

- Routes phone calls between phones and the outside world (through connections with analog phone lines or a SIP trunk)

- Manages voice mail for the system

Typically, each time a phone powers on, it contacts the PBX and downloads its configuration. The PBX can identify each phone by its MAC address. The PBX can be directly connected to each phone or connected to the same network as each phone.

Some VoIP phones operate in the cloud, and do not require a PBX. Cloud-based VoIP phones do not function with analog phone lines.

An example of a PBX is below.

VoIP Endpoint

A **VoIP Endpoint** is a device that connects a user to a VoIP network. In other words, it's a fancy name for a phone. Other devices that could be endpoints are ATAs (allows an analog device such as a fax machine or alarm system to connect to a VoIP system) and conference room phones.

A VoIP Endpoint connects directly to a switch. A VoIP endpoint may operate on a separate physical network from the rest of the LAN or may operate on a separate VLAN.

Some VoIP phones support **IP Passthrough**. Passthrough is useful when the building does not have enough ethernet wiring to support the installation of phones and computers. For example, a desk may have only one ethernet cable, but a user must connect both a phone and a computer. The solution?

The phone connects to the network and to the computer. The phone acts like a little switch. It passes the ethernet connection through to the computer. Notice on the back of this Cisco phone, there are two ethernet ports (the port on the far left is used to connect an expansion module). The port in the middle connects to the ethernet. The port on the right connects to a computer. The traffic for the phone can be on a separate subnet (VLAN) from the traffic for the computer.

Printer

A printer can connect to the network (as opposed to via USB or serial). A network printer can accept print jobs from local and remote users. If equipped, a user can also scan documents from the printer direct to a network folder or to e-mail.

Physical Access Control Devices

An access control device is part of an access control system. An access control system is used to track and restrict access to different buildings or rooms. It typically has four parts

- A card reader and/or biometric reader – this device is installed next to each doorway and scans user proximity cards or biometrics

- A door lock – an electronic door lock that allows the door to be unlocked automatically. This might be known as a door strike.

- A controller – the controller connects to both the card reader and the electronic door lock. When a user scans a card at a card reader, the card reader reports the user's information to the controller. The controller checks the time and decides whether the user is permitted to access that door. If the user is permitted, then the card reader sends a signal to the lock to unlock the door.

- The wiring between the controller and the card reader.

The access control system can be wired as follows (depending on the make and model of the system)

- The controller is connected directly to the network and power. The controller powers the card reader and door lock. The controller connects to each card reader and door lock via a proprietary cable. The door lock and card reader communicate with the controller via the proprietary cable. The controller may have a software program or web-based interface where it can be programmed.

- The controller is connected directly to the network. Each card reader and door lock are also connected to the network and receive power via PoE. The card reader and door lock use the network to communicate with the controller. They might be on a separate VLAN or on a separate physical network.

Cameras

IP Surveillance cameras can be connected to the network. There are several components

- The camera – several makes, and models of cameras are available with different types of lenses, zoom, quality, and weather ratings

- The NVR (Network Video Recorder) – video from the camera is recorded onto the NVR. The NVR is available in various storage capacities. Some NVRs have a built in PoE switch which can power the cameras and provide them with IP addresses.

- The network – the physical network infrastructure consists of ethernet cables (cat5e or cat6 between the NVR and the camera. It may also consist of the underlying network switches and routers that connect the cameras with the NVR.

There are several scenarios

- We can connect an analog camera to a coaxial cable. The analog camera has no way to communicate with the network. A network encoder is a device that converts the analog signal from the coaxial cable into a digital signal. The digital signal can be sent to an NVR where it can be recorded.

- We can connect an IP camera directly to the NVR. Many NVRs have switches that can power the cameras and provide IP addresses.

- If our NVR does not have capacity to directly connect all of the cameras, or if the distance between the NVR and the camera is too far, we can connect the NVR and the cameras to our network switch (or to multiple network switches if our network is large).

  If we have multiple cameras, they can all connect to the same switch. The surveillance camera system can have a separate VLAN from the remainder of the network.

  In most scenarios, the NVR has two VLANs: one VLAN for the camera and one VLAN for managing the NVR and viewing the recorded or live video.

- We might use a combination of the above scenarios. If we have a combination of analog and IP cameras, some might connect via ethernet and some might connect via converters.

Heating, Ventilation, and Air Conditioning (HVAC) Sensors

Traditionally, a building's ventilation system consisted of the following

- A rooftop unit – this brings cool air from the outside and warms it as necessary

- Exhaust fans – exhaust fans export stale air from the building

- Ducts – ducts transport air throughout the building

- Fans – fans blow air through the ducts

- Temperature sensors – sensors measure the temperature throughout the building.

- Controller – the controller makes the system work. Each temperature sensor reports the local temperature back to the controller. If an area is too cold, the controller instructs a nearby fan to turn on and blow more air into the area. The controller also instructs the rooftop unit to heat more air up for the building.

A temperature sensor is typically connected to the controller via a single-pair thermostat wire. Newer, IP based systems use Ethernet. The controller connects to the network via an ethernet cable, and so do the sensors. The controller and the sensors can connect on a separate physical network or can connect to the building's main network and use a separate VLAN. The controller might also have a web interface that can allow a building operator to remotely program it or view its status.

Internet of Things (IoT)

The Internet of Things is a new concept that relates to devices that connect and communicate independently. It refers to devices other than computers. Many of these devices use Wi-Fi to connect to the internet. They do so to provide users with updates and to download firmware updates.

The internet has created a catch-22 scenario in that

- Devices have become complicated enough to connect to the internet

- The software required to run the devices has become more complicated

- Complicated software frequently experiences additional security holes

- To patch the additional security holes, the devices must stay connected to the internet to download software updates

Some of the devices include

- **Refrigerator** – an example of a smart refrigerator is the Samsung with the Family Hub. The Hub is a touch screen, built in to the refrigerator, that allows family members to share updates and calendars in a way that mimics the use of fridge magnets. The Hub also allows users to view recipes, watch television, and play music while cooking.

- **Smart Speakers** – Smart Speakers refers to a general set of devices with artificial intelligence. A smart speaker can include a device such as a Sonos, which is a battery-powered Wi-Fi connected speaker. When you link the speaker with your cellular phone, you can stream music to it.

  More advanced speakers have "tablet" screens. They include Google Assistant, Amazon Alexa, and the Amazon Echo. These smart speakers can display content that you request, including news, videos, and music. They can also connect with other devices such as thermostats and doorbells.

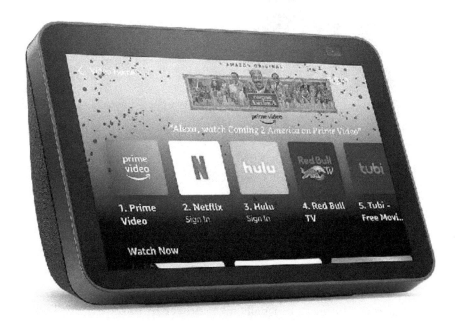

- **Smart Thermostats** – A smart thermostat is a device that uses artificial intelligence to regulate the temperature of a location.

  A traditional thermostat has two functions. A user sets the desired temperature on the device. The thermostat continually monitors the temperature of the location. It also directly connects to the heat source. If the temperature of the location is too high, the thermostat does nothing. If the temperature of the location drops below the set temperature, the thermostat instructs the heat source to power on. When the temperature reaches the set point, the thermostat instructs the heat source to power off.

  A smart thermostat does the same thing as a traditional thermostat. The only difference is that it monitors the environment and user habits to independently adjust the set temperature. For example, the smart thermostat might lower the temperature when nobody is home to reduce the cost of heating the building. The thermostat might set the temperature based on the user's physical location.

- **Smart Doorbells** – A smart doorbell is a device that replaces a traditional doorbell. A traditional doorbell has two components: a button and a speaker. When a person presses the button, the speaker inside the house generates a sound.

  A smart doorbell replaces the button. It usually takes power from the doorbell wiring.

  A smart doorbell may have the following features

  - Camera that a user can view on their phone or computer

  - Two-way communication (speaker and microphone) to communicate with visitors

  - Motion sensor

  The most popular smart doorbell is the Ring doorbell. Most doorbells have limited power, so they only record video when they sense motion.

Industrial Control Systems / Supervisory Control and Data Acquisition (SCADA)

SCADA stands for **Supervisory Control and Data Acquisition** while **ICS** stands for **Industrial Control System**. These systems are found at power plants, factories, utilities, and other critical forms of infrastructure.

An ICS is designed to operate reliably 24 hours per day, 7 days per week for many years, without interruption. Multiple ICSs can be combined to operate redundantly. An ICS may consist of many PLCs – Programmable Logic Controllers. A PLC is a special type of industrial computer that collects input from sensors, uses an algorithm to make decisions, and send an output to different control units.

For example, a PLC could be connected to a water pump that is filling a tank with water, and a sensor that is monitoring the tank's water level. The PLC continuously monitors the tank's water level. When the tank is empty, the PLC directs the pump to pump water, and when the tank is full, the PLC directs the tank to turn off.

Multiple ICSs can be connected to a SCADA system. The SCADA system collects data regarding a process. For example, the SCADA system can collect data from an oil refinery to determine the quantity of crude oil being turned into gasoline and can collect data from thousands of steps along that process. This data is typically sent to a control room where operators can analyse the data and detect discrepancies.

The different components of the SCADA system can be housed close together or may be far apart. SCADA system components may communicate over a standard IP network via copper or fiber links.

Ideally, a SCADA system should be air gapped and isolated from any commercial network. This is not always possible because a SCADA system may control facilities that are physically separated by hundreds of kilometers. For example

- SCADA system that controls the traffic lights in a major metropolitan city

- SCADA system that controls the power grid in the North Western United States

- SCADA system that monitors multiple oil refineries in a state

The SCADA system's communications should be

- Securely encrypted

- Air gapped and isolated from any commercial network, where possible

- On a dedicated WAN connection where air gapping is not possible due to distances

Yet there are many SCADA systems in use today that are accessible remotely (due to the negligence of the installer or manufacturer), some without a password. It is possible to locate these systems simply by running a port scan.

SCADA should be physically isolated from the commercial network. For example, a nuclear plant should not allow any part of the SCADA network to interact with the plant's commercial network. SCADA systems should not communicate wirelessly unless necessary, and where extreme precautions have been taken to ensure that all data is encrypted.

Many components inside the SCADA system may communicate without encryption. An air-gapped SCADA network can be easily disrupted if a malicious user has physical access to any SCADA network equipment or wiring. A malicious individual could splice the wiring between two SCADA system components and

- Disrupt the communication. For example, a conveyor belt is being used to load a truck with fertilizer. A hacker could cut the wire between the PLC and the conveyor belt motor, in which case no trucks could be filled. This behavior would disrupt operations.

- Spy on the communication. For example, a hacker could spy on the content of the communication to determine the quantity of oil being refined; the hacker could use this data to predict oil prices on the open market and place trades.

- Substitute inaccurate data inside the communication. For example, SCADA systems are used to control traffic lights in many major cities. These systems connect over unencrypted wireless systems or analog telephone lines. A hacker could disrupt the traffic patterns and bring intersections to a halt.

According to **NIST Guidelines for SCADA Systems** (**NIST Special Publication 800-82**), good SCADA security should

- Restrict logical access to an ICS network (using firewalls, multiple network layers, a DMZ, and unidirectional gateways)

- Restrict physical access to an ICS network

- Protect ICS from exploitation (install and test patches when available, disable unused ports and services, restrict user privileges to only those that need it, monitor and audit use of the system, check for file integrity)

- Restrict modification of data

- Detect security incidents (detect security events before they become incidents, detect failed ICS components and overloaded resources)

- Maintain functionality during adverse conditions (ensure that there is no single point of failure, that critical components have redundant counterparts, that the failure of a specific component does not create additional traffic or cascading effects, that if the system is to operate in a degraded state it does so gracefully)

- Restore the system after an incident (organization should have an incident response plan which includes key roles for all individuals involved, a well documented system, back up of all configuration, readily available replacement parts, and support from manufacturers and vendors)

An example of a virus that affects SCADA systems is Stuxnet. The Stuxnet virus

- Infected computers and hid its presence through a root kit

- Infected the firmware on USB drives inserted on those computers (the firmware on a USB drive does not contain any user storage and is typically inaccessible by any form of operating system or antivirus program)

- Searched for and infected any computer running the Siemens Step7 software application (which controls PLCs)

- Once locating a PLC, modified the code on the PLC so that it would cause damage, but returned normal values to the computer (so that the operator was unaware as to the harm that was being caused)

2.2 Compare and contrast routing technologies and bandwidth management concepts

- *Routing*
  - *Dynamic Routing*
    - *Protocols*
      - *Routing Internet Protocol (RIP)*
      - *Open Shortest Path First (OSPF)*
      - *Enhanced Interior Gateway Routing Protocol (EIGRP)*
      - *Border Gateway Protocol (BGP)*
    - *Link State vs Distance Vector vs Hybrid*
  - *Static Routing*
  - *Default Route*
  - *Administrative Distance*
  - *Exterior vs Interior*
  - *Time to Live*
- *Bandwidth Management*
  - *Traffic Shaping*
  - *Quality of Service (QoS)*

Okay, now that we know a bit about internal networks, we should learn something about external networks. Let's say you need to access Google.com. How does data from Google.com get to your computer and vice versa? Remember that we already talked about DNS.

The internet is a bunch of cables, and different sections are owned by different internet service providers. Thus, your data must pass through many routers controlled by many companies. The internet is a massive spider web. It's like the highway system. On a long trip, there are many routes you could take and arrive at the same destination. How does the data packet know which route to take? It uses a routing protocol.

In other words

- The router receives a packet

- It asks, what is the destination for this packet

- Based on the final destination, where do I send this packet?

There are three types of routes

- **Static**. A static route is programmed into the router. We tell the router that packets addressed to a specific destination (or range of destinations) take this specific route. We can provide one static route or many.

- **Dynamic**. The router figures out routes on its own using one of the routing protocols.

- **Default**. The default route is used when there are no other destinations for the packet. When the router receives a packet, it first checks the static route table. If it can transmit the packet via a static route, it does. If the packet's destination does not match a static route, then the router sends the packet over a dynamic route. If the packet does not match a dynamic route, then the router sends the packet over the default route.

There are four main dynamic routing protocols: RIP, OSPF, EGRIP, and BGP.

RIP – Routing Information Protocol. The router calculates the number of "hops" between the source and the destination. For example, if you are in Florida, and your data passes through a router in Atlanta, a router in Nebraska, and a router in Nevada before reaching California, that is four hops.

Each router maintains a table, known as a routing table. The router records the best route for each destination in this table. For example, google.com has a route, cnn.com has a route, facebook.com has a root, etc. (more accurately, each IP address has a route; the router doesn't care about or look at domain names).

The router doesn't care about the entire route; it only cares about the address of the next router, or the "next hop". When a router receives a packet, it asks, "which router should I send this packet to next?" and sends it off. Each router makes its own decision about the next destination without considering the source of the data.

The problem with RIP is that every router must update its routing table every 30 seconds, and that RIP supports routes with a maximum of 15 hops. As the internet grew, so did the routing tables, and eventually the system broke down. There were too many routers per pathway and too many routes per router.

RIP communicates over port 520 via UDP. A router that just powered on can use RIP to ask a neighboring router to send over its routing table. A router needs neighboring routers to cooperate so that it can understand the total "hop" length of a route. The router is constantly asking "how many hops does this data packet need to travel through to reach its destination?". Cisco devices used the proprietary **IGRP (Internet Gateway Routing Protocol)** to communicate and have now switched to the **EIGRP (Enhanced Interior Gateway Routing Protocol)**.

OSPF – Open Shortest Path First. Unlike RIP, OSPF not only considers the number of "hops", but also the speed between each hop, known as a link. Each link can be given a cost that factors the speed of each link. An administrator can manually set a different priority for each link.

Each router advertises its link cost to other routers. It does so by sending a "hello" message. This information travels through the network because a router will pass on information that it received from one router to its neighboring routers (a router is considered to be a neighbor if it is directly connected).

OSPF works with multiple redundant routers. It can detect a failed link and create a new link within seconds (remember that because the internet is a spider web, there are usually many pathways to the same destination).

Each router within a network will go through the following phases

- **Down** – this is when the router first joins the network. It hasn't said or heard anything

- **Attempt** – the router is trying to establish a connection with another router

- **Init** – the router received a "hello" from a neighboring router

- **2-Way** – the router is communicating with another router

- **ExStart** – the routers are establishing that they are adjacent. This happens right after the 2-Way

- **Exchange** – the router sends its **link state database** to a neighboring router. It is telling its neighbor about all the routers it knows about. The Link State Database tells us what routes a router knows about.

- **Loading** – the router requests the link state database from a neighboring router. It is telling its neighbor about all the routers it knows about

- **Full** – the routers are fully adjacent

This way, each router can learn about how all the routers are connected, and then each router can decide as to the best pathway to send a packet.

OSPF uses an IP packet to send data. The following types of data are sent

- **Hello** – this is when a router wants to talk to an adjacent router. The router always sends hello messages to its neighbors. If it does not receive a reply, it assumes that the neighbor stopped working, and will stop sending traffic through it

- **Database Description (DBD)** – this contains the link state database of an adjacent router

- **Link State Request (LSR)** – a router sends this to request information so that it can update its link state database

- **Link State Update (LSU)** – a router sends this in response to the request

- **Link State Acknowledgement (LSAck)** – the requesting router sends this to acknowledge receipt of a Link State Update message

The problem with OSPF is that there are millions of routers. That means every router will eventually learn all the routes for all the routers. To make it simple, we can divide the networks into areas.

All the areas must belong to the same **autonomous system** (a network that is under the control of a single internet service provider). This is important because there is another system that determines routes between two or more internet service providers.

- **Backbone area** – this forms the core OSPF network. The backbone distributes routing information between other areas. This is known as area 0. All the other areas connect to the backbone directly or through another router.

- **Stub area** – the stub area does not receive route advertisements from other routers. A router in this area must send traffic through a default route. Thus, the routers here do not have to maintain link state databases. There are mode advanced types of stub areas, which are proprietary to Cisco

  - **Totally stubby area** – this is like a stub area. Traffic can only be routed outside this area through a default route.

  - **Not-so-stubby area** – this area can import external routes and send them to other locations but can't receive external routes for itself.

  - **NSSA totally stubby area** – this area can import some types of external routes and send them to other locations but can't receive external routes for itself.

- **Transit area** – area with at least two border routers. The transit area passes traffic from one location to another but is not the source or the destination of the traffic.

Types of OSPF Routers

- **Internal router** – all the interfaces belong to the same area

- **Area border router** – connects an area to the backbone. That is all its interfaces belong to the area except for one that belongs to the backbone.

- **Backbone router** – connects to the backbone (may also be an area router). A backbone router may connect to other backbone routers and not to any areas.

- **Autonomous system boundary router** – this router connects networks from multiple autonomous systems. Such a router will use another routing protocol to send traffic between itself and another system.

BGP – Border Gateway Protocol. BGP allows routers to exchange data between two or more autonomous systems. Unlike OSPF, routers using BGP must be programmed to learn their neighbors, known as **"peers"** (it is not automatic). Every minute, a router sends a "keep alive" message to the neighboring routers to ensure that they are still available. Within an autonomous system, the BGP is known as **Internal BGP**, otherwise it is known as **External BGP**. A router that is exchanging data with another network is known as a border router. BGP uses TCP to exchange information.

Once programmed, a router can have the following states

- **Idle** – the router does not accept any new connections. The router begins to initiate a connection with its peer.

- **Connect** – the router is willing to accept negotiation messages with a peer

- **Active** – if the router is unable to connect with the peer, it turns to the active state and tries to start a new session. If the router is not able to connect, it might switch to the idle state.

- **OpenSent** – the router is listening for an open message from its peer. If the message is valid, then it establishes a connection

- **OpenConfirm** – the peer is waiting for a Keepalive message from its peer

- **Established** – the connection is established and the routers exchange information about their capabilities

How does the router decide which routes are best?

- Unlike OSPF, BGP needs to be able to detect loops in the routing. Thus, it needs to be able to detect the entire pathway between the router and the destination. It would not be possible to store this much information. Therefore, the solution is to keep track of the autonomous systems that a packet will travel through to reach its destination.

- By default, the BGP will choose the route that crosses the least number of Autonomous Systems

- An administrator can change the weight given to a route.

- Since BGP is used to move traffic between different ISPs, one ISP may prefer other ISP networks due to cost or contractual obligations.

- An administrator might not want to transport "transit" traffic. Transit traffic is traffic that did not originate in his network and that has a destination outside of his network. In other words, it is traffic that does not belong to any of his customers. Why should he transport it for free?

- Thus, the router does the following

  - Imports all of the routes

  - Eliminates any routes with loops

  - Gives each route a weight (known as the **local preference**) based on the number of autonomous systems and administrative rules

  - Picks the best routes based on the distance and other criteria

  - Advertises only the best routes to the neighbors

All the routers using Internal BGP must be configured in a full-mesh (that means that every router must have a connection to every other router). To reduce the amount of work a router must do

- One router can be designated as a **Route Reflector**. This router stores all the routes, while other routers peer to it.

- A large Autonomous System can be split into multiple smaller Autonomous Systems. The group of systems is known as a **Confederate**. Routers within each smaller Autonomous System are fully meshed. Routers in different autonomous systems are not fully meshed. The entire confederate appears to be a single autonomous system to any external routers.

Traffic Shaping is a method of throttling different forms of traffic. Let's say we have an office and half the people are on YouTube. They are slowing down the network for employees who are trying to work. What do we do? We can block YouTube, but that might be a bad idea because some employees might have a legitimate reason to access it. Or we can perform traffic shaping. Each type of traffic follows a pattern. We use a router to "fingerprint" the different types of traffic – websites, videos, file sharing, VoIP calls, etc.. Then we tell the router how much bandwidth each one can have. We might say that 10% of our bandwidth can go to web traffic, or 1Mb/s can go towards video streaming.

Traffic shaping is also used by internet service providers. If the ISP has limited bandwidth and a few customers are streaming Netflix in 4K, forcing others to wait for their e-mail to download, that's not fair. The ISP might use traffic shaping to give business-oriented traffic a larger portion of the bandwidth. Traffic shaping by ISPs is controversial, and the opposition is known as "net neutrality".

There are several traffic shaping algorithms. In general, each time a packet reaches the traffic shaping router

- The router figures out what kind of application it belongs to

- Based on the intended shape, it decides whether to hold the packet or send it

- Packets are held in a buffer until they are ready to be sent. Each type of traffic has its own buffer. The rate that packets leave the buffer is fixed. This is known as the "leaky bucket" problem. Imagine if we made a hole in the bottom of a bucket and pored water into the top. It doesn't matter how fast water enters the bucket, it leaves the bottom at the same speed.

- What happens if the buffer fills up with packets? No buffer is infinite. In that case, the buffer drops (ignores) the remaining packets.

To summarise, there are three ideas for choosing the best next hop destination

- **Link State** – the router chooses a destination using an algorithm that includes gathering information from the other connected routers

- **Distance Vector** – the router chooses a destination based on the shortest pathway to the final destination; this might be the number of routers or the number of autonomous zones that the traffic will pass through

- **Hybrid** – the router chooses a destination based on a combination of factors including the link state, the distance, and the local policies of the internet service provider

If our router has multiple routes to the same final destination learned from different sources (OSPF, BGP, static, etc.), how does it decide which one to use? It assigns each route an **administrative distance**, also known as a route preference. The following are some administrative distances are assigned to routes on Cisco routers (smaller distances are preferred)

Directly Connected Interface	**0**
Static Route	1
External BGP	20
Internal EIGRP	90
OSPF	110
RIP	120
Internal BGP	200
NHRP	250
DHCP	254

Quality of Service (**QoS**) is a concept regarding how well a specific network service is performing. We can measure different things like bandwidth (speed), packet loss (what percentage of data is reaching its destination), jitter (does the data we send show up in the same order or is it all mixed up).

QoS is most important in VoIP and live video applications. Why? Remember that TCP follows a three-way handshake? If I send you a file, you must acknowledge that you received it. If a computer sends a packet to another computer, the recipient must acknowledge receipt. If something happens to the packet along the way, it could always be retransmitted. A small amount of packet loss is a minor annoyance. Maybe the users don't even notice. If the packets don't arrive in the correct order, the receiving computer puts them back together.

With VoIP and live video however, imagine that each word you say is a packet. The phone or video screen on the other side must play those packets back to the other party in real time. It doesn't have time to correct for errors. If some packets go missing, then the person on the phone with you doesn't hear some of the words you said. If packets arrive in the wrong order, then the words you say are heard in the wrong order on the other side. Too much of that and the users become frustrated.

What are some things we measure when we say Quality of Service?

- How much **bandwidth** are we getting? This is known as throughput, or **Goodput**. Goodput is the useable bandwidth (actual bandwidth minus overhead for protocols). It's like the weight of the mail without the envelopes.

- **Packet loss**. What percentage of packets are lost in transmission?

- **Errors**. What percentage of packets arrive without errors?

- **Latency**. How long does a packet take to reach its destination?

- **Out-of-Order delivery**. Are the packets arriving in the same order that they were sent?

A customer and his internet service provider may enter into an agreement to obtain a specific level of service. How can the ISP meet this obligation? Over-provision the network so that it has much more capacity then is required.

But a single service provider doesn't own the entire internet! Your traffic first reaches your ISP and then it reaches your ISP's ISP, and then your ISPs ISPs ISP…therefore, the ISPs must negotiate a way to prioritize certain types of traffic so that customers who pay more experience better service. Otherwise, an ISP's ISP will turn on the BGP and not allow much of your traffic through their network.

One way to do this is called **DiffServ** or **Differentiated Services**. Remember that each packet has a header with information about its destination, size, etc.. Well, there is also an optional spot for a **Differentiated Services Code Point (DSCP)** value. The most common values are

- **Default Forwarding** – the data will be delivered with a "best effort"

- **Expedited Forwarding** – the data will be given priority

- **Assured Forwarding** – the data will be guaranteed to arrive within a specific time

You can think of DiffServ like a courier service. You can ship something that could arrive within a week. Or it could be guaranteed by the end of the next business day. Or it could be guaranteed to arrive by 10:30AM the next morning. Data that is sent through a slower method might arrive quickly if the network has spare capacity. But when the network is overwhelmed, more important traffic is given priority.

When an ISP sees a packet marked with Expedited Forwarding or Assured Forwarding, it knows to prioritize it. How much priority to give a packet is up to each ISP.

CoS or **Class of Service** is like QoS, but on an internal network. CoS tags an ethernet frame with a priority from zero to seven.

I could write an entire book on traffic shaping. It is an art, not a science because every ISP must balance the needs of all its customers. Giving many customers a lousy experience because a few people are paying more may not be in their best interests.

2.3 Given a scenario, configure and deploy common Ethernet switching features

- *Data Virtual Local Area Network (VLAN)*
- *Voice VLAN*
- *Port Configurations*
    - *Port Tagging/802.1Q*
    - *Port Aggregation*
        - *Link Aggregation Control Protocol (LACP)*
    - *Duplex*
    - *Speed*
    - *Flow Control*
    - *Port Mirroring*
    - *Port Security*
    - *Jumbo Frames*
    - *Auto-Medium-Dependent Interface Crossover (MDI-X)*
- *Media Access Control (MAC) Address Tables*
- *Power over Ethernet (PoE) / Power over Ethernet Plus (PoE+)*
- *Spanning Tree Protocol*
- *Carrier-Sense Multiple Access with Collision Detection (CSMA/CD)*
- *Address Resolution Protocol (ARP)*
- *Neighbor Discovery Protocol*

I mentioned VLANs and switches earlier, but now let's take a closer look. We already said that if we have a single physical network with an IP address range, we can break it up into multiple subnets. And we can assign different types of devices to different subnets (for example, computers, phones, security cameras, etc.).

When we have different devices with different subnets connected to the same physical switch, we need to make sure that their traffic stays separate.

We could create a **VLAN** or **Virtual Local Area Network**. We could assign each switch port to a single VLAN. Any device connected to that port belongs to that particular port's VLAN.

A host such as a phone, computer, or switch will belong to a single VLAN.

Simple switches do not support VLANs. These are commonly known as unmanaged switches. On an unmanaged switch, all the ports belong to VLAN 1 and there is no option to add additional VLANs.

What if we have a large network with multiple switches? Let's say we have one core switch and ten edge switches. And let's say we have ten VLANs. If I want a device on VLAN 1 switch 1 to be able to talk to a device on VLAN 1 switch 2, then I need to choose a port on the core switch and a port on switch 1, set each of them to VLAN 1, and connect them with a patch cable. I could do this for the other nine VLANs and the other nine switches, but then I'd run out of switch ports. My core switch might only have 48 ports. Clearly this is not a good solution.

How can we transport traffic from multiple VLANs between the same set of switch ports? We can use a trunk port. We choose a port on the core switch, and a port on switch one, and connect them with a patch cable. Then we configure them as trunk ports. We tell the switch which VLANs are permitted to transport their traffic through that trunk port.

A **Trunk** port carries traffic for multiple VLANs. Each frame is tagged with its VLAN. Ports that are not trunk ports are known as **Access** ports. An Access port belongs to a single VLAN. The switch assumes that traffic through that port belongs to the VLAN assigned to the port. The standard for VLANs is called 802.1Q.

This brings us to our next point: Tagging and Untagging ports. An access port is known as an **untagging port** or **untagged port**, because it strips the VLAN tags off any traffic it receives and because traffic passes through the port untagged. A trunk port is known as a **tagging port** or a **tagged port**, because it adds VLAN tags to any traffic it receives, and because traffic passes through the port tagged.

Now we have three scenarios for traffic flow within the switches

- Traffic moving between two devices on the same VLAN and on the same switch. This traffic moves from one access port on the switch to another access port on the same switch.

  - The switch receives the frame

  - The switch realizes that the destination device is directly connected to the switch

  - The switch realizes that the source port and the destination port are assigned to the same VLAN

  - The switch forwards the traffic out of the destination port

- Traffic moving between two devices on the same VLAN but connected to different switches.

  - The switch receives the frame

  - The switch realizes that the destination device is connected to another switch through a trunk port

  - The switch tags the frame with the VLAN ID of the port it was received on

  - The switch forwards the frame through its trunk port to the appropriate switch

  - The receiving switch receives the tagged frame

  - The receiving switch realizes that the destination is directly connected to it

  - The receiving switch removes the VLAN ID from the frame and sends the frame to the correct destination

- Traffic moving between two devices on a different VLAN

  - The switch will forward the traffic to the router and the router will decide whether to forward the traffic back to the switch

  - If the switch is a Layer 3 switch, it may apply its own rules to forward the traffic

It is important that we configure the same VLANs on every switch. If VLAN one on switch one is VLAN two on switch two, it takes little to imagine what kind of problems that would cause.

Every port can be assigned to one VLAN only. There is one exception. Access ports on a Cisco switch can be configured with two VLANs. Why? In a large organization using VoIP, the VoIP phones are connected on one VLAN and the computers are connected on another VLAN.

This is known as **IP Passthrough** because the phone passes the computer's traffic through to the switch. The main advantage is that the organization only requires one cable per user. The Cisco switch knows how to separate VoIP and user traffic.

Each switch port can have several attributes that can be configured

- **Port Tagging** – whether the port is an access port or a trunk port

- **Port Aggregation** – whether multiple ports can work together to transmit data

- **VLAN** – the VLAN assigned to the particular port, or the VLANs allowed to be transported over that port if it is a trunk

- **Duplex** – whether the port operates at **full duplex** or at **half duplex**. That is, whether it talks and listens at the same time (full duplex), or whether it waits for the other device to stop talking before it starts.

- **Speed** – we can manually set the speed of the port. Available options depend on the switch, but the most common are 100 Mbps and 1 Gbps. Slower switches had the ability to choose either 10 Mbps or 100 Mbps. Newer, faster switches offer 2.5 Gbps, 5 Gbps, 10 Gbps, and 40 Gbps. These faster speeds might require an SFP.

  If we don't manually configure a duplex and/or speed, the switch and the other device connected to it will automatically agree on a speed and duplex through a process called **autonegotiation**.

  If we manually set a speed and duplex on only the switch or on the other device, the device that is not manually set will try to figure out the correct speed and duplex setting and attempt to communicate via the correct setting.

- **Flow Control** – flow control allows a switch to tell the sender to slow down the amount of data it is sending. The purpose is to allow the switch to catch up when it is overwhelmed with the amount of data being received; the alternative being that the switch will begin dropping the traffic, resulting in data loss.

- **Port Mirroring** - Port Mirroring is a feature where the switch passes the same traffic on two different ports. For example, if we wanted to monitor Port #4, we could tell the switch to mirror Port #4 onto Port #8. Now the switch will duplicate traffic leaving Port #4 onto

Port #8. We can monitor Port #4's traffic by connecting a monitoring device onto Port #8.

Port Mirroring is known as **Switched Port Analyzer (SPAN)** or **Remote Switched Port Analyzer (RSPAN)** on Cisco devices. We can monitor incoming and outgoing traffic. Why would we want to monitor traffic? We could detect intrusions or ensure that the network is performing as expected.

- **Port Security** – Port Security is a method for controlling the devices that are permitted to talk to the switch. There are a number of settings and we will discuss port security in greater detail.

- **Jumbo Frames** – Jumbo Frames is a setting that permits or denies a port the ability to send or receive a packet larger than 1500 bytes

- **Auto-Medium-Dependent Interface Crossover (MDI-X)** – in the early days of ethernet, when we connected two switches together, we used a crossover cable (the pins are swapped). When we connected a router or other user device to a switch, we used a straight through cable.

  If we enable the MDI-X feature, a switch port will automatically determine the type of cable that is connected and switch the pins that it uses to send and receive. Thus, users don't have to worry about whether they are using a straight through or crossover cable. MDI-X is enabled by default, but only applies to speeds of 10 or 100 Mbps. Faster speeds use all four pairs and do not have dedicated transmit or receive pairs.

- **PoE** – we can determine whether the port will provide power over ethernet (to power devices such as cameras, wireless access points, and phones)

Now we know that the switch receives a frame and tags it or untags it depending on the VLAN, etc. But how does the switch know what all of the devices connected to it are and which ports they are actually plugged in to?

Introducing the **MAC Address Tables**. A switch remembers the MAC address of every device that is connected to it. Well, the switch has a huge table called the MAC Address Table. When the switch first powers on, this table is completely blank. Each time the switch receives a frame, it checks the source MAC address on the frame.

Let's say the switch received a frame on Port 27, from a device with the MAC address AA:AA:AA:AA:AA:AA. It now knows that a device with the MAC address AA:AA:AA:AA:AA:AA is connected to Port 27 (it doesn't matter if it is directly connected or connected through another switch). The switch updates the table to reflect this information. Each time the switch receives a frame, it updates the table.

Second, when the switch is ready to forward that frame, it checks the table. Every frame has a destination. If the switch later receives a frame addressed to a device with MAC address AA:AA:AA:AA:AA:AA, it knows from the table that it should forward that frame out of Port 27. Remember that since a switch can be connected to other switches, and since each of those switches can be connected to dozens of devices, a single port on a core switch could see frames coming from dozens or hundreds of MAC addresses.

If the switch receives a frame addressed to a MAC address that is not in the table, then it sends that frame out all its ports, except for the one on which it received the frame. This is known as flooding. If VLANs are configured, then the switch only sends the frame out of the ports that match the VLAN on which it was received. But, but, but, then a whole bunch of devices will receive frames that aren't addressed to themselves? Yes, but that isn't a big deal. Legitimate network devices ignore frames that aren't addressed to themselves.

The entries in the table only last about five minutes. If the switch doesn't see traffic from a specific MAC address after five minutes, it deletes the entry in the table. The default time can be adjusted by an administrator.

The MAC address is the core of all switch logic.

How does a device know what MAC address to send its frame to anyways? That's where ARP or **Address Resolution Protocol** comes in.

Let's say my computer has a MAC address of AA:AA:AA:AA:AA:AA and an IP address of 192.168.1.2, and my printer has a MAC address of BB:BB:BB:BB:BB:BB and an IP address of 192.168.1.3. My computer knows my printer's IP address (an administrator may have programmed it), but it needs to find out its MAC address so that it can send it a document.

My computer sends out a message known as an **ARP request message**. It addresses the message to the generic MAC address FF:FF:FF:FF:FF:FF. All network devices by default can read messages addressed here. My computer's message in effect says, "if your IP address is 192.168.1.3, then tell me your MAC address". This message is flooded over the entire network, but only the printer responds (because only the printer has that IP address). The printer sends an **ARP response message** back to my computer, indicating that its MAC address is BB:BB:BB:BB:BB:BB, basically saying "hey, my IP address is 192.168.1.3 and my MAC address is BB:BB:BB:BB:BB:BB".

My computer maintains a table called the **ARP table**. It adds the information learned from the ARP response to the table. The ARP table contains a list of device MAC addresses and their corresponding IP addresses. Next time my computer wants to talk to the printer, it doesn't need to follow the ARP process. It just checks the table. In fact, every time a computer needs to send an

ARP message, it checks the ARP table first. If it doesn't find an entry in the ARP table, then it sends out an ARP request message.

Now let's say we did something stupid and connected two switches together with two cables. We now have a loop because the top switch sees all the MAC addresses from devices connected to the bottom switch (due to the blue cable), and all the devices connected to itself (due to the red cable). The same applies to the bottom switch.

Any frame that the switch attempts to transmit enters the loop and goes in circles. This results in unpredictable network activity. One common result is a **broadcast storm**. Remember that a broadcast is sent to everybody? Well, if the top switch receives a broadcast packet, it sends it to the bottom switch, which sends it back. The two switches send packets to each other until they crash.

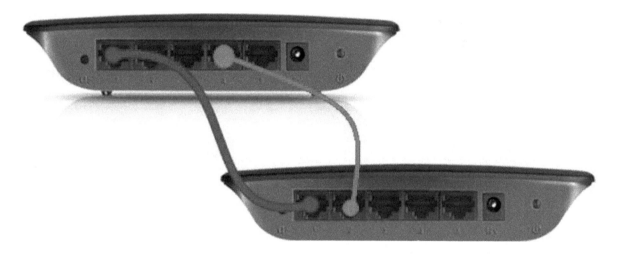

How do we avoid this? We use a **Spanning Tree Protocol (STP)**. The switches figure out how many connections they have amongst themselves. If two switches discover that they have multiple links, they turn all of them off except for one. STP works on small networks of just two switches and large networks that could have dozens or hundreds of switches. How does it work?

- First all the switches pick one switch to be the "**root bridge**". The root bridge is switch with the smallest bridge ID. An administrator would manually configure a bridge ID on each switch. If there is a tie with the bridge ID, then the switches pick the switch with the lowest MAC address.

- Each of the remaining switches figures out how it is connected to the "root". If a switch has multiple connections, it assigns a cost to each one. The greater the bandwidth, the lower the cost. For example, a 100 Mbit/s link costs "19", while a 1 Gbit/s link costs "4". The switch turns off the most expensive links. The switches communicate the cost through **Bridge**

Protocol Data Units (BPDUs).

- Remember that the topology can become complicated. There may be several switches between an edge switch and the root switch. Thus, the pathway to the root may involve several links, each of which has its own "cost". Consider the following diagram. If the black switch (on the top) is a core switch and the yellow switch (on the bottom) is an edge switch, the yellow switch has two links back to the root (one through the switch on the left and one through the switch on the right). It must calculate the cost of the entire pathway.

  If the pathway through the switch on the left was least expensive, the bottom switch would turn off the link to the switch on the right. What if the bottom switch needed to send traffic to a device connected to a switch on the right? It would have to send it through the switch on the left, and the switch at the top.

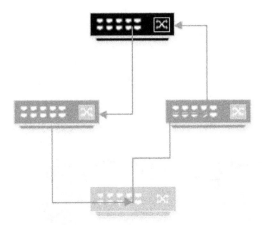

- If multiple pathways have the same cost, then the switch chooses the pathway containing the neighboring switch with the lowest bridge ID.

- A port can have any of the following statuses:

  o **Blocking.** The switch determined that this port will cause a loop. It does not send or receive any traffic on this port, except for BPDU data.

  o **Listening.** The port does not transmit data, nor does it learn MAC addresses, but it is still watching for BPDU data that would make it switch to a blocking state.

  o **Learning.** The port does not transmit data, but it still learns MAC addresses of devices that could be connected to it, and adds them to the MAC address table.

- **Forwarding**. A normally operating port. All data is transferred. The port is still watching for new BPDU data that would make it switch to a blocking state.

- **Disabled**. The port was manually turned off or turned off due to a security incident. We'll talk about security incidents later. No data is transferred, not even BPDU data.

- When the port first activates (when something is first connected to it) the port will first enter the listening state and then the learning state. It will remain in this state for about 15 seconds, although the value can be changed by an administrator. If it doesn't find any adverse information from the BPDU data then it will switch to a forwarding state.

- The switches continually revaluate their connections and recalculate the cost of each link. Switches exchange Bridge Protocol Data Units every two seconds.

- The switches also continually test their data links. If a link fails, the switch activates a more expensive link. If a less expensive link starts working again, the switch returns to sending traffic over it. A switch tests its link by sending a "hello" message every two seconds. If the switch does not receive a reply after three "hello" messages (six seconds), it assumes that the link is defective and chooses a new link.

We might call this **Rapid Spanning Tree Protocol (RSTP)**. RSTP is an improvement over the original STP and is proprietary to Cisco.

- In RSTP, there are three port states

  - **Discarding**. The port does not send or receive any traffic.

  - **Learning**. The port does not send any traffic, but it does learn MAC addresses of devices connected to it.

  - **Forwarding**. The port is sending and receiving traffic normally.

What if I had a really big network and I decided that one cable between my switches wasn't enough to handle all the traffic? What if I needed two or three cables? How can I make such a connection without creating a loop?

We could use **Link Aggregation Control Protocol**, or **LACP**. Link Aggregation is also known as **Port Aggregation** or **Channel Bonding**. Link Aggregation allows us to combine multiple physical ethernet links into a single logical link. LACP has automatic failover detection. We could choose between two and eight ports to use in the link.

The links must be assigned to the same logical switch and they must all have the same speed.

How does the switch decide which packet to send down which physical link? It uses a scheduling algorithm that looks at the source and destination IP addresses and MAC addresses. The goal of the algorithm is to randomize the use of each link so that the load is balanced.

Finally, let's say we wanted to connect a VoIP phone, an access point, or a surveillance camera to the switch. These devices require power. But it's a hassle to connect the device to an ethernet cable and to a power outlet. That's where **PoE (Power Over Ethernet)** comes in. PoE lets a switch power a network device over the same ethernet cable that it communicates on.

PoE is governed by the 802.3af standard and delivers up to 15.40 W. PoE+ delivers up to 30W. Type 4 PoE delivers up to 100W. A switch capable of delivering PoE is called a PoE switch and is typically more expensive than a non-PoE switch. You must choose a switch that has enough overall capacity to power all the devices connected to it.

If you only had one or two devices that required PoE, you might connect a **power injector** instead. A power injector sits between the switch and the device requiring power. It takes data from the switch, adds power, and sends it to the device.

You can enable or disable PoE on a per-port basis. Devices that require PoE have a resistor inside their network card between two of the pins. When you connect a PoE-capable device to a switch, the switch will detect the high resistance and send it power. This prevents the switch from sending power to a device that doesn't require it, which could potentially damage the device.

What if all the devices want to talk at the same time? What if one device wants to send a message to many devices at the same time? We can learn some concepts

- **Broadcast Domain**. A broadcast domain is a network segment. Your entire office (everything behind the router) is one broadcast domain, even if it has many switches.

  If one device wants to talk to all the other devices, it sends a message known as a **broadcast frame** (or **broadcast packet**). The switch receives the broadcast frame and passes it on to all the devices connected to it that are in the same VLAN. These devices make up the broadcast domain. A router will ignore broadcast frames.

  We can separate a local network into multiple broadcast domains by implementing VLANs.

  Why do we have broadcast domains? For example, a computer joins the network and chooses an IP address. It sends a broadcast message to the network to verify that no other device shares its IP address. Or a printer joins the network and announces its presence so that computers can find it.

- **CSMA/CD**. **Carrier Sense Multiple Access with Collision Detection**. What happens if two devices want to talk at the same time on the same cable? Each device transmits a frame at the same time and a collision takes place.

  A collision is bad, but at least we know that it happened. Both devices stop talking immediately. Each device sends a "jam signal"; a message to the other devices that tells them to be quiet. Each device picks a random amount of time to wait and then resends its frame. Hopefully, the next time, the line is free.

  The collision detection method depends on the type of ethernet wiring in use.

  In modern networks, CSMA/CD is not required. Collisions only took place on the old form of ethernet wiring, where many devices were connected to the same cable.

- **CSMA/CA**. **Carrier Sense Multiple Access with Collision Avoidance**.

  A device "listens" to the channel it is attempting to transmit on. If another device is transmitting, we wait a random amount of time and then listen again. The device might ask for permission to send its data, or it might just wait until it knows the line is clear. If the line is clear, or if the device is told that it can transmit the data, then it sends the data.

- **Collision Domains**. All the devices that are at risk of having a collision make up a collision domain. In the modern world, collisions are not possible; therefore, each collision domain consists of a single device. Consider a computer connected to a switch via an ethernet cable. Only the switch and the computer can communicate over that cable. It is not possible for another device to send data along that physical ethernet cable.

- **Protocol Data Units**. A Protocol Data Unit is the smallest unit of information that can be transmitted on a layer. Remember I said that a computer breaks the data into chunks before sending it? Each chunk has an address and some other metadata to help it get to its destination. Well, on Layer 2, the chunk is called a frame, and contains the MAC address of the sender/recipient. If that chunk (frame) makes it to the router, the router adds some more metadata (like an IP address) to it so that it can get to its destination. That frame becomes a packet.

  A PDU is like a letter. If you write a letter and put it in an envelope, the mailman uses the address on the envelope to decide where it goes. If you wrote a letter to your neighbor, the mailman might take it there himself. This envelope is like a Layer 2 PDU.

  If you wrote the letter to a friend in another city, it might go into a mailbag that is thrown onto a truck and driven there. The mailbag has its own address (that of the post office in the other city). When the mailbag gets to the destination, the envelope is taken out and delivered to the recipient. The mailbag is like a Layer 3 PDU. Notice that the metadata for the previous layer is still present.

  If you wrote the letter to a friend in another country, that mailbag might go into a shipping container. The shipping container is addressed to the central post office of the receiving country. The container is like a Layer 4 PDU. The container is opened at its destination and the mailbag is removed. The letter is removed from the mailbag and taken to its final destination. Notice that the metadata for the previous two layers is still present.

- **MTU**. The **Maximum Transmission Unit** is the largest size PDU that can be transmitted over a particular layer and protocol. Each layer and each protocol has different limitations.

  Remember that each PDU has metadata, and the amount of metadata is not affected by the size of the actual data. It's like a letter. The letter has a to address, a from address, and a stamp. It doesn't matter how long the letter is. If we send a document in one envelope or if we break it up into twenty envelopes, we must include the same addresses (metadata) on each envelope.

If the MTU is small, then a large portion of the data being transmitted is metadata. Thus, it is more efficient to have the MTU as large as possible. Each network device has physical limitations; therefore, the size of the MTU can be affected by the types of devices in use. When two devices establish a connection, they may agree on an MTU size.

- o IPv4 – between 68 bytes and 64 kilobytes
- o IPv6 – between 1280 bytes and 64 kilobytes
- o Ethernet – up to 1500 bytes

2.4 Give a scenario, install and configure the appropriate wireless standards and technologies

- *802.11 Standards*
    - *a*
    - *b*
    - *g*
    - *n (Wi-Fi 4)*
    - *ac Wi-Fi 5)*
    - *ax (Wi-Fi 6)*
- *Frequencies and Range*
    - *2.4GHz*
    - *5 GHz*
- *Channels*
    - *Regulatory Impacts*
- *Channel Bonding*
- *Service Set Identifier (SSID)*
    - *Basic Service Set*
    - *Extended Service Set*
    - *Independent Basic Service Set (Ad Hoc)*
    - *Roaming*
- *Antenna Types*
    - *Omni*
    - *Directional*
- *Encryption Standards*
    - *Wi-Fi Protected Access (WPA) / WPA2 Personal / Advanced Encryption Standard (AES) / Temporal Key Integrity Protocol (TKIP)*
    - *WPA/WPA2 Enterprise (AES/TKIP)*
- *Cellular Technologies*
    - *Code-Division Multiple Access (CDMA)*
    - *Global System for Mobile Communications (GSM)*
    - *Long-Term Evolution (LTE)*
    - *3G, 4G, 5G*
- *Multiple Input, Multiple Output (MIMO) and Multi-User MIMO (MU-MIMO)*

All Wi-Fi protocols are regulated by IEEE (Institute of Electrical and Electronics Engineers). Collectively, we call them 802.11. As the demand for technology increases, new standards are released. The current standard is 802.11ac.

An access point or client (computer, phone, Wi-Fi adapter) may support multiple standards. The standards are backwards compatible (for example, an 802.11ac device will work with an 802.11a device).

Six standards have emerged

802.11a

1999 Standard

Supports up to 54 Mbps in the 5GHz range

802.11b

1999 Standard

Supports up to 11 Mbps in the 2.4GHz range

802.11g

2003 Standard

Up to 54 Mbps in the 2.4GHz range

If all the devices on a network are at the 802.11g level, then the network operates at 54 Mbps. Otherwise, it operates at 11 Mbps to support the older devices.

802.11n (Wi-Fi 4)

2009 Standard

Supports **multiple-input, multiple-output** (**MIMO**) – an access point device with multiple antennas
Up to 72.2 Mbps with one send and one receive antenna
Up to 450 Mbps with three send and three receive antennas
Also supports **transmit beamforming** which focuses the signal so that there are no dead zones

It has a better way of supporting older devices. It can operate in one of three modes
- **Legacy** means it sends separate packets for older devices, which is not efficient
- **Mixed** means it sends out standard packets that support older devices and newer devices. We might also call this

high-throughput or **802.11a-ht** or **802.11g-ht**.
- **Greenfield** means that it sends out 802.11n packets that support newer devices, but not older devices

802.11ac (Wi-Fi 5)

2014 Standard

Supports **multiuser multiple-input, multiple-output (MIMO)**

Up to 433 Mbps per antenna, or 1.3Gbps with three antennas

802.11ax (Wi-Fi 6)

2021 standard

In addition to all the features of Wi-Fi 5, Wi-Fi 6 offers a 400% improvement in throughput and a 75% drop in latency. It has the best performance in high-density areas such as offices.

It takes advantage of cellular technology called orthogonal frequency-division multiple access, which optimizes the radio signal.

While the previous Wi-Fi standards operated in the 2.4Ghz and 5Ghz bands, Wi-Fi 6 also operates at 6Ghz (technically 5.925Ghz to 7.125Ghz).

The standard provides guidelines that manufacturers of wireless devices use when making devices. With a reliable standard, products from different manufacturers all work together. Just think about it – it doesn't really matter what brand laptop or phone you have, it generally works with the Wi-Fi at your office, your home, the airport, the mall, your friend's house, etc. That's because the Wi-Fi card in your device follows the same standard as the Wireless Access Points installed everywhere.

Which Wi-Fi device should you select? Obviously, the latest version is the best! Technology will continue to improve, and you don't want to be stuck with something that is obsolete by the time you install it.

A radio signal (like the one used in Wi-Fi and cell towers) is like a wave. It goes up and down.

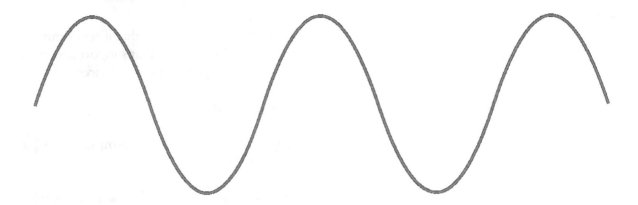

The height of the wave is called the **Amplitude**. The width of the wave is called the **wave length**. No matter the height or the width, the wave travels at the speed of light. You can think of a Wi-Fi signal like light that you can't see, because scientifically, that's exactly what it is. Thus, the wider the wave (the larger the wavelength), the less waves will pass through each second. We call this the **frequency**, measured as the number of waves that pass through per second. We measure frequency in **Hertz (Hz)**.

If you had special glasses that would let you see waves in the air, it would look like a big mess of waves travelling everywhere. So, each device is programmed to "look" for waves at a specific frequency and ignore the rest.

The government regulates the frequency that each type of technology can use. If everybody could broadcast signals at any frequency they wanted, the air would be a mess and wireless systems would not be able to function.

Wi-Fi signals travel at a frequency of 2.4GHz and 5GHz (and 6Ghz soon). Older cordless phones use a signal with a frequency of 900MHz.

If we change the Amplitude of the wave over time (up and down), we can use it to convey information.

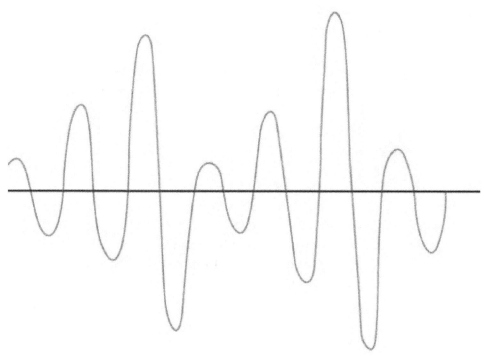

The range of a Wi-Fi signal is between 50 and 300 feet. It is affected by signal interference (noise) from neighboring networks. Different wall types can block or reduce the signal (glass, concrete, steel will block signals more than drywall).

The 2.4GHz range has eleven channels. It has a longer range and is less vulnerable to noise than the 5GHz range, which has twenty-three channels. Older devices use the 2.4GHz range. What's a channel?

When two waves with the same frequency collide, they cancel each other out and the signal is lost. If I have a Wi-Fi network and my neighbor has a Wi-Fi network, the signals will interfere, and nobody will be able to understand anything. To solve this problem, we divide the 2.4GHz spectrum into 11 channels: Each channel is 22MHz wide, spaced 5MHz apart.

Therefore, a 2.4GHz network is not actually broadcasting at a frequency of exactly 2.4000000GHz, but instead at 2.412GHz, 2.417GHz, or 2.422GHz, etc.

If two neighboring networks choose different channels, they will each broadcast on a slightly different frequency – different enough that their signals won't interfere. We can manually select the channel that we want to broadcast on, or we can let our wireless system choose it for us. We should survey the neighboring networks to see what channels they are broadcasting on and select a different channel from all of them. If we have multiple access points in a building and their signals overlap, we should select a different channel for each of them.

The channel concept applies to 5GHz networks as well. A 5GHz spectrum is divided into 23 channels, each is 20MHz wide. A 5GHz spectrum can broadcast on 5.150GHz, 5.1570GHz, etc.

There are more regulations for the 5GHz network and some countries do not allow some frequencies (they could interfere with weather radar and other systems).

If our network does not have enough bandwidth, we can bond two adjacent channels together to double its capacity. This is known as **channel bonding**. We combine two 20MHz channels into one 40MHz channel. One of the channels is the primary channel, and the other is secondary. Client devices that use channel bonding will transmit and receive on both channels, while client devices that don't support it will only use the primary channel.

5GHz has one complication. Some of the frequencies in the 5GHz range are also used by government weather radar systems. If your device is using a frequency in the range of a government radar system, it must first scan to see if such a device is present. If it is, your device must switch to a different channel for at least an hour and then scan again. That is, the government devices get first dibs on some of the 5GHz channels and don't allow interference from consumer devices. Devices have a feature called **dynamic frequency selection (DFS)**, which allows them to detect the nearby signal and switch over.

- Channels in the range of 5.150Ghz to 5.250Ghz are always permitted

- Channels in the range of 5.170Ghz to 5.740Ghz are only permitted when not in use by a government device. A device using this range must have dynamic frequency selection so that it can switch to another channel once it detects a government device.

- Channels in the range of 5.735Ghz to 5.815Ghz are always permitted.

- Channels in the range of 5.815 to 5.895 are permitted for indoor use only

High end devices such as smartphones and wireless access points will use dynamic frequency selection. Cheaper devices will not. If a wireless access point switches to a DFS channel, cheaper devices will not be able to detect the signal and will switch to the 2.4Ghz range instead.

Every country regulates the use of wireless signals and some channels that are available for use in the United States are not available in other countries. When you set up a wireless device, you must check the regulations in your country and verify that you are broadcasting in a range that is permitted. Regulations are subject to change and a channel that was legal before may become illegal later.

There are two general types of networks

- An **ad hoc network** is when two devices try to connect to each other directly. For example, when you connect to a wireless printer, or a wireless access point, you are using an ad hoc network.

- An **infrastructure network** is one with wireless access points. Devices, known as clients, connect to the network through the wireless access points

The **SSID** is or **Service Set Identifier** is the name of the network. An SSID is mapped to a WLAN (Wireless Local Area Network), and a WLAN is typically mapped to a VLAN (Virtual Local Area Network). Multiple SSIDs/WLANs can be mapped to the same VLAN. The purpose of an SSID is to allow us to separate wireless traffic the same way that we can separate wired traffic.

A single wireless access point can broadcast multiple SSIDs. For example, we might have a "Guest" SSID for guests, a "Staff" SSID for staff, and an "IoT" SSID for smart devices. If we have a large office with multiple wireless access points, each wireless access point can be configured to broadcast all the SSIDs.

If I have a large office, one wireless access point won't be able to provide a good signal across the entire floor. I might place my access points like this, and give each of them a different channel (or the controller might assign each one a different channel automatically). Each access point has its own MAC address, but all are broadcasting the same SSIDs.

What happens when I connect to the "Staff" SSID and I'm standing at the top left corner of the office? My laptop will probably connect to the closest access point (because it has the strongest signal). It might see "Staff" SSIDs from other access points nearby with weaker signals and different channels. As I move throughout the office, the signal from the first access point I connected to will become weaker, but my laptop will automatically move its connection to another wireless access point that is broadcasting the "Staff" SSID. This process is called **roaming**. When multiple access points create a seamless SSID, it is known as a **ESSID** or **Extended Service Set Identifier**.

The **BSSID** or **Basic Service Set Identifier** is the name (or MAC address) of the physical access point that I am connected to. Thus, within a given SSID, there can be one or multiple BSSIDs. If an access point is broadcasting multiple SSIDs, then that access point will also have multiple BSSIDs. That is, an access point will have multiple MAC addresses assigned to it by the manufacturer – one physical MAC address that it uses to communicate with the wired network, and multiple wireless MAC addresses that it can assign to each SSID. The number of SSIDs that a wireless access point can broadcast is limited to the number of wireless MAC addresses that are assigned to it.

The portion of the access point that broadcasts the signal is called the **radio**. An access point can have multiple radios. Having multiple radios allows the access point to communicate with multiple devices at the same time. An access point will need a unique MAC address for each radio-SSID combination. Thus, if an access point can broadcast 32 SSIDs and has two radios, it will have 64 wireless MAC addresses.

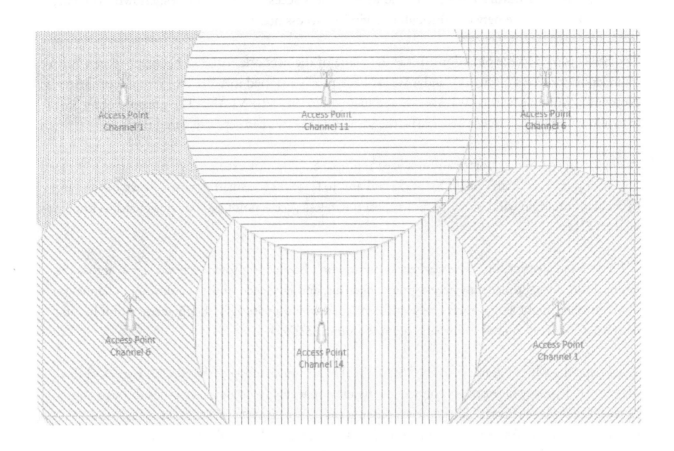

Below is a common Wireless Access Point, the Cisco Aironet 1142N. This access point has antennas concealed inside it. It's considered **omnidirectional**, because it broadcasts in all directions. Most access points are omnidirectional. We can mount it to a ceiling and it will provide good coverage in an office.

What if I have a problem where I need to point a Wi-Fi signal in a specific direction? I could attach external antennas to the access point and mount them facing the direction that I require. This is known as **unidirectional** transmission. Antennas are available in different shapes and sizes. Antennas also increase the signal strength of the access point.

An example of an access point with antennas is below

Another example of powerful directional antennas is the Ubiquiti AirFiber. It allows us to send a strong Wi-Fi signal long distances by pointing it in a specific direction. For example, I could use the AirFiber to connect two far away buildings via a wireless connection.

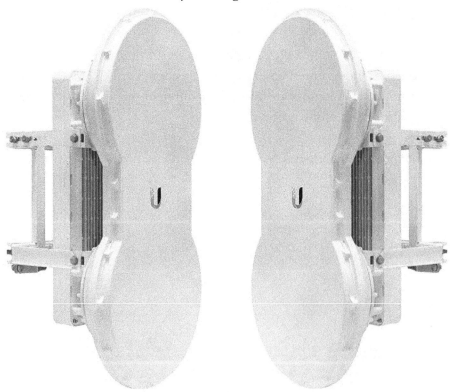

There are many other types of antennas, each of which has a different pattern and purpose.

How do we secure the communication between the wireless access point and the wireless device? How do we ensure that unauthorized users can't connect? There are several forms of wireless encryption.

- **WEP (Wired Equivalent Privacy)** encryption uses a password to authenticate the host with the access point.

  o An administrator configures a password on the wireless access point

  o The authorized users are provided with the password, which they use to authenticate with the access point

  o All further communications are encrypted with the provided password

  o A packet sniffer can intercept packets and easily crack the password.

  o WEP has been known to be insecure since 2005 but is still in use today.

  o WPA keys were 64-bits long.

  o WEP is not recommended

- **WPA (Wi-Fi Protected Access)** and **WPA2** use a password to create a handshake (which creates a unique one-time password) between the host and the access point.

  o An administrator must create a WPA or WPA2 password and configure it on each access point

  o The authorized users are provided with the password, which they use to authenticate with the access point

  o When a device first connects to a wireless access point, the device and the WAP follow a handshake process to create a unique one-time key that the two parties use to encrypt all further communications

  o WPA is more secure than WEP because the key is much longer and because every connection is encrypted with a different password

  o A packet sniffer can intercept packets during the handshake process and identify the password.

o WPA uses 256-bit keys

o WPA2 uses AES encryption algorithms and has replaced WPA

- **WPA Enterprise** uses a RADIUS server to authenticate the identity of the host attempting to connect. The host will typically present a digitally signed certificate to the RADIUS server (i.e. the host computer must have a certificate installed to connect to the network). Another option is for the host to sign in to the wireless network by entering a username and password. Certificate-based WPA Enterprise is difficult to break, provided that the certificates are digitally signed using a strong algorithm and that there are no other flaws in the access point or RADIUS server. Username/password based WPA Enterprise can be broken if the username/password are intercepted. An attacker could set up a rogue access point broadcasting the same SSID and then intercept usernames/passwords.

- **WPA3** is under development but is expected to replace WPA2.

- **TKIP (Temporal Key Integrity Protocol)** was a standard that was introduced to temporarily replace WEP.

  o WEP had been broken and the Wi-Fi alliance needed a quick solution to replace it without forcing customers to replace physical hardware

  o TKIP is no longer considered secure

  o TKIP uses the same functions as WEP, except that it

    ▪ Adds an initialization vector to the secret key

    ▪ Uses a sequence counter to prevent replay attacks

    ▪ Uses a 64-bit Message Integrity Check

    ▪ Encrypts every data packet with a unique encryption key

Remember that Wi-Fi is considered a "one-to-many" connection. One antenna talks to many devices. But as I said before, a wireless access point can only communicate with one device at a time.

Access points use **Time Division Multiplexing**. The access point sends data to one device, pauses, sends data to the next device, pauses, sends data to the third device, pauses, etc. until it has sent data to all the devices. It is also receiving data from each device in the same pattern.

To send data to multiple devices at the same time, an access point must have multiple antennas and engage in advanced signal processing. This technology is known as **Multiple Input, Multiple Output (MIMO)**.

How does it work?

- Remember that if we send multiple radio signals at the same time, they can either merge and become more powerful, or they can cancel each other out. Whether they merge or cancel each other out depends on the way that they are sent.

- **Beamforming** is an idea that we can send out signals from multiple antennas in a way that they can all combine at the receiver as a more powerful signal. The receiver uses an algorithm to amplify amplifies the different signals by giving each one a different weight.

- There are three ways

  o **Precoding** – the access point sends out the same signal through multiple antennas. Each signal is given a different phase and weight so that the signals combine at the receiver to have the maximum power.

  o **Spatial Multiplexing** – the access point splits a high-bandwidth signal into multiple low-bandwidth signals. Each signal is transmitted from a different antenna. Spatial multiplexing is good when there is a high level of noise. The receiver splits the signals into channels and interprets the data.

  o **Diversity Coding** – the access point sends the same signal through multiple antennas, but each signal is sent orthogonal to the other ones (at right angles). That means, regardless of how the receiver is facing, it will receive at least one signal correctly.

We can take this a step further and use a **Multi-User MIMO (MU-MIMO)**. What happens when we want to use MIMO with multiple users at the same time? The access point can divide the signals spatially so that it can serve multiple users at the same time, provided they are some distance apart. When multiple users close together, the signals cannot be separated easily, and those users must share the bandwidth.

Wi-Fi 6 allows MU-MIMO to function in both directions. Previous versions allowed multiple users to be served quickly when downloading, but Wi-Fi 6 allows multiple users to upload data at the same time.

When selecting wireless devices, consider the following

- Purchase wireless access points that support Wi-Fi 6 and MU-MIMO

- As the use of Wi-Fi increases, consider purchasing wireless access points that support a 2.5 Gbit/s or 5 Gbit/s ethernet connection.

- Determine the range of each access point and the area that you must cover; this will allow you to calculate the number of access points required

- Determine the number of devices or users that need to be served and the maximum capacity of the wireless access point

- Consider whether the area that requires coverage has a basic layout or whether specific directional antennas are required

A cellular antenna in a tower can only talk to one phone at a time. How do we connect multiple phones to a tower at the same time? What if everybody is at the Super Bowl and texting and talking and tweeting?

There are three types of cellular network connections – **GSM (Global System for Mobile Communications), TDMA (Time Division Multiple Access),** and **CDMA (Code Division Multiple Access).**

A cellular phone connects to a tower through its cellular modem. The phone will contain a SIM card that allows it to authenticate with that network. Some laptops and routers also support cellular connections.

A cellular phone may be locked to a specific cellular network (Bell, Telus, AT&T, Verizon, etc.) or unlocked (in which case it can connect to any network). You pay for a cellular plan with a specific carrier (Bell, Telus, AT&T, Verizon, etc.), which could include any number of features.

Some cellular phones have room for two SIM cards. A cell phone with two SIM cards can connect to two networks at the same time (or maintain two separate connections to the same network).

When a phone is outside the range of its default network (for example, when it is in another country), it is roaming, and will attempt to connect to any number of available networks. The user may incur additional charges for roaming.

GSM and CDMA are the two main types of cellular radio networks. Most cellular networks are GSM, except for those maintained by Sprint and Verizon. Some phones can operate on both GSM and CDMA networks. A carrier will operate their radios on several different frequencies (for example, Sprint operates over the CDMA 800 MHz and 1900 MHz frequencies). For a phone to connect to a carrier's network, it must have a modem that operates on at least one of that carrier's frequencies.

TDMA was an older cellular technology that has been incorporated into GSM. With TDMA, a cellular antenna would give each cell phone a time slot. The width of each slot is measured in milliseconds. Each phone would only listen during its slot. This way the tower can connect multiple phones at the same time. It's like a person trying to have a conversation with several other people: say a few words to person one, say a few words to person two, say a few words to person three, come back to person one and say a few words, etc.. Each of the other people only needs to listen when they are being talked to.

GSM continues to use the same time slots that TDMA did. GSM data uses the GPRS (General Packet Radio Service) protocol, which is no longer considered secure.

CDMA is more complicated. It involves complicated math, linear algebra to be specific. You can think of the signal from a cell tower to a phone like a wave. Each phone agrees on a code with the tower. The tower creates a signal that is a mash of all the messages that it wants to send each phone; the messages are coded so that they don't cancel each other out. Every phone receives the same signal but extracts its own portion from it. It's like if I hid French words between all the English words in this book. An English-speaking person would read the English words and a French-speaking person would read the French words. Now imagine that I hid words from eighty different languages in this book. Every person could see all the words but only understand their own language.

There are several cellular network technologies/speeds

- **3G** – 3G is also known as **Third Generation**. It provides data transfer rates of at least 144 kbit/s.

- **4G** – 4G is also known as **Fourth Generation**. 4G must use an underlying IP network, and provide data speeds of up to 100 Mbit/s for moving users and 1 Gbit/s for stationary users.

- **5G** – 5G is also known as **Fifth Generation**. It provides data rates of up to 1 Gbit/s. 5G is supposed to provide enough bandwidth to allow devices to function as primary internet connections. 5G broadcasts signals at 24 Ghz to 40 Ghz.

- **LTE** – LTE is also known as **Long Term Evolution**. It is an advancement of the 3G network, but does not meet the standard of 4G. LTE provides download speeds of up to 299 Mbit/s. It also requires IP packet switching for both data and voice calls.

Some phones support both GSM/CDMA and either 3G/4G/5G/LTE. GSM/CDMA are becoming less popular as 5G takes over.

When selecting a phone

- Ensure that the phone's modem is compatible with the chosen carrier

- Ensure that the carrier has adequate network coverage in the areas you plan to visit

- Ensure that the cost of the cellular data and voice plan is known in advance

Cellular (data-only) connections are used by mobile workers and by cellular modems. It is common for an organization to install a primary broadband modem and a back up cellular modem. If the primary connection fails, the cellular back up will take over.

Part D: N10-008 3.0 Network Operations

3.1 Given a scenario, use appropriate statistics and sensors to ensure network availability

- *Performance Metrics/Sensors*
  - *Device Chassis*
    - *Temperature*
    - *Central Processing Unit (CPU) Usage*
    - *Memory*
  - *Network Metrics*
    - *Bandwidth*
    - *Latency*
    - *Jitter*
- *SNMP*
  - *Traps*
  - *Object Identifiers (OIDs)*
  - *Management Information Bases (MIBs)*
- *Network Device Logs*
  - *Log Reviews*
    - *Traffic Logs*
    - *Audit Logs*
    - *Syslog*
  - *Logging Levels/Severity Levels*
- *Interface Statistics/Status*
  - *Link State (Up/Down)*
  - *Speed/Duplex*
  - *Send/Receive Traffic*
  - *Cyclic Redundancy Checks (CRCs)*
  - *Protocol Packet and Byte Counts*
- *Interface Errors or Alerts*
  - *CRC Errors*
  - *Giants*
  - *Runts*
  - *Encapsulation Errors*
- *Environmental Factors and Sensors*
  - *Temperature*
  - *Humidity*
  - *Electrical*
  - *Flooding*
- *Baselines*
- *NetFlow Data*
- *Uptime/Downtime*

If the network is unavailable or the performance is poor, the business will not be able to function? How can we properly monitor the network so that we can detect issues and resolve them before they get out of control? We should not wait until a user complains.

At the hardware level, we can monitor three things

- **Temperature** – if the device (router, switch, server, etc.) is operating at a higher temperature than is normal, it might be overloaded, or it may have a hardware problem (a fan is not functioning) or the room that it is in may not be cooled properly. In general, devices should operate at a temperature of less than 90 F, but we should check the manufacturer's specifications for each device.

  When we see that a network device has a higher than normal temperature, we should check the CPU usage. If the CPU usage is not high, then the device may have issues with cooling or may need to be replaced. It is also possible that it has a faulty thermometer. A device that overheats may automatically shut down (if equipped with that feature) or may just fail.

- **CPU Usage** – when a device has a high CPU usage, it means that

  o It is receiving more traffic than it was designed to handle. We should verify whether the traffic is legitimate. If it is, then we should upgrade the device or replace it with a more powerful model. If the traffic is not legitimate, then it is possible that the device is under attack. We should find the source of the increased traffic and block it.

  o There is a software bug that is causing the device to overload. We should upgrade or downgrade the device software, firmware, or configuration to reduce the CPU load. For example, an administrator may have written a new configuration that causes the device to make calculations in an endless loop, which could explain the high CPU usage.

- **Memory** – when a device has a high memory usage, it means that

  o It is receiving more traffic than it was designed to handle. It is possible that the device is receiving traffic but is not able to send it out fast enough. Thus, it is storing the traffic in a buffer. The device is either receiving more traffic than was expected or the devices downstream are not able to accept the traffic. We should upgrade the devices as necessary.

  o There is a software bug that is causing the device to occupy too much memory. We should upgrade or downgrade the device software, firmware, or configuration to reduce the memory load. We can also try rebooting the device to clear the memory and see if the issue returns.

At the network level, we can monitor three things

- **Bandwidth** – Bandwidth is the maximum data transfer rate on a connection. It is also known as throughput, or **Goodput**. Goodput is the useable bandwidth (actual bandwidth minus overhead for protocols). It's like the weight of the mail without the envelopes.

  Bandwidth is like how wide a highway is. If I was monitoring the highway between New York and Florida, bandwidth would be the number of lanes. The more lanes there are, the more vehicles that can get through per second.

  If we are playing a video, the greater the bandwidth, the higher the quality of video we can broadcast.

- **Latency** – Latency is how long it takes to get a packet from the source to the destination. When we are sending a stream of packets, and bandwidth is good, our main concern is how long it takes for the first packet to arrive.

  If we are playing a video, the latency is the time it takes for the video to start playing after we press play.

  Going back to the highway, the distance is kind of like the latency. If a group of bikers started their trip in New York, how long it takes for them to reach the destination is the latency.

  Latency is based on distance and it's also based on how many twists and turns the data must take. If the data can take a direct route to the destination, the latency will be lower than if it has to stop through other networks and routers.

  If we're experiencing high latency, we can run a tracert to see where the data is passes through. On a residential network, there isn't much we can do, but on a commercial network, we can negotiate a better plan (like a WAN or MPLS) with our ISP so that they can prioritize our traffic. Areas with high latency might be called **bottlenecks**.

- **Jitter** – Does the data we send show up in the same order, or is it all mixed up? If some cars started the trip in New York, do they show up in the same order in Florida or a different order?

  If we are playing a video, a high jitter would make the video frames show up in an incorrect order.

At the interface level, we can look at several items. We can check these on a router, switch, or client device (laptop, desktop, wireless access point, server, etc.) Chances are, if a device is experiencing connectivity issues, we are going to check at the router or switch first – the client device will be offline, but we will probably still be able to access the switch.

- **Link State (Up/Down)** – is the physical connection up or down? If the link is up (i.e. there is traffic) then we can look at other areas to troubleshoot. If the link is down, then that means at least one device is not communicating. Possible causes

  o The port has been disabled on the switch/router or client device

  o The client device is powered off

  o The cable between the two devices is damaged

- **Speed/Duplex** – is the speed and duplex setting on each device correct? If the speed or duplex is mismatched, then the devices will not be able to communicate.

- **Send/Receive Traffic** – how much traffic is being sent and how much traffic is being received? If we are not receiving any traffic, but sending lots, then the other device may not be configured correctly. For example, if our router interface has the wrong IP address, it may be sending traffic to the wrong destination, which would explain why it is not receiving any in return.

- **Cyclic Redundancy Checks (CRCs)** – each time a packet is received, the device performs a check to verify that it was received correctly. If a high number of packets fail the check, then we know that there is a transmission error.

- **Protocol Packet and Byte Counts** – this tells us how many packets have been sent/received and the total number of bytes being sent/received.

- **Giants** – a giant is a frame that is larger than the maximum permitted size of 1500 bytes.

- **Runts** – a runt is a frame that is smaller than the maximum permitted size of 64 bytes. Giants and runts are caused by

  o Malfunctioning network interface cards

  o Electrical interference on the cable

  o Collisions on the cable (only common on half-duplex)

- **Encapsulation Errors** – a router interface may be misconfigured

Networks generate a lot of information to collect and monitor. **SNMP** or **Simple Network Management Protocol** is the standard for collecting data from network devices and for updating their configuration.

- An **SNMP Monitor** is a tool that automates this data collection and configuration.

- Each device that is subject to monitoring contains software called an **Agent**. The Agent sends data back to the monitor. The Agent might be pre-installed by the manufacturer or it might be something that an administrator must install manually. A device can be read only (can only be monitored) or read-write (can be monitored and configuration can be changed).

- The types of data collected are known as variables. SNMP does not determine the variables. Rather, each device can set the variables that it wishes to share.

- A manager must typically request the data from the agent.

- If a significant event occurs, the device can send unsolicited data to the agent. This type of data is known as a **trap**. An administrator will configure the types of events that constitute a trap (for example, a security breach, a power outage, etc.).

- We can manage all this data in a **management information base**, or **MIB**. The MIB has a hierarchy that spans all layers of the OSI model. The MIB identifies each stored variable with an **object identifier** or **OID**.

  There are hundreds of different types of MIBs spanning all aspects of networks and devices. You must choose a MIB or set of MIBs that is right for your organization.

Devices also store data in logs

- A log is a record of different events generated by the device. For example, a switch may log each time it powers up, each time a port status changes to active, each time a user logs in, and each time it blocks traffic for security reasons

- A device may have one or multiple logs

- A device might store the logs on its internal storage or upload them to a server or cloud application

- An administrator may be able to determine what types of information is stored in the logs. A device may categorize issues by severity and then only log the most severe ones.

- When an incident takes place, we might obtain the logs from the affected devices and review them to determine the cause. It is important that the logs are backed up to a safe place if possible.

  - A **syslog** is a tool that allows a device to send its logs to a central server. Each time an event occurs, syslog sends a message to the central server.

  - We can use syslog in conjunction with SNMP. Why do we need both? SNMP messages use variables, which are predefined by the administrator. Syslog allows a system to send messages that are not predefined.

  - If we have a device with custom applications (such as a web server or database), it will not be possible for an administrator to predefine all the possible variables that each of them would generate. Thus, we might use syslog. Any message generated by an application can be sent to the logging server.

- A traffic log keeps track of traffic entering and leaving the system

- An audit log keeps track of each user or administrator who logged into the system, when they logged in, and what changes they made.

Physically, the room where our network equipment is kept should have sensors for the following

- **Temperature** – the room should have a separate heating/cooling system if large enough. If the room is too hot, then equipment will overheat and likely get damaged or have a shorter lifespan. People will disagree on the ideal temperature. Many say that the most optimal temperature is 20-21°C (68-71°F). According to ASHRAE (American Society of Heating, Refrigerating and Air-Conditioning Engineers), the ideal temperature is 18°C-27°C (64.4°F-80.6°F).

  It is better to run the room on the cooler side of the range rather than the hotter side. If the air conditioner were to fail, you would have more time to react. Running the room hotter will reduce energy costs.

  Google runs its data centers at 26.7°C (80°F), but Google's data centers are designed for optimal air flow and they use proprietary hardware that has been designed for the warmer temperatures. Your company probably does not have the same setup as Google.

- **Humidity** – humidity is a measure of the amount of moisture in the air and should run between 40% and 60%. Too much humidity is bad because it will result in corrosion, which will lead to a shorter equipment life span. Too little humidity will create static electricity, which will also damage the equipment.

- **Electrical** – we should monitor the electrical consumption. Too much or too little consumption could indicate that equipment is malfunctioning.

- **Flooding** – we must monitor the environment for flooding and react accordingly. A flood can come from an air conditioner condenser or from a leaky pipe or sprinkler. We can monitor flooding through a sensor. The most common sensor looks like a rope. It is placed on the floor and when it detects moisture it will send an alert to a control unit.

  This system is only good for detecting floods that start at the ground level. There is not much we can do to prevent a water pipe in the ceiling from bursting and damaging equipment. Having said that, we should attempt to locate our server rooms away from sources of water.

The **Baseline** tells us how the network is performing on a regular basis. We can measure bandwidth, latency, jitter, and other factors. Once we have set a baseline (i.e. the expected performance of the network), we can compare the actual performance against it. If the actual performance is worse, we know that there is an issue with the network. We must always have something to compare the actual performance to.

We can also measure network performance with a tool called **NetFlow**. NetFlow is a feature in Cisco routers that measures traffic source, traffic destination, and protocols. We can use NetFlow to determine sources of congestion. NetFlow will show us how many different connections are present on our network and the amount of traffic generated by each one.

Uptime/Downtime.

- We can measure uptime as the amount of time that the network has been up consecutively. For example, if the network has been up for ten hours in a row, then we could say that the uptime is ten hours. If the network has been up for three months in a row, then we could say that the uptime is three hours. The uptime shows us how long it has been since the service has been interrupted.

- We can also express uptime as a percentage. For example, if our network uptime is 99.9%, then that means it only goes down for approximately 40 minutes per month. We might have a specific uptime percentage that we want to achieve.

- We can measure downtime the same way. If an incident takes the network down, we might want to measure how long the network is down.

3.2 Explain the purpose of organizational documents and policies

- *Plans and Procedures*
  - *Change Management*
  - *Incident Response Plan*
  - *Disaster Recovery Plan*
  - *Business Continuity Plan*
  - *System Life Cycle*
  - *Standard Operating Procedures*
- *Hardening and Security Protocols*
  - *Password Policy*
  - *Acceptable Use Policy*
  - *Bring Your Own Device (BYOD) Policy*
  - *Remote Access Policy*
  - *Onboarding and Offboarding Policy*
  - *Security Policy*
  - *Data Loss Prevention*
- *Common Documentation*
  - *Physical Network Diagram*
    - *Floor Plan*
      - *Rack Diagram*
      - *Intermediate Distribution Frame (IDF) / Main Distribution Frame (MDF) Documentation*
  - *Logical Network Diagram*
  - *Wiring Diagram*
  - *Site Survey Report*
  - *Audit and Assessment Report*
  - *Baseline Configuration*
- *Common Agreements*
  - *Non-Disclosure Agreement (NDA)*
  - *Service-Level Agreement (SLA)*
  - *Memorandum of Understanding (MOU)*

A policy tells users how to what actions to take in each situation so that they are not guessing. Some policies that might apply to networks include

- **Change Management** – Change Management is the process for managing changes to assets and systems. Change management is also known as configuration management.

  In a large organization, a single employee cannot make a change on his own. For example, an IT technician can't just decide to change all the Cisco routers to Juniper routers without getting permission.

  Changes cost money, and changes affect other parts of the organization both in the short-term and the long-term. It is important to document each change so that others can be aware of it in the future.

  Before implementing a change, we must seek approval from a committee, which may be known as the Change Control Board. The CCB decides whether a change is approved or denied.

  If it is approved, the CCB ensures that the employee who performs the change does so in accordance with the organization's policies. When the change is complete, the CCB documents the change.

  If it is denied, the CCB will document the reasons for denying the change.

  An organization will have policies for who must approve each type of change depending on what it affects and the level of risk. For example, a change that presents a low-level risk may require approval from the department head, and a change that presents a high level of risk may require approval from the CEO.

  In an IT environment, change management applies to network hardware configuration, switch configuration, security policies, the physical location of infrastructure, and many other items.

  Some of the things that might require a change management procedure

  o Replacing a piece of network equipment (switch, router, wireless access point)

  o Change in the configuration of a piece of network equipment

  o Installation of a new network cable drop

  o Installation of a new internet connection

- o Installing new network cable drops

- **Incident Response Plan** – An Incident is an event that is not normal and that causes disruptions. For example, the failure of an internet connection or a security breach is considered an incident. An organization must maintain an Incident Response Plan that is reviewed and practiced regularly. The plan will include:

  - o Documented Incident Types/Category Definitions

    - The organization should maintain a list of different types of incidents and categorize them based on the business lines that they affect

    - The plan should allow a user to determine the severity of an incident (Critical, Serious, Minor, etc.) based upon its impact to the business, human life, clients, etc.

    - Each category and severity should have a standard response procedure

    - It should state who is notified in each scenario (executives, customers, government agencies, 911)?

    - It should state the people who will be involved in the incident response and describe the role of each one

  - o Why do we do this? When an incident occurs (and incidents will occur!), we don't have to panic. We categorize the incident based on its severity and impact, and then we follow the appropriate procedure.

  - o Roles and Responsibilities

    - Each department is specifically tasked with a responsibility for each incident category

    - When an incident occurs, a team composed of each departments' representatives is summoned. Each person on the team will have reviewed the plan and knows exactly what to do.

  - o Reporting Requirements/Escalation

    - We use the plan to determine the response, if any

    - Does the organization have to respond to the incident at all? Do they have to report the incident to a higher level in the organization (vice president,

CEO, board of directors, shareholders, etc.)? This depends on

- The severity of the incident

- How long it takes to resolve the incident

- The impact to the business and its customers

- Organization may have to report the incident to the government if it involves a

  o Data leak

  o Chemical spill

  o Public health matter

  o Contamination of a food product or pharmaceutical

o Cyber-Incident Response Teams

  - An organization may maintain a Cyber Incident Response Team that is dedicated to responding to a cyber incident. This team may travel to the physical of the incident or work remotely.

  - Other third parties also have cyber response teams. We might choose to outsource our incident response to a third party that is more experienced, especially when it involves a security breach or when we require an independent investigation. The FBI has a cyber response team that can deploy to any cyber incident location within 48 hours.

o Exercise

  - It is impossible to know how a person will react to a real crisis until it happens. Nevertheless, the organization should practice its response to each type of incident on a regular basis. The more people practice, the better they will respond when the crisis occurs.

  - No plan ever failed on paper. The exercise also allows an organization to identify errors that made it through the planning phase.

- After a real incident, the organization should evaluate its response and modify the plan accordingly.

- **Disaster Recovery Plan** – A disaster recovery plan allows the organization to resume normal operations after a discovery.

  o What is a disaster? A disaster is a serious event that causes grave disruption. It could include a natural event like a fire, flood, earthquake or hurricane. It could also include a man-made event like a war or an industrial accident.

  o Our disaster recovery plan should

    - Consider all the different causes of disruption that affect our operations in each geographic area. For example, an organization located in Florida should consider hurricanes, but an organization in Wyoming should not.

    - Identify the amount of downtime the organization can accept before having to resume normal operations. An organization such as an insurance company may not accept any disruption to its operations. A retail store may accept a disruption of one or two weeks. The shorter the disruption, the more expensive the recovery plan.

    - Specifically state the sources of vendors, equipment, parts, and supplies that are required to implement the recovery.

    - Describe the roles of each person who will assist with the disaster recovery effort.

    - For example, if a fire in our server room occurs, our disaster recovery plan might include the following

      - Contacting the insurance company to file a claim

      - Salvaging any available equipment or materials

      - Construction of a server room, either in the same location or in a new location

      - Installation of new equipment and of salvaged equipment

      - Testing equipment

- The people who would be involved

  - Accountant to mange the budget and file the insurance claim

  - Project manager to oversee the new construction

  - Engineer or architect to provide advice regarding applicable building codes

  - Procurement to obtain new equipment

  - Network technicians to configure and install the new equipment

- **Business Continuity Plan** – A business continuity plan allows the organization to continue operating in the event of a disaster. We can combine the Business Continuity Plan and the Disaster Recovery Plan so that our business can keep operating while working to get back to normal operations.

  - The number one rule is to not let people panic, but most people forget about this. It is more important than fixing the actual problem. When people panic, they behave irrationally, and things get worse.

  - What does the plan include?

    - We first must cut up the organization into different departments and decide which ones are crucial

    - We must also look within each department to determine whether the entire department is critical or whether a subset of its employees is critical

    - We must then determine the types of disasters that can affect each organization. We could possibly make a table, where roles are columns and disasters are rows. Then each cell would be a plan.

    - Ask the following questions

      - If the disaster causes the person in that specific role to die or get injured or otherwise become unavailable, how can we replace them? Are there other employees in the department who are trained to perform in that person's role? Or are there contractors who can?

- If the disaster affects the person's workspace, can the person work from home? Does the person have adequate equipment to do their job from home?

- Does the company have other offices where it can carry out the same functions?

- Can customers interact with the company remotely?

- For example, say we manufacture toilet paper. We might have the following roles

  - People who operate the manufacturing equipment. Some people add raw pulp to the mixing machines. Some people operate the packaging machines. Some people operate the forklifts, etc.

    - We can't shut down the manufacturing plant and people can't work from home. People can't make toilet paper at home.

    - If the plant is damaged by a natural disaster, we cannot continue operating unless we had a second manufacturing plant in another region. Distributing our critical operations is a good idea, but if the business is small, it might not be possible or efficient.

    - We might be able to run the plant with fewer workers than we have (for example if many workers must quarantine due to an illness)

    - We should document the role of each person so that it is easier to train a new person to fill their role. Sometimes people keep the knowledge in their heads and not on paper.

  - People who purchase materials

    - People who purchase materials can work from home

  - People who maintain the manufacturing equipment

    - People who maintain the manufacturing equipment are critical, just like those who operate them, but it is possible that a contractor could perform their task

  - People who sell toilet paper to stores

- Sales people are important, but the business can continue to serve existing customers until they recover

- Sales people can work from home

- People who deliver toilet paper to stores

  - Delivery services can be outsourced to a contractor

- Management

  - Management can work from home

  - If a manager dies, we might be able to have another manager step into their role. That means we should have the managers trained to understand the entire business.

- Financial people who pay bills and invoice customers

  - Financial people can work from home

- The organization should practice the disaster recovery plan and business continuity plan, holding regular drills with the key responders.

- The organization should review and revise the plans to take advantage of new technologies and consider new threats.

- The more effective the disaster recovery plan, the more it will cost. The disaster recovery plan may cost the organization, even when no disaster has taken place. For example, maintaining a second office for emergency use may cost the organization tens of thousands of dollars per month. Is the potential harm caused by the disaster (multiplied by its likelihood) more expensive than the cost of maintaining the office? The organization must decide about the types of risks that it is willing to accept.

- With respect to networks, the focus is on

  - How do we make sure that the data is secure and accessible (i.e. not permanently lost during a disaster)?

    - Is the data backed up to multiple sources?

- How do we make sure that the users can continue to connect to the network and access their software?

  - Do we have spare network equipment, redundant power, cooling, etc.?

  - Do we have documentation of the network, how it is configured, and how everything is connected?

  - Have we documented all of the vendors that need to be notified (electrical, HVAC, internet, networking, servers, etc.)?

  - Which pieces of network equipment are critical and which ones are not?

- **System Life Cycle** – A system life cycle outlines how long a component remains in the organization, how it is introduced, and how it is removed. It usually consists of the following phases

  - Investigation/Design – in this phase, we consider the requirements of the component. We then decide what the best component is for the job. For example, if we want to purchase a switch, we would look at

    - The makes and models of switches available. We might have to select from an approved vendor.

    - Whether we require a 24-port switch, a 48-port switch, or multiple switches

    - Whether we require a switch that supports SFPs, Gigabit Ethernet, 10G Ethernet, etc.

    - Whether we require a layer 2 or layer 3 switch

    - The budget of the organization

    - The time frame for purchasing the switch

    - Who will configure the switches

    - Where the switches will be installed

o Installation – once we have purchased the component, we must install it. We might use the Change Management to obtain approval for the installation. We should obtain approval prior to expending funds (in case the change is rejected). We might also use a standard operating procedure. For example, we have now purchased the switch

  - We set up a date and time to replace the existing switch

  - We ensure that we have a valid configuration for the new switch

  - We assign a technician to replace the switch and configure the new switch

  - The old switch is decommissioned

o Operational – the item is now in use. We must identify how long the item will last in our organization. There are five possibilities

  - The item will continue to function until it fails. This is common with items that fail quickly due to the harsh environment, items that are low cost, or items that are obsolete.

    For example, we might allow the coffee maker or microwave to run until it fails. It can be replaced quickly and with little disruption to the business. We do not want to allow a router or other critical network component to run until it fails.

    We might have a local server that is being replaced by a cloud device but want to maximize our cost savings. If the failure of the local server does not cause disruptions, we might allow it to operate until it fails.

  - The item will last a specific period. This is common with items that wear out after some time, or items that present a safety risk when they fail.

    For example, many organizations specify that their laptops or desktops are replaced every three or four years. When a laptop is three years old, it must be replaced with a newer model. This reduces the risk of a failure (which could be expensive). It also reduces maintenance costs associated with repairing old laptops. It also ensures that users have access to the latest technology.

    We should replace critical safety equipment such as hard hats, steel toed boots, and safety harnesses well before they could be expected to fail.

- The item will last until newer technology is becomes available. For example, we might specify that switches with 10/100 ports are to be replaced with Gigabit switches. We might not want to replace Gigabit switches with 10 Gigabit switches until the cost is low enough.

- The item will last until it wears out.

  For example, we replace vehicle tires once they are worn out. It is based on the depth of the tread, not the age of the tire. Electronics usually fail catastrophically, not gradually, but some devices start to overheat as they age. We might replace a device once it becomes prone to overheating.

- The item is no longer required. The organization has decided that it no longer wants to use this item. For example, the organization has switched from Cisco routers to Juniper routers. The Cisco router is still functional, but the organization no longer wants to use it.

  o Decommission – we remove the item from service. The item has reached the end of its useful life, it has failed during operation, or it is no longer required. We should start the planning phase for the replacement well ahead of time so that the new item is available.

  The decommission phase must also include disposing of the old item and wiping any sensitive data from it.

- **Standard Operating Procedures** - A Standard Operating Procedure a set of instructions for common tasks that an organization performs. Employees, vendors, and contractors are required to follow standard operating procedures when those procedures exist. A standard operating procedure is designed to reduce risk, reduce uncertainty, and improve safety. A large organization may have many different procedures for things like

  o Climbing a ladder

  o Operating a company vehicle

  o Booking travel

  o Obtaining a corporate credit card

o   Paying an invoice

o   Issuing a purchase order

IT Standard Operating Procedures can exist for

o   Creating new user accounts

o   Disabling terminated user accounts

o   Acquiring software and hardware

o   Replacing network equipment

Standard Operating Procedures are based on laws and security practices. An organization will revise the procedures when they acquire new information about risks.

Some policies that apply specifically to information technology ideas

- **Password Policy** – a password policy may include the following

    o   A statement that users should not share passwords or write them down

    o   How often a user should change his password

    o   Password complexity requirements (number of characters, special characters, numbers, etc.)

    o   How many times a password must be changed before it can be reused

    o   Whether an account is locked out after the password has been entered incorrectly, and how many incorrect tries are permitted

    o   Whether an account must use two-factor or multi-factor authentication

- **Acceptable Use Policy** - the Acceptable Use Policy (AUP) describes what the user may do and what they may not do while on a company's system. The user may be an employee, contractor, or guest. In general, the user should

    o   Only use the computing resources for purposes that benefit the employer (a guest may not be subject to this restriction)

- Not use the computing resources for illegal purposes

- Not access games, social media, pornography, or racist content

- An employer may allow an employee to use the devices for non-commercial purposes if the impact to the business is minimal (this is a work life balance choice that the employer may make). For example, a user may be permitted to access social media on their work computer during their lunch break.

- The AUP must clearly state that the employer's systems are subject to monitoring and recording, and that the employee has no reasonable expectation of privacy. In the event the employee is terminated for violating the AUP, the employee will not be able to exclude evidence of wrongdoing in a wrongful termination lawsuit.

- The employer's computer systems should clearly state that the system is subject to monitoring and recording.

- **Bring Your Own Device (BYOD) Policy** – A BYOF Policy permits each employee to bring their own personal device (subject to restrictions) and connect it to the corporate network.

  - With BYOD, an employee can use their own personal device and not have to carry two devices. They can use a device that they like.

  - The organization must be able to provide technical support for a wide range of manufacturers and models. The organization may limit the support that they provide for BYOD devices to only basic technical support.

  - The organization must be able to ensure that all employee-owned devices can be secured. They may do this with special software that allows the employer to remotely lock or wipe the device. Increasingly, they also use software that can separate the employer's data from the employee's data.

  - There may be legal restrictions on what the organization can do with an employee-owned device (such as GPS tracking, data erasing, encryption).

  - The organization may be required to reimburse employees for the use of their phones.

- **Remote Access Policy** – The Remote Access Policy determines which users have access to the employer's system, and how they may access the system. Both employees and contractors may have access. The policy should describe

- o Which people have access to the remote network

- o What resources each user has access to. A user should only have access to the specific resources that they require to perform their job.

- o Whether specific resources are not accessible remotely

- o How a user can access the network. Do they use a web-based application, or a VPN? Different applications can have different types of access.

- o Whether the user must use a username/password, a smart card, or multi-factor authentication to access the network

- o Whether the user may access the network through a personal device

- **Onboarding and Offboarding Policy** – Onboarding refers to hiring an employee and offboarding refers to firing an employee. The Onboarding Policy should include

  - o Creating the user's accounts (including the user's e-mail account)

  - o Assigning the user devices such as a desktop, a laptop, a telephone, and a mobile phone

  - o Setting up the user's devices

  - o Assigning appropriate privileges to the user based on his role

  - o Training the user regarding security precautions and the use of the electronics

  - o Ensuring that the user signs the acceptable use policy and is aware of the employer's policies regarding the use of technology

The Offboarding Policy should include

  - o Disabling the user's account (the user's account should be disabled prior to informing the user about his termination; otherwise, a disgruntled user may attempt to delete data or cause other damage to the network)

- Instructing the user to return his company-owned devices

- Deleting employer data from any employee-owned devices

- Forwarding the user's email to another user, and creating an auto-responder to inform senders that the user is no longer employed

- An exit interview to remind the user of his obligation to keep the employer's data confidential

Onboarding and Offboarding can be trigged automatically from a request made by the Human Resources department when a user is hired or terminated.

- **Security Policy** – The Security Policy describes how the organization keeps its infrastructure secure. A good approach to security includes multiple layers. It should include

  - A description of which users have access to each type of resources

  - The type of physical security measures in use at each facility (for example, security guards, cameras, biometric readers, etc.)

  - How the organization handles security breaches (how security breaches are reported, how security breaches are investigated)

  - The type of encryption in use on each device

  - How network devices are configured to prevent unauthorized access

  - How devices are secured to prevent local access to unauthorized users

- **Data Loss Prevention** – The Data Loss Prevention policy tells us how we keep the company data from leaving the organization. It should be noted that most data leaves the organization through the brains of the employee. It should include

  - The types of data that are considered sensitive, and who has access to each type

  - Whether there are specific legal requirements that require the organization to protect some types of data (for example health data or client personal information) o   Whether data is encrypted in transit and/or at rest

o   Whether a data leak prevention appliance or other applications is installed and how it is configured

o   Whether users are permitted to copy data to personal devices, to mobile devices, or to portable devices such as USB drives

o   Whether attempts to access specific types of data is logged and/or monitored

o   How the organization investigates and reports data leaks

o   How long does the organization need to store data

We should create some documents and update them each time a change is made. Documents should be available electronically and on paper.

- **Physical Network Diagram** – The Physical Network Diagram shows us where things are located.

    o   **Floor Plan** – the floor plan shows how rooms are arranged and includes

        ▪   Location of network outlets

        ▪   Pathways of the ethernet and fiber optic cables and cable trays/cable support system

        ▪   Location of the IDFs and MDF

        ▪   Location of devices such as wireless access points, cameras, and access control system devices

    o   **Rack Diagram** – a rack diagram shows us each device and what rack unit it is installed in. A rack diagram is a physical representation of the rack and a paper copy should be in each server room. It should include

        ▪   The name and description of each device in the rack

        ▪   The physical rack unit that the device is installed in

        ▪   How the device connects to other devices

- How the device connects to power (and which power outlet on a PDU it connects to)

    o **IDF and MDF Documentation** – each IDF and MDF should have documentation that includes

        - A Rack Diagram of each rack installed in the room

        - User manuals for each device installed in the room

        - Instructions for maintaining other devices in the room such as the UPS and air conditioner

- **Logical Diagram** – a logical diagram is one that shows how devices are connected. For example, it might show that router port 1 is connected to switch port 48, or that access point 4 is connected to switch port 8. The logical diagram might also show the different VLANs configured and the and IP addresses of each device. We can use a logical diagram to connect devices, but it does not show where the wiring is physically located.

- **Wiring Diagram** – a wiring diagram shows the physical location of the wiring. It includes the physical location of network outlets and cable support systems such as conduit and pull boxes.

- **Site Survey Report** – a site survey report is a document that is prepared after a site survey. A site survey is a review of the building conditions to identify features such as wall types, ceiling types, dimensions, outlet locations, wiring locations, etc.. We might complete a site survey prior to installing network equipment; this will allow us to determine whether the building conditions are adequate. We might also complete a site survey prior to moving in to a new facility.

    Site surveys are commonly completed prior to installing Wi-Fi. A wireless site survey tells us the type of walls in the facility and whether they will block or reduce the wireless signal.

- **Audit and Assessment Report** – the audit report describes whether the organization is in compliance with a policy. The report shows us the areas where we are compliant and the areas where we need improvement. The report might contain recommendations for improving the deficiencies. The report might be created internally, prepared by a third-party contractor, or prepared by a government organization. We should maintain a copy of the report so that we can keep track of improvements.

    For example, we might conduct an audit of the organization's security policy. The report might indicate that we have excellent surveillance camera coverage but that some doors were propped open.

- **Baseline Configuration** – the baseline shows us how devices are configured and what level they normally operate at. We can compare the actual state of the devices to the baseline to determine whether our system is operating correctly. For example, if the baseline

Some Common Agreements we can expect to see in an organization

- **Non-Disclosure Agreement (NDA)** – An NDA is a Non-Disclosure Agreement. Each employee, contractor, or vendor with access to any sensitive data must read and sign the Non-Disclosure Agreement prior to being provided with access to any data. The NDA may be revised from time to time. The NDA contains the following features

  o Prohibits employees from disclosing any sensitive data to any person outside the organization

  o Identify how the organization marks sensitive data

  o Describes how the employee should store sensitive data (encrypted USB, laptop, not taking data home, use of personal mobile devices

  o The NDA may have exceptions for legal reasons such as in response to a court order or other legal process

  o Describes how an employee should report the inadvertent disclosure of sensitive data

  o The obligations under the NDA do not stop when the employee leaves the organization

- **Service Level Agreement (SLA)** – A Service Level Agreement details the required level of performance and penalties for not meeting those levels. For example, if an organization purchases web hosting services, the hosting company may guarantee that services will operate 99.99% of the time. If the web hosting is available less than 99.99% of the time, the organization may be entitled to a refund. The SLA holds the service provider accountable because downtime costs the organization money.

  An SLA is typically signed by the organization and a vendor, but an SLA can be created between the organization and the IT department. This ensures that the IT department's objectives are aligned with those of the business.

  The SLA could include

- Response time for different issues, depending on their impact and priority. For example, two business day response for non-critical issues, one-hour response time for critical issues

- Uptime guarantee for web hosting, servers, internet connections, and other services

- Geographical location where the SLA applies. For example, urban locations may have a two-hour response time, while rural/remote locations could have a two-day response time

- Penalty for not meeting the response time or uptime guarantee. The penalty could be structured as

  - A refund of 10%, 25%, or 100% of the monthly fee paid for a service outage exceeding 1%, 2%, or 5%. This structure is common for web hosting and cloud compute service providers. An outage of more than 5% would not typically entitle the customer to a larger refund, but the customer may reconsider using that particular vendor.

  - A penalty for each violation. The service provider could be required to pay a penalty for each violation.

  - The service provider could be required to reimburse the customer for actual damages caused by the outage. This not a typical structure because most agreements prohibit indirect or consequential damages. The service provider's liability is typically limited to the fees paid by the customer.

- **Memorandum of Understanding (MOU) MOU** – An MOU is a general document that outlines the reasons that two parties have for pursuing an agreement (i.e. how each party will benefit from the agreement). It is not an actual agreement, but it provides a framework for further negotiations. We might sign an MOU when we are negotiating the purchase of a WAN or a large amount of computer equipment. Once the MOU is in place, then the parties can negotiate more detailed terms.

In the event of a dispute in a formal agreement signed after the MOU is created, a court may look at the original purpose outlined by the MOU, but an MOU is generally not legally binding

300

3.3 Explain high availability and disaster recovery concepts and summarize which is the best solution

- *Load Balancing*
- *Multipathing*
- *Network Interface Card (NIC) Teaming*
- *Redundant Hardware/Clusters*
  - *Switches*
  - *Routers*
  - *Firewalls*
- *Facilities and Infrastructure Support*
  - *Uninterruptible Power Supply (UPS)*
  - *Power Distribution Units (PDUs)*
  - *Generator*
  - *HVAC*
  - *Fire Suppression*
- *Redundancy and High Availability (HA) Concepts*
  - *Cold Site*
  - *Warm Site*
  - *Hot Site*
  - *Cloud Site*
  - *Active-Active vs Active-Passive*
    - *Multiple Internet Service Providers (ISPs) / Diverse Paths*
    - *Virtual Router Redundancy Protocol (VRRP) / First Hop Redundancy Protocol (FHRP)*
  - *Mean Time to Repair (MTTR)*
  - *Mean Time Between Failure (MTBF)*
  - *Recovery Time Objective (RTO)*
  - *Recovery Point Objective (RPO)*
- *Network Device Backup/Restore*
  - *State*
  - *Configuration*

In the previous section, we mentioned disaster recovery and general ideas for keeping a business operating even in the event of a disaster. We are now going to look at some specific ways that this can be accomplished.

Fault Tolerance is the ability of a system to continue operating even when encountering an error. An example of a fault tolerant system is a RAID array. RAID is a system where multiple hard disk drives in a server store the same data. If a single drive in a RAID array fails, the system continues to operate without data loss. We can then replace the failed drive, and the server will copy the data to it.

Fault tolerance is expensive, and the organization must weigh the cost of fault tolerance against the cost of not having it (data loss, disruption to its operations, damage to its reputation).

High Availability is the state that Fault Tolerance gives us. Fault Tolerance is simply a design goal that results in a system with High Availability.

High Availability means that the system continues to operate even when there is a disruption.

One system that provides High Availability in a server environment is VMware VSphere – Fault Tolerance. VSphere is a hypervisor that allows a user to create multiple virtual servers on a physical machine. High Availability by VMware distributes the virtual server workload on multiple physical machines, which can be in different geographic locations. In the event of a failure of a server component, or even a physical server, the system continues to operate as normal.

For example, I could set up a virtual database server that is physically hosted on a server in Florida and a server in Oregon. Users think that they are connecting to a single physical server but if a hurricane destroys the server in Florida, VMware will ensure that the server in Oregon continues to host the server without any disruption.

We can ensure availability by reducing or removing single points of failure.

We can calculate the percentage of time that a system is available for. The percentage might be expressed as a number of "nines". For example, if the system is available 99% of the time, it is called "two nines". If the system is available for 99.999% of the time, it is called "five nines". Below is a table of the most common uptimes.

Availability %	Downtime per year	Downtime per quarter	Downtime per month	Downtime per week	Downtime per day (24 hours)
99% ("two nines")	3.65 days	21.9 hours	7.31 hours	1.68 hours	14.40 minutes
99.9% ("three nines")	8.77 hours	2.19 hours	43.83 minutes	10.08 minutes	1.44 minutes
99.99% ("four nines")	52.60 minutes	13.15 minutes	4.38 minutes	1.01 minutes	8.64 seconds
99.999% ("five nines")	5.26 minutes	1.31 minutes	26.30 seconds	6.05 seconds	864.00 milliseconds
99.9999% ("six nines")	31.56 seconds	7.89 seconds	2.63 seconds	604.80 milliseconds	86.40 milliseconds
99.99999% ("seven nines")	3.16 seconds	0.79 seconds	262.98 milliseconds	60.48 milliseconds	8.64 milliseconds
99.999999% ("eight nines")	315.58 milliseconds	78.89 milliseconds	26.30 milliseconds	6.05 milliseconds	864.00 microseconds
99.9999999% ("nine nines")	31.56 milliseconds	7.89 milliseconds	2.63 milliseconds	604.80 microseconds	86.40 microseconds

When a system is down for planned maintenance, that time is not factored into the downtime calculation because users are notified in advance, and the maintenance is scheduled after hours when few users are likely to be logged in (on a Saturday night for example).

Some ways that we can eliminate single points of failure in a network

- **Load Balancing** – a load balancer is a device that takes traffic and distributes it to multiple devices. For example, if a web server can handle 1000 visits per hour, but our website receives 3000 visits per hour, we need at least three web servers. We can put a load balancer between the internet and the servers. The load balancer distributes the traffic equally among the three servers. If we add a fourth server, then our website will continue to operate even if one fails because the load balancer will continue to distribute traffic among the other three.

  We might put each server in a different physical location.

  The load balancer itself can become a single point of failure. We can prevent this by

  o Installing multiple load balancers, each with a unique IP address

  o Giving the set of load balancers a hostname

  o Registering the hostname with a DNS server and configuring all the load balancer IP addresses under that hostname o   Configuring the DNS server to return all the IP addresses in a lookup request, but to return them in a random order

When a client attempts to connect to a resource

o   It looks up the hostname in the DNS server

o   The DNS server returns a list of IP addresses corresponding to the hostname (actually corresponding to the load balancers)

o   The list appears in random order. The client tries the first IP address on the list. The randomness of the DNS response load balances the load balancers.

o   If a load balancer stops working, the client will not receive a response on its IP address. The client will attempt to access the resource by visiting the second IP address on the list.

- **Multipathing** – Multipathing is a technique to create more than one pathway between a resource and the clients. Multipathing ensures that if a device in the pathway fails, the resource is still accessible.

- **NIC Teaming** – NIC Teaming is a form of load balancing that allows a server to maintain multiple network connections. Remember that a server can have multiple network interfaces. Consider the following server. I have connected it to two switches. Each interface is assigned a different IP address (192.168.0.10 and 192.168.0.11).

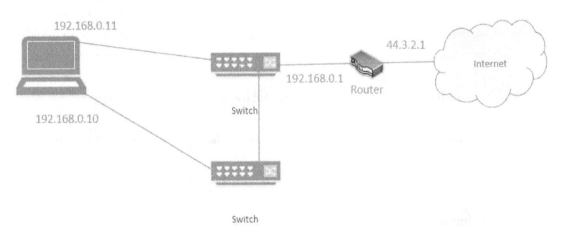

You may think that it is fault tolerant because it has two connections. If 192.168.0.11 fails, the server will continue to accept traffic on 192.168.0.11, but this is not fault tolerant because devices connected to the server on 192.168.0.10 will lose their connections. Some clients know to connect to 192.168.0.10 and some know to connect to 192.168.0.11. So, what can we do?

We group the network interfaces into a "team". We assign the team a single IP address even when the server is connected to multiple switches. This is known as **Switch Independent Teaming**. One interface is active, and one is passive. The active team assumes the IP address. When the active interface fails, the passive interface takes over and assumes the IP address.

Right now, the bottom link is active with IP address 192.168.0.10

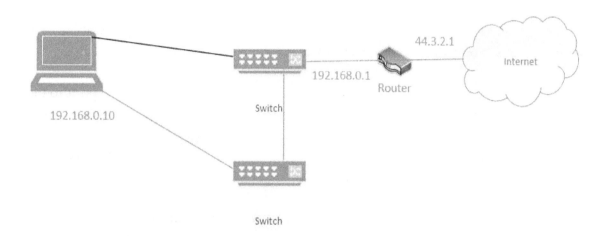

If the bottom link fails, the server assigns 192.168.0.10 to the top link

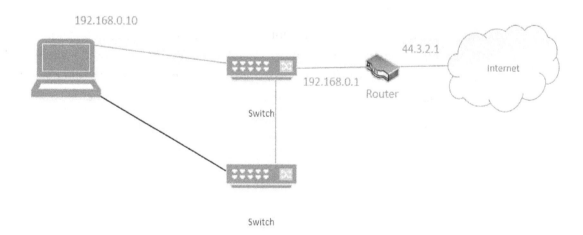

- Redundant Hardware – Redundant Hardware means that we eliminate single points of failure from our network infrastructure.

  o Switches – most devices have only a single ethernet connection (cameras, computers, access points, etc.). Thus, it is not possible to have a redundant ethernet connection unless we have more than one ethernet port on the device.

    When we have many devices, we can split them onto multiple switches. For example, if we have twenty wireless access points, we can connect ten to one switch and ten to another switch. In the event of a failure of one switch, half of our wireless access points will continue to function.

    High end switches will have two power supplies. That ensures that the switch continues to operate when one fails (or when one power source fails).

    We should configure our switches so that we have enough open ports to move connections from a failed switch to a working switch.

  o Routers – it is possible to configure two routers in parallel, so that the failure of one router does not affect the network.

  o Firewalls – it is possible to configure two firewalls in parallel, so that the failure of one firewall does not affect the network. This depends on having enough internet connections

Below is a setup I have made. On the right, we have two internet connections (one broadband and one cellular). Each internet connection connects to both of the firewalls. Each firewall connects to both routers. Each router connects to both switches. Half of the wireless access points connect to one switch and half connect to the other switch. The switches connect to each other, and the routers connect to each other.

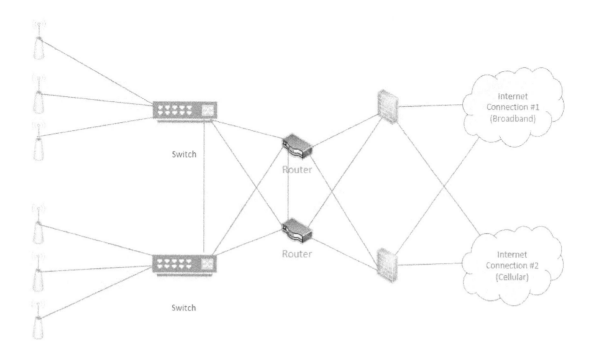

When things are operating normally, the data probably uses the black route. That is, the internet connection #1 is used, the top firewall is used, the top router is used, and both switches are used.

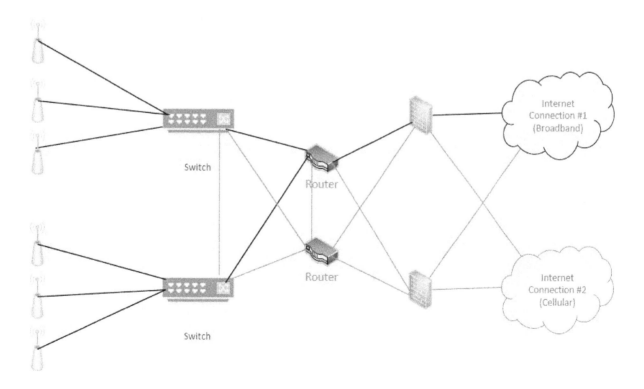

If an internet connection fails, a router fails, and/or a firewall fails, the system will continue to operate.

In my example, we connected each router to both internet connections. One router acts as primary and one router acts as secondary. Remember that every computer on the network has a "default gateway"? That is, if I connect a computer to the switch, how does it know which router to connect to when it wants to access the internet?

We can use the **First Hop Redundancy Protocol** (**FHRP**) to create a "virtual router". We configure FHRP on all the routers. The routers then elect one router to be the primary. The primary router assumes the configuration and becomes the default gateway. If the other routers detect that the primary router has failed, they elect a new router to become the primary. The newly elected router assumes the configuration and becomes the default gateway.

FHRP is a generic idea and can be used to ensure high availability of other services that require a single IP address (such as a web server, DHCP server, e-mail server, etc.). **Virtual Router Redundancy Protocol (VRRP)** is an FHRP that is proprietary to Cisco devices. Other network equipment manufacturers have their own protocols.

Our devices should each have two power supplies, if possible (the ISP modems usually will not have more than one power supply). We can connect each device to two separate UPSs.

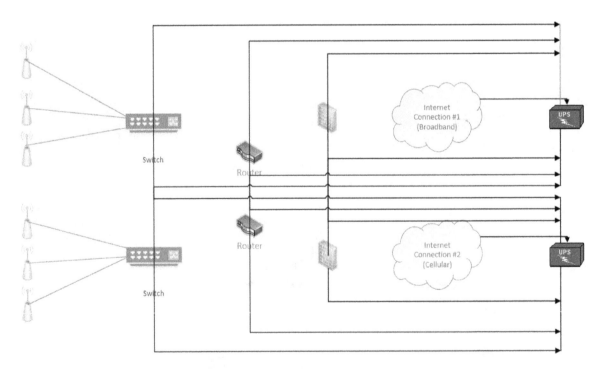

- Facilities and Infrastructure Support – depending on the size of the building and/or infrastructure, we may have some or all of the following

- **Uninterruptible Power Supply (UPS)** – Between the electrical supply and our equipment, we install a **UPS** or **Uninterruptable Power Supply**. In simple terms, a UPS is a giant battery. We connect our equipment to the UPS, and we connect the UPS to the municipal power supply. If the municipal power supply fails (a blackout) or decreases (a brownout), then the UPS takes over. The UPS must be able to take over so quickly that our equipment doesn't notice and shut down. A UPS may also protect against power surges (when too much power rushes into the building, which could damage the equipment). When the municipal power supply is active, the UPS charges its batteries. When it fails, the UPS supplies the connected equipment from the battery.

  The size of the UPS that we need depends on the quantity and type of equipment that we have. When you purchase electrical equipment, the manufacturer must specify how much power it consumes (in Watts). A Watt is a unit of energy consumption. Equipment may use more power when it is busy than when it is idle. Therefore, we should calculate the maximum power consumption of all our equipment.

  A UPS is rated in Watts. We should not exceed the Wattage rating of the UPS. We should consider purchasing a UPS that can handle 20% to 50% more capacity than we are consuming, in case we need to add new equipment in the future. Also, no UPS is 100% efficient.

  The second factor we should consider is the **runtime**. The runtime tells us how long the UPS can power our equipment for. We should think about how much time we need to properly shut down our equipment. If shutting down the equipment is not an option, then we should think about how much time we need until our power generator takes over.

  A UPS can be a small unit that sits on a shelf, a rack-mounted unit, a unit that is the size of a rack, or an independent unit.

  This is a small UPS. It might sit on the floor under your desk. It is good for powering a single device or a few small devices. It costs approximately $50. If we have a single switch or router, this might be acceptable.

This is a rack-mount UPS. It takes up 2Us in a rack and is good for powering a rack full of devices. It costs approximately $2000. If we have a single rack full of equipment, this might be acceptable. It would be a good idea to purchase two separate UPSs for redundancy.

This is a full rack UPS. It comes as a full rack and can sit in an MDF or IDF. If we have multiple racks full of equipment, this might be a better solution than using multiple 2U UPSs.

This UPS requires an electrician to install. Equipment will not connect directly to this UPS. Instead, this UPS is connected to an electrical panel. From the electrical panel, we install multiple electrical circuits. We then connect our equipment to the electrical circuits.

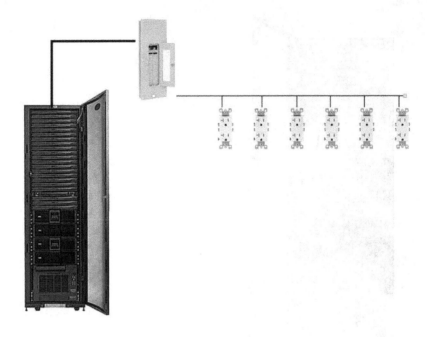

UPSs can be much larger. A large building such as a school, shopping mall, or hospital may have a UPS that is connected to the electrical panel and electrical outlets.

o **Generator** – What if we have a power outage that lasts three days and we need to keep operating, but our UPS only lasts one hour? We install a **power generator**, which is a device that can produce electricity. When the power outage takes place, the UPS supplies power from its batteries, and the generator produces new power to recharge those batteries.

A typical power generator burns diesel. Generators can be portable or fixed. It is better to have a power generator and not need it then to need it and not have it. The power generator should be maintained regularly to ensure that it is operating and that it contains an adequate supply of fuel. The organization should also make sure that it has a contract to receive additional fuel deliveries during a long power outage.

o **Power Distribution Units (PDUs)** – Finally, to avoid any single point of failure, it is important to select network devices and servers with redundant power supplies. If we have two UPSs, we connect one power cord from each device to the first UPS, and we connect the second power cord to the second UPS. That way, if a UPS fails, the devices continue to receive power. Most devices with dual power supplies offer power supplies that are hot swappable. Electronics use power that is DC (Direct Current), while a UPS or municipal power supply provides power in AC (Alternating Current). An electronic device will contain an adapter that converts from AC to DC. This adapter may fail during operation. When it is hot swappable, it can be replaced even while the device is powered on.

In a data center with hundreds of devices, it can become difficult to identify which plug goes to which power supply. As a result, manufacturers produce power cables in different colors such as red, green, and yellow. You can use these cables to tell different circuits apart.

o **HVAC** – HVAC stands for Heating, Ventilation, and Air Conditioning. Engineers typically follow standards published by ASHRAE (American Society of Heating Refrigeration and Air Conditioning Engineers) when they design ventilation systems.

- Heating the room is not typically a concern because the equipment will generate more than enough heat. If the room needs to be heated, we need to decide how the building is heated

  - If the building has a boiler (water is heated and pumped throughout the building), we will extend the heating loop into the room. This only provides heat.

  - If the building has an air handling unit (air is heated and circulated throughout the building), we extend the duct work into the room. This provides heat and fresh air.

  - We can install a portable heater.

- Ventilation is a concern, but it depends on how much time people spend inside the room. If it is an MDF or IDF, it may not require much ventilation. It may be acceptable that the room receives fresh air through the doorway. If it is a data center, then fresh air is required. Fresh air can be pumped in through a make up air unit.

- Air Conditioning is a very important concern because the equipment will generate heat that needs to be removed. The air conditioner can also bring fresh air into the room.

  A typical setup for a small server room is to install a split system. It is technically a "heat pump" not an air conditioner because it does not exchange any air with the outside world.

Inside the server room, we install an evaporator unit on the wall. On the roof, we install a condenser unit. The evaporator and condenser are connected with refrigerant lines.

The evaporator unit takes warm air from the room and extracts the heat. It empties the heat into a liquid called refrigerant. The warm refrigerant is pumped to the condenser on the roof, where the heat leaves. The refrigerant cools down and is pumped back into the server room.

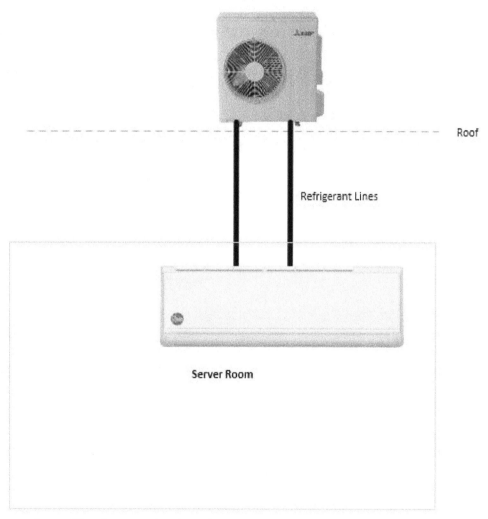

- o **Fire Suppression** – Fire Suppression is an important concern. How do we stop a fire?

  - ▪ A fire extinguisher – the most basic fire suppression is to install a fire extinguisher. If a person sees a fire, and they can put it out safely, they can spray it with a fire extinguisher.

A fire extinguisher only prevents small fires that start when a person is watching. We must be careful to use an ABC fire extinguisher, which is one that can put out fires burning wood, flammable liquids, and electrical equipment.

A fire extinguisher must be inspected yearly.

- Sprinkler system – a traditional sprinkler system (also known as a wet pipe system) can automatically put out a fire. It consists of sprinkler heads that are installed throughout the building, connected to water pipes. The water pipes used for the sprinkler system are pressurized. Each sprinkler head contains a small piece of metal that melts under low temperatures (in the photo below it is red). If a fire occurs under the sprinkler head, the metal melts and water is released.

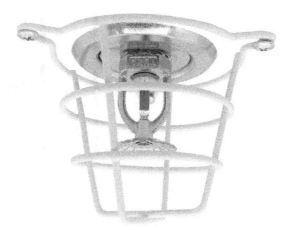

A sprinkler system will put out the fire, but it will damage the equipment. We don't want the sprinkler head to activate accidentally, and we can use the following measures

- If we install a sprinkler head, we should install a cage around it so that it is not accidentally broken. If somebody breaks the sprinkler head, it will leak water.

- We can install high temperature heads in the server room. Sprinkler heads are manufactured to activate at different temperatures (100°F, 150°F, 225°F, etc). We should select a head that is rated for a high enough temperature so that it does not accidentally activate.

- We do not need to install a sprinkler system in a building that is not combustible (for example a building made of concrete). The actual determination of whether a building is combustible or non-combustible is complicated. It may be possible to build the server room out of materials that are fire rated, and then not have to install sprinkler heads (even if the rest of the building is sprinklered).

- We can install a pre-action system

- Sprinkler system with pre-action – a pre-action system is a system that does not activate until at least two signals trigger the system. We would install a normal sprinkler system. We would then install a heat detector in the server room, next to the sprinkler head. We would install a valve in the pipeline that feeds the sprinkler heads.

  If the heat detector is senses heat, it opens the valve and allows water to flow to the sprinkler head. If there is a fire, the sprinkler head melts and water is sprayed onto the fire.

  If the heat detector does not sense heat, the valve remains closed and no water reaches the sprinkler head. The sprinkler head will not release any water, even if it is broken.

- Dry system – a dry system is a sprinkler system that does not release water, but some other chemical such as Nitrogen or Carbon Dioxide. The gas flows through the entire room and forces the Oxygen out. Since fire needs Oxygen to continue burning, the lack of Oxygen puts out the fire.

  A dry system is better because it can penetrate areas that water won't. For example, if the fire starts at the bottom of the rack, underneath the UPS, the water from the sprinkler will not be able to reach it. The water will fall on top of the rack and puddle underneath the floor.

  A dry system also won't damage equipment.

  We will need to install an alarm that warns people when the fire suppression system is activated so that they can quickly leave the room.

  3M™ Novec™ 1230 Fluid is a special fluid that can put out a fire 50 times faster than a water-based system without damaging electronics.

The dry systems are more expensive than traditional sprinkler systems.

- Hypoxic system – a hypoxic system is one that reduces the level of oxygen in the room to a point where humans can breathe but a fire cannot start. Normal air is 21 percent oxygen, 78 percent oxygen, and 1 percent other gases.

  If we change the air so that it is 15 percent oxygen and 85 percent nitrogen, then humans can breathe but a fire cannot start.

  This system is currently not permitted by government regulations unless the employer provides workers with respirators, although studies have shown no adverse health effects.

  This system is an active system because it must constantly remove oxygen from the air (fresh air coming from outside will continue to increase the oxygen levels).

- Sprinkler system with water mist – water mist systems are newer, but their popularity is increasing. A water mist system is one that generates an aerosol from the water instead of discharging a high-pressure stream.

  The smaller droplets of water cool the air and create steam, which displaces the oxygen. This serves to put out the fire quickly. The mist also reduces the amount of water damage caused when compared with a traditional fire sprinkler system.

  Water mist systems are more expensive than traditional systems. They may also be more expensive than pre-action systems.

- What type of fire suppression should you choose? Consider

  - The cost of the sprinkler system, the cost of a fire damaging the equipment or burning down the building, the cost of the replacing the equipment, and the building codes

  - It is better for the sprinkler system to damage the equipment in the server room than having a fire damage the equipment in the server room and spreading to the rest of the building

- It is always cheaper to design the sprinkler system before the building is built

- Always have a fire extinguisher handy – it is usually required by the local fire code. The fire extinguisher should be mounted to the wall and have a sign that people can see.

- If your building is still under construction or in the design phase and non-combustible, it will not have a sprinkler system

  - Consider having the MDF and IDF built out of materials that can withstand a fire for one hour or two hours

  - A dry or water mist sprinkler system may be installed only for the IDF and MDF. This will protect the equipment if a fire starts in one of these rooms. The cost of a dry system for a single room will not be much more than the cost of a traditional system for a single room.

- If your building is still under construction or in the design phase, and combustible, it will have a sprinkler system

  - If your building code allows it, you may build the IDFs and MDF out of materials that can withstand a fire for at least two hours, and not have a sprinkler head in those rooms

  - Otherwise, you may be required to extend the sprinkler system into the IDF and MDF. This type of sprinkler system will damage the equipment. It is unlikely that the entire building will have a dry system.

  - A dry or water mist sprinkler system may be installed only for the IDF and MDF. This will protect the equipment if a fire starts in one of these rooms, but the cost may be too high. It may cost $30,000 to install a dry system in a single room, so the business must consider whether the cost outweighs the risk.

- If your building is existing construction and non-combustible, then the building will not have a sprinkler system

- The business must consider whether they need a fire suppression system for the IDFs and MDF.

- Since only a single room is affected, the cost of a traditional system may be almost as much as the cost for a dry system.

- If your building is existing construction and combustible, it will already have a sprinkler system that extends into the IDFs and MDF

  - The existing sprinkler system will likely be a traditional system.

  - Consider whether you can use fire proof materials to insulate the rooms and remove the sprinkler heads, and whether the cost is worth the reduction in the risk.

  - Consider whether the cost of replacing the existing sprinkler heads with a pre-action or dry system is worth the reduction in risk of damaging the equipment

- Redundancy and High Availability (HA) Concepts – now that we know how to keep a building running in the event of an isolated issue (like a power outage), what do we do to keep the entire business running when an entire building is inaccessible? We can maintain a second site (a second location). There are four types of back up sites

  - **Hot Site** - A **hot site** is a site that is continually running. With the use of a hot site, an organization has multiple locations that are operating and staffed. For example, an insurance company may have a call center in New Jersey, a call center in Florida, and a call center in California. The insurance company staffs all three centers 24/7. If the California call center is affected by an earthquake, the insurance company diverts calls to New Jersey and Florida, and operations are not disrupted.

    In the case of a data center, the organization will maintain data centers in multiple geographic locations. These data centers are connected to each other over WAN links. Data is replicated across multiple data centers, so that damage to one data center does not compromise the data. For example, an insurance company stores customer data in data centers at California, Utah, and Virginia. The Virginia data center is hit by a tornado, but all the data has been replicated to the other two centers. The organization and its customers can continue accessing their data.

    A hot site is expensive to maintain. The organization must decide whether it is worth the cost. In the example of the insurance company, they can staff the three sites cost-effectively. A smaller organization (such as a restaurant or warehouse) that operates out of a single location may not find it cost-effective to operate a second site.

Key staff (like the CEO) who operate from one site can be moved to the hot site during a disaster.

- o **Cold Site** – A **cold site** is a location that does not contain staff or equipment. An organization hit with a disaster must send employees to the cold site, bring in supplies, and configure equipment. The cold site does not contain any data; the organization must restore its data from back up.

  A cold site is cheaper to operate than a hot site. In the event of a disaster, the cold site can be used to operate the business. The cold site may be an empty office, an abandoned warehouse or a trailer.

  Organizations such as Regus provide immediate short-term office space that companies can rent in the event of a disaster.

- o **Warm Site** – A **warm site** is a compromise between a cold site and a hot site. A warm site may contain some hardware and preconfigured equipment. The organization may need to bring in staff and/or specialized equipment for the warm site to become operational. The warm site may contain copies of data, but they will not be current.

- o **Cloud Site** – A cloud site is where we replicate our physical infrastructure in the cloud. An organization may want to maintain physical control of its data and devices but may compromise during a disaster and redirect employees to the cloud. The cloud will likely be set up as a warm site that can mimic the infrastructure and data of the existing operation. Employees can connect to the cloud site from home or from an actual cold/warm/hot site.

We should also make sure to maintain multiple internet connections at each site

- • Active-Active vs Active-Passive

  - o An **Active-Active** connection is where we set up two or more internet connections and use both or all of them at the same time. The router will choose which internet connection to route traffic to based on an algorithm.

o An **Active-Passive** connection is where we set up two or more internet connections and use only one of them. The internet connection that we prefer to use is called the primary internet connection. The other internet connection is called the failover.

o Some scenarios that we can have

- WAN and Broadband

  - The active connection is a WAN link – traffic between offices passes over the WAN

  - The second active connection is a broadband link – traffic from an office to the internet passes through the broadband link. This is good when we have an expensive WAN and we don't want to waste it on traffic that does not need to pass through it

  - If the WAN fails, the router can create a VPN tunnel to the other offices through the broadband connection

- Broadband and Cellular

  - The active connection is a broadband. If the business has only one location, all of the traffic passes through the broadband.

  - If the business has multiple offices, they might set up an SD-WAN. Traffic to another office passes through the broadband and into the SD-WAN. Traffic to the internet passes through the broadband and straight into the internet.

  - If there are two or more broadband providers in the area, we might set up an SD-WAN with two broadband connections.

  - The failover connection is a cellular modem. If the broadband fails, traffic passes through the cellular modem.

- WAN and Broadband and Cellular

  - The active connection is a WAN link – traffic between offices passes over the WAN

- The second active connection is a broadband link – traffic from an office to the internet passes through the broadband link.

- A cellular link provides back up for the WAN and the broadband. This is good when the same ISP provides the WAN and the broadband (i.e. where physical damage to the wiring would shut down both the broadband and the WAN)

Some ways that we can measure our recovery

- **Mean Time to Repair (MTTR)** – **MTTR**, or the **mean time to repair** is the average time from when a failure is detected/reported until it is repaired. For example, if a server breaks down at 11AM and is repaired at 1PM, the time to repair is two hours. If we have multiple breakdowns, we can average them to obtain the MTTR.

  The MTTR is the time to resolve to the issue, not the time to respond the issue. For example, if a server fails, and a repairman arrives within three hours, but it takes an additional hour to troubleshoot and repair the issue, then the repair time is four hours.

  When determine an MTTR, the shorter the MTTR the more money it will cost. To ensure a short MTTR, the we (or our vendor) may need to have more technicians on call whether they are performing useful work or not, and the we (or our vendor) may need to stock spare parts whether or not they are required.

  Different types and severities of incidents can have different response times. The organization must weigh the response time against the impact to the business. Critical incidents may require response times measured in hours while trivial issues may allow response times measured in days or even weeks.

$$MTTR = \sum \frac{TOTAL\ DOWNTIME}{NUMBER\ OF\ FAILURES}$$

The system's availability is the time that it is available.

$$AVAILABILITY = \sum \frac{MTBF}{MTBF + MTTR}$$

- **Mean Time Between Failure (MTBF)** – **MTBF** is the **Mean Time Between Failures**. This is the average amount of time between failures of a device. Some devices can be repaired, and some devices cannot. For example, a hard disk drive that fails irreparably after 300,000 hours has a MTBF of 300,000 hours. A computer server that fails (but can be repaired) after 100,000 hours and then again after 300,000 hours has an MTBF of 200,000 hours (average of 100,000 and 300,000).

The MTBF of electronics and industrial equipment is usually measured in operating hours (since a device sitting on a shelf is less likely to fail). Some devices have a failure rate that is measured in cycles or per use (for example airplanes are rated based on the number of times they take off and land, and not the amount of time they spend in the air – take offs and landing put more stress on the airplanes' components than the actual flying).

A manufacturer will should disclose the MTBF on each device that they manufacture so that customers can make informed purchasing decisions. If a device is inexpensive but has a high failure rate, then the long-term cost may be much higher.

For example, if an organization purchases hard drives with a 300,000-hour MTBF, but they have deployed 100,000 hard drives, then they can expect that (on average) one hard drive will fail every three hours (or about eight per day). They can use this to plan their replacement strategy.

Electronic devices usually fail on what is called a bathtub curve (high failure rate at the beginning and end of their life span, and low failure rate in the middle).

$$MTBF = \sum \frac{START\ OF\ DOWNTIME - START\ OF\ UPTIME}{NUMBER\ OF\ FAILURES}$$

- **Recovery Time Objective (RTO)** – The Recovery Time Objective is how much time we have from the disruption to get things back to normal. If we exceed the RTO, then the business will begin to suffer severe consequences.

  For example, a chemical plant I worked with had an RTO of four hours. If a critical issue was not resolved within four hours, the plant would lose one million dollars per hour after that. That is not to say that they did not suffer any consequences the first four hours, just that they were tolerable.

  The less time we have to restore our services, the more the restoration will cost. We must weigh the cost of the recovery against the cost of the harm to the business.

- **Recovery Point Objective (RPO)** – The Recovery Point Objective is the amount of data the business can afford to lose without suffering severe consequences. It is typically measured from the time of the last back up until the incident occurs.

  For example, if we can afford to lose a maximum of 24 hours worth of data, then we should back up our data at least once per day. If we back up our data at 12:01AM, and we have a crash at 11:59PM, we would lose 24 hours of data. If we back up our data once per week at 12:01AM on Monday and we have a crash at 2:00PM on Friday, we would lose several days of data, which would be unacceptable.

We must weigh the cost of the back ups against the cost of losing the data.

- **Availability** – The system's availability is the time that it is available to the end users. It can be calculated from the MTBF and the MTTR.

$$AVAILABILITY = \sum \frac{MTBF}{MTBF + MTTR}$$

- Network Device Backup/Restore

  - **Configuration** – we should maintain a back up of the configuration of each network device. This can be completed automatically each time a change is made. In the event that a device is replaced, the configuration can be easily transferred to the new equipment.

    We should always make a back up of the configuration before making any changes.

  - **State** – it is more difficult to back up the state of a network device. The state includes things like active sessions and connections, MAC address tables, and routing tables. If we are using a software defined network, then we can take snapshots of the device states and restore them to exactly the way they were before.

Part E: N10-008 4.0 Network Security

4.1 Explain common security concepts

- *Confidentiality, Integrity, Availability (CIA)*
- *Threats*
  - *Internal*
  - *External*
- *Vulnerabilities*
  - *Common Vulnerabilities and Exposures (CVE)*
  - *Zero-Day*
- *Exploits*
- *Least Privilege*
- *Role-Based Access*
- *Zero Trust*
- *Defense in Depth*
  - *Network Segmentation Enforcement*
  - *Screened Subnet (DMZ)*
  - *Separation of Duties*
  - *Network Access Control*
  - *Honeypot*
- *Authentication Methods*
  - *Multifactor*
  - *Terminal Access Control-Access Control System Plus (TACACS+)*
  - *Single Sign-On (SSO)*
  - *Remote Authentication Dial-In User Service (RADIUS)*
  - *LDAP*
  - *Kerberos*
  - *Local Authentication*
  - *802.1X*
  - *Extensible Authentication Protocol (EAP)*
- *Risk Management*
  - *Security Risk Assessments*
    - *Threat Assessment*
    - *Vulnerability Assessment*
    - *Penetration Testing*
    - *Posture Assessment*
  - *Business Risk Assessment*
    - *Process Assessment*
    - *Vendor Assessment*
- *Security Information and Event Management (SIEM)*

Now that we have explored network redundancy, let's take a look at security. The principles of data security follow three concepts: **Confidentiality, Integrity, and Availability** (CIA)

Confidentiality means that sensitive data is only seen by authorized users.

We link data (objects) and users (subjects) so that only authorized subjects have access to objects. We evaluate confidentiality according to the following ideas

- **Sensitivity** – what is the value of the information? How much damage could it cause if it were leaked?

- **Discretion** – does a user have the ability to leak the confidential data? How much ability? Is it easy or difficult to leak the data?

- **Criticality** – how important is the information to the business?

- **Concealment** – can we hide the data so that unauthorized users can't see it?

- **Privacy** – if the data is leaked, what harm can it cause to a specific individual?

- **Seclusion** – can we store the data in a remote location?

- **Isolation** – can we store the data away from other types of data?

Data could be leaked intentionally or unintentionally, but a leak is still a leak.

Integrity ensures that the data is not modified by unauthorized users while in transit or at rest. That means that the data that is received is the same as the data that was sent. We should be able to verify that an object has not been changed.

We evaluate integrity according to the following ideas

- **Accuracy** – the information is correct.

- **Authenticity** – the information has not changed since it was created

- **Nonrepudiation** – the person who created the information cannot deny that he created it. That is, we are certain of the identity of the author.

- **Completeness** – the information is not missing any component.

- **Truthfulness** – the information is realistic

- **Validity** – the information is logically sound

- **Accountability** – a person is responsible for the accuracy of the information

- **Comprehensiveness** – the information is complete

If an unauthorized user can access an object, he can probably change it too. Integrity can be affected by human users and by malicious programs such as viruses.

Availability ensures that the resource is available when it is needed.

We evaluate availability according to the following ideas

- **Usability** – the information is easy to understand

- **Accessibility** – many people can view the information regardless of the type of equipment they have or their background

- **Timeliness** – the users can access the data quickly

Availability can be affected by a lack of resources (too many users and not enough computing hardware/bandwidth) or by attacks such as Denial of Service.

The Threats to the data can be **Internal** or **External**. An internal threat is an employee, a vendor or somebody that we trust. An External threat could be a hacker, a foreign government, an activist, or a competitor.

A **vulnerability** is a weakness in a system, such as a misconfigured firewall or an operating system that is not patched. A threat will take advantage of a vulnerability to gain access into our system. When this happens, it is known as an **exploit**.

The end goal of security is to reduce or eliminate the exploits. We can't stop external threats, but we can reduce internal threats and we can reduce the number of vulnerabilities. Because it is not always possible to eliminate every vulnerability, we must create multiple layers of security. The more important the asset, the more layers of security we should have.

Think about a bank. A burglar is a threat. If the bank leaves the vault unlocked at night, that is a vulnerability. But the bank has multiple layers of security – a locked door, a surveillance camera, a motion sensor, a security guard, a locked vault. Even if one of those items fails, it is still difficult for the robber to get the money from the vault.

Our network might have a firewall with access control lists, a VPN with two factor authentication, and a server with complicated passwords and limited privileges. Even if the server was unpatched (a vulnerability), a hacker wouldn't be able to access it because the firewall would block him, and he wouldn't be able to connect to our network through the VPN. These layers might be known as **defence in depth**.

A group sponsored by MITRE and the US Department of Homeland Security created a database of vulnerabilities called Common Vulnerabilities and Exposures, or CVE.

Each time a vulnerability is discovered in a commercial device, it is listed in this database. You can search the database for devices in use at your organization and determine whether one or more of them contains a vulnerability. You can then patch the device or take it out of service if it cannot be patched, or remove it from the network (or put it behind a firewall) if it cannot be patched and is critical to your operations.

A **Zero Day** exploit is a vulnerability in a software program or system that has just been discovered; therefore, there is no patch. Day Zero is the day that the exploit is first discovered by the public. An attacker might know about the vulnerability before the public and can take advantage of it for days, weeks, months, or even years.

When a company discovers a serious vulnerability in their system, they may choose to develop a patch and ensure that their largest customers have installed it before disclosing the vulnerability to the public. This will reduce the risk that hackers become aware of the vulnerability before it can be patched.

Some of the things we can do to protect our network

- Enforce the **Principle of Least Privilege** – A user account should be granted only the least privileges/access required for the user to perform his/her job (or function in the case of a generic account).

  o User accounts should be audited to ensure that users are not granted permission to objects that they do not require

  o An account can be restricted so that it can only access the system (or specific system resources) during specific times of day or specific days.

  o Workers who operate on a fixed schedule should only be permitted to access the system when required to perform their job

  o In a large organization, assigning privileges to each account manually can be time consuming and lead to security vulnerabilities (when too many privileges are assigned) or disruption to the business (when not enough privileges are assigned)

Instead, groups can be created. A group is a role that a user plays in the organization. Each group can be assigned specific privileges consistent with that role. A user can be assigned to one or more groups. The user then inherits the privileges that were assigned to each group.

For example, an organization may create an "engineers" group. The engineers' group is given the privilege of accessing AutoCAD files. When a new engineer is hired, he is added to the engineers' group. He now has access to AutoCAD files automatically.

- A location-based policy is one that provides a user with privileges based on his physical location at the time of log in, or based on his office location

  When accessing the network through a mobile device, the user's GPS location may be used to determine the appropriate policy

- Enforce **Role Based Access Control** – Permissions are not assigned to individual users or to objects. Instead, permissions are assigned to operations/actions (known as roles)

  - A user can be assigned to a specific group (the user is given a role); the user inherits the permissions assigned to the role

  - The organization can define the operations and actions that are relevant to their organization. For example:

    - Sales person (can access sales data)

    - Accountant (can enter data into the accounting system)

    - Accounts payable clerk (can approve invoices and issue payments)

- Enforce **Zero Trust** – Zero Trust is a new concept that tells the network not to trust anything regardless of whether it is inside the network or outside. Any device connected to the network must prove that it is worthy of accessing a resource. In a way, it is an idea of installing a firewall between the internal users and the network, not just between the internet and the network.

  The Zero Trust system works at Layer 7. It must deeply examine the data that is being transferred, not just the source and recipient.

A common implementation

- o We don't trust anything connected to our network, not even computers. Even though they are probably corporate owned, we can't immediately verify that they haven't been exploited or placed there by a hacker.

- o When a user logs in to a computer connected to our network, we verify that the computer is legitimate and that it has the proper security patches. We might do so through an endpoint management application or security certificate.

- o We also verify that the user is legitimate and has authorization to log in to that specific computer at that specific time. We might do so through a smart card or other credential.

- o We also verify that the computer is connected to the network at the correct location.

- o We now give the user access to the specific resources that he is entitled to.

- o We continue to monitor the user and the computer.

- **Network Segmentation Enforcement** – earlier we talked about setting up VLANs to segment the network. We could have a VLAN for security cameras, a VLAN for user computers, a VLAN for servers, etc. When a user wants to access a resource inside another VLAN, the firewall must decide whether such an action is permitted. An administrator can configure firewall rules to give users access to the resources that they require.

  The problem with this approach is that we must create many firewall rules (tens of thousands for a large network), and that a user can access all of the devices on his own VLAN, even though such actions may not be necessary. It is not possible for an administrator to manage all those rules.

  Think about a scenario where a user downloads a virus (either accidentally or on purpose) and it spreads to all the other computers in the office due to an unpatched vulnerability. The VLAN could not prevent it.

  A new idea is called **micro-segmentation**. With virtualization and software defined networking, we can monitor and inspect the contents of every packet travelling East-West (on the same VLAN). We can also create a firewall on each device (user computer, virtual server, physical server, etc) to determine whether a packet is permitted, and configure policies to adapt to changes in activities or user behavior.

- **Screened Subnet** (DMZ) - The **DMZ** is the **Demilitarized Zone.** The DMZ is a zone where devices that need to access the internal and external network can be placed.

  Hosts that require internet access and that are vulnerable to attack (such as e-mail servers, web servers, and VoIP servers) should be placed in the DMZ.

  The best setup is to install a firewall between the internet and the DMZ, and another firewall between the DMZ and the internal network.

  Always assume that a device in the DMZ has been compromised. Building on the concept of our redundant network from earlier, now we have installed a DMZ, and one server within the DMZ. The firewalls on the right protect our DMZ servers from external threats, and the firewalls on the left protect our internal network from external threats and potential threats from the DMZ.

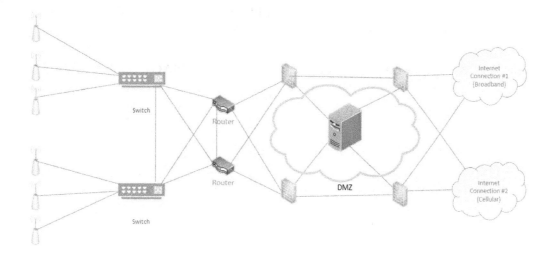

  Devices in the DMZ may have a public and a private IP. Their private subnet is known as the screened subnet.

- **Separation of Duties** – No single employee can or should do everything. For example, an employee who approves invoices should not also be the one to create/sign the checks. If the employee who approves invoices submits a fraudulent invoice and attempts to pay themselves, they would be caught.

  In the IT world, we want to reduce the risk that a malicious administrator can introduce a vulnerability to our system. Some ways that we can separate duties

  - No employee should have "super admin" access to every system; the system can be segmented, and each employee can be given a role. Multiple employees should share each role. This prevents a rogue employee from locking out other administrators.

- o The work of any employee should be verified by another employee
    - Have one employee install patches and another employee verify that the patches are operational

    - Have one employee write configurations and have another employee verify that the configurations are correct

    - Have one employee update configurations on a device and have another employee verify that the configurations have been correctly updated

    - Have multiple employees jointly investigate security incidents, and have other employees review their findings

- o Require multiple administrators to approve the creation of an administrator account or changes to an administrator's privileges

- **Network Access Control** – Network Access Control or **NAC** is an idea that we should verify the security status of a device before permitting it to access the network. It is related to Zero Trust. Some of the properties that our network will seek to verify

    - o Security patches

    - o Antivirus protection

    - o User authentication

We usually need to be able to give a non-compliant device limited access to the network so that it can obtain the required software updates and become compliant. Otherwise, devices that are offline for some time will become bricks.

- **Honeypot** - A Honeypot is a network device that appears to be vulnerable but is in fact designed to detect hackers. A network security administrator creates a honeypot to identify hackers and/or to distract them from legitimate network resources. A honeypot allows an organization to understand the motives behind the attacks (which can be used to better protect network and other resources), and the type and sophistication of the hackers.

There are several types of honeypots

- o **Pure honeypot** – a production system with a monitoring device on the network interface. The pure honeypot can be detected by a hacker.

- High interaction honeypot – runs on a physical or virtual machine and imitates many production systems. The high interaction honeypot consumes a substantial amount of resources. When run on a virtual machine, the honeypot can be quickly killed and regenerated.

- Low interaction honeypot – simulates only necessary services, allowing more honeypots to operate with fewer resources.

- SPAM honeypot – spammers will locate servers that use open relays (an open relay is an e-mail server that allows an unauthenticated user to send an e-mail) and use them to send e-mails. The spammer will attempt to send e-mail test messages through the SPAM honeypot; if successful, the spammer will continue to send e-mail through the honeypot. The honeypot can detect the SPAM messages and also detect the spammer.

Authentication Methods are ways for us to verify the identity of a user. Some of the methods include

- **Multifactor** – In the past, you would authenticate with a server by providing a username and password. The problem with that method is that people can steal your username/password combination and log in as you.

  The principles of **multifactor authentication** (formally two-factor authentication) are important. The three main factors are Something You Are, Something You Have, and Something You Know. Basic authentication methods combine Something You Have (a username/access card) with either Something You Know (a password) or Something You Are (biometric).

  - **Something You Are** – something you are refers to a biometric identity such as facial recognition, fingerprints, voice recognition, or a retinal scan. Select the best type of biometric for your environment. A construction site or hospital may have employees with gloves, who cannot scan into a fingerprint reader, so a retinal scan will be more appropriate.

  - **Something You Have** – something you have refers to a smartcard, identification card, or username; it could also refer to a randomly generated password (such as an RSA SecurID or authenticator app)

  - **Something You Know** – something you know refers to a password or PIN o **Somewhere You Are** – somewhere you are refers to your physical location. In the case of connecting to the internet, somewhere you are is your IP address or GPS location. If a hacker compromises a username/password and logs in through a computer or network location that is not recognized, then the login may be denied. Websites have sophisticated ways of detecting users – IP address, web browser version, computer version, date/time of the login, other user behaviors. If the username/login is correct, but the other factors aren't it could be that the account was compromised, or it could be that the user is travelling/bought a new computer. The site can ask the user for additional verification (such as through an automated phone call) if it determines that the account may be compromised.

o **Something You Do** – something you do is an observation of the user's action's or behaviors. In Windows a user can choose a picture password; in an Android phone the user can interact with a pattern.

Consider that we have a large network with multiple devices (servers, switches, routers, etc.). We need a centralized method for managing user authentication. Why?

- We want an administrator to be able to log in to multiple devices without having to keep track of a different username/password combination for each one.

- We also want to log each time the administrator logs in.

- We want to be able to disable an administrator's account without having to manually log in to each device.

How can we accomplish the above? There are a few methods

- **Terminal Access Control-Access Control System Plus (TACACS+)** – TACACS or Terminal Access Controller Access-Control System is a protocol for accessing/managing network devices. It was developed by UNIX.

  TACACS+ was developed by Cisco and is a separate protocol from TACACS. Most systems use TACACS+ or RADIUS.

  TACAS uses port 49 to communicate.

  TACACS+ encrypts the full content of each packet while RADIUS encrypts only the user passwords. TACACS+ uses TCP, while RADIUS uses UDP (therefore RADIUS has more errors). Cisco continues to support RADIUS, but TACACS+ is recommended.

TACACS+ uses the **AAA (Authentication, Authorization, Accounting)** architecture, where each element is separate. Therefore, a system could use a different form of authentication (such as Kerberos) with TACACS+ authorization and accounting. Some forms of user authentication include

- o Point-to-Point

- o PAP

- o CHAP

- o EAP

- o Kerberos

Authentication – the server is trying to determine who you are

- o The client sends a START message to the server

- o The server sends a REPLY message

- o The client sends a CONTINUE message, if additional information is required for authentication

- o Otherwise, authentication is complete

Authorization – the server is trying to determine if you are permitted to access the resource

- o A default state of "unknown user" is created if the user's identity is unknown

- o Otherwise, the TACAS+ server responds with a RESPONSE message, which contains the restrictions on the user

Accounting – the server is making a record of your access

- o A START message records when the user started the connection

- o A STOP message records when the user stopped the connection o An UPDATE message says that a task is still being performed

TACACS+ allows an administrator to configure different privilege levels for each user (for example a user may not be permitted to modify an ACL on a router). RADIUS does not allow different privilege levels (all users are effectively superadmins).

- **Single Sign-On (SSO)** – Single Sign-On uses a central system to authenticate users across multiple applications.

  For example, a user logs in to his computer via his Windows Active Directory password. He is then able to access the corporate intranet, procurement application, online library, payroll, and e-mail without having to re-enter a username or password.

  Once logged in, the remaining applications understand that the user is already authenticated. In the background the applications receive authorization from the Active Directory server.

  A user (and the organization) does not have to maintain separate usernames/passwords for each application.

  If the single sign on system fails, then the user will not be able to access any of the applications.

  Increasingly, social media sites such as Google and Facebook provide SSO services to other websites. For example, a user can use their Facebook account to log in to another site. Using Facebook for Single Sign On is a bad idea because Facebook will collect data about your visits to other websites and the websites will collect data from your Facebook account.

- **Remote Authentication Dial-In User Service (RADIUS)** - RADIUS, or Remote Authentication Dial-In User Service, is a server that has three components

  o Protocol

  o Server

  o Client

The **Network Access Server** is a Client of the RADIUS Server. When a user attempts to log in to the client, the client sends user information to the RADIUS server. The client and server encrypt their data with a shared secret, but the communication between the user and the client are not encrypted.

The RADIUS server receives connection requests and authenticates the user. RADIUS does not allow different privilege levels (all users are effectively superadmins). A RADIUS server combines authentication and authorization.

Authentication

- o Many methods are possible including PPP, PAP, and CHAP

- o The client sends the RADIUS server the user's username and encrypted password

- o The RADIUS server replies with

  - Accept – the user is authenticated

  - Reject – the user is rejected (credentials invalid)

  - Challenge – the user must provide additional information

Authorization

- o Authorization tells the client what privileges to assign to the user

Accounting

- o Accounting data is transmitted at the beginning and end of a session

- **LDAP** - LDAP stands for **Lightweight Directory Access Protocol** or **LDAPS** (for secure access). LDAP is essentially an address book. LDAP is governed by the X.500 standard.

  LDAP includes a server called a **Directory Server Agent**, which typically speaks on port 389 or 636 for LDAPS. A client connects to the server.

  A client can do the following (a client may have permission to do only some of these)

  - o Add

  - o Delete

  - o Modify

o   Search

For example, a photocopier with "scan to email" capabilities would connect to the LDAP server and obtain e-mail address entries for the various users in the office.

- **Kerberos** - Kerberos is a protocol that allows clients and servers to authenticate with each other and prove their identities. The server knows that the client is legitimate, and the client knows that the server is legitimate.

  The Kerberos protocol protects against eavesdropping and replay attacks. Kerberos uses UDP port 88. Kerberos provides encryption over an unsecure network.

  Kerberos' current version is V5. It was developed by MIT and made available for free.

  All versions of Windows including Windows 2000 and later use Kerberos for authentication by default (although other protocols can be used). Kerberos is used by Windows to join a client to a Windows domain.

  Most common versions of UNIX also use Kerberos.

  If a client wishes to connect, the following procedure is followed.

  o   The client calls the Authentication Server (AS) to obtain authentication.

  o   The authentication server takes the client's username and sends it to another server called the **Key Distribution Center** (**KDC**).

  o   The KDC runs a service known as the **Ticket-Granting Service** (**TGS**), which maintains a secret key.

  o   The KDC issues a ticket known as the **Ticket-Granting Ticket** (**TGT**) and encrypts it with the secret key.

  o   The encrypted key is sent back to the client.

  Let's look at how a user would log in to a Windows machine

  o   A user would like to log in to a local Windows machine (the client), with a username and password. Even on a corporate network, the password should not be sent to the server (domain controller) in plain text.

o The local Windows machine encrypts/hashes the password.

o The client sends the user ID to the authentication server (in plain text), but not the password.

o The Authentication Server verifies that the client is in the database. The AS creates a secret key from the hash of the user's password (that is stored on the server) and returns to the client the following messages

  ▪ A TGS Session Key, which is encrypted with the newly created secret key (Message A) – i.e. encrypted with a hash of the user's password

  ▪ A TGT, which includes an expiry date and the client's network address, all encrypted with the TGS's secret key (Message B)

o The client takes the TGS Session Key and decrypts it with the hash of the password that the user entered earlier. If the user entered the wrong password, then the client will be unable to decrypt the TGS Session Key. If the user entered the correct password, then the client will be able to decrypt the TGS Session Key.

o The client uses the decrypted TGS Session Key to communicate with the TGS

o If the client wants to request additional services

  ▪ The client sends additional messages to TGS

    • Specifically, the client sends Message C, which is the TGT from Message B and the ID number for the requested service

    • The client also sends message D, which is the authenticator (client ID and time stamp), encrypted with the Client/TGS

  ▪ TGS obtains Message B from Message C and decrypts it (Only TGS has the encryption key for Message B). TGS uses this to decrypt Message D.

  ▪ If the Client ID in Message C and Message D match, then the client is authenticated

  ▪ TGS sends additional messages

- Message E is the Client-to-Server Ticket, which includes the client ID, network address, and expiry, encrypted using the service's secret key

- Message F is the Client/Server Session Key, encrypted with the Client/TGS Session Key

- The client takes Message E and Message F and uses them to authenticate with the Service Server

- The client sends

  - Message E from before

  - Message G, which is an authenticator, including the client ID, and timestamp

- The Service Server decrypts Message E with its own secret key and obtains the Client/Server session Key. It uses this key to decrypt Message G. If they match, then the client is authenticated with the service

- The Service Server sends Message H to the client, which includes the timestamp in Message E, encrypted with the Client/Server Session Key

- The client decrypts Message H. If the timestamp on Message H is correct, then the client knows it can trust the server. A rogue agent could issue a fake message but would not be able to match the timestamp.

The encrypted key will expire, but if the user is logged in, the key will renew (the client will automatically contact the server and obtain an updated key).

To communicate with another node, the ticket is sent back to the service. The TGS verifies that the user is permitted to access the service and then sends the ticket to the Service Server (SS).

Kerberos has a single point of failure, which is the authentication server.

Kerberos also requires the clients, servers, and services to be responsive (since timestamps must match on all devices). That means that all devices must have synchronized clocks. If a client/server issues a ticket/message with a timestamp that doesn't match due to a clock that is out of sync, then the system will fail. Clocks must not be more than five minutes apart (they don't have to have the exact time).

- **Local Authentication** – Local Authentication means that we store the username and password on the local device.

  Every device comes with the option to store a local username and password, which can be used if the remote authentication server is unavailable.

  To avoid security issues, we should create a unique local username and password on each device and store them in a secure database. We should not use the default local username.

  There are tools (especially on Windows machines) that automatically change the local username and password on a daily or monthly basis, according to a predefined formula. An administrator needing to log in with a local account can use a tool to determine the current local password. The local username and password can be unique for each computer.

- **802.1X** – IEEE 802.1X is a standard for Network Access Control. It allows a device to authenticate when connecting to a LAN or WAN.

  There are three devices involved

  - The **supplicant** is the device that chooses to connect to the LAN/WAN. It could be a laptop, desktop, smartphone, tablet, or other computing device

  - The **authenticator** is a network device that allows/denies access. It could be a switch, a router, a firewall, or a proxy server.

  - The **authentication server** is a server that decides whether a device should be granted access

- The procedure

  - The supplicant connects to the network

  - The authenticator (switch) detects the new supplicant and automatically sets the port to an unauthenticated status. Only traffic related to 802.1X is permitted while the port is set to an authenticated status.

  - The authenticator sends frames to the supplicant. These frames demand that the supplicant provide credentials such as a user ID. The frames are sent on the local network segment to a specific address (01:80:C2:00:00:03). The supplicant listens for messages on this address.

o The supplicant replies to the message with an EAP-Response Identity frame

o The authenticator sends the supplicant's response to an authentication server

o The authentication server and the supplicant negotiate an authentication method. The server and the supplicant may support different methods of authentication and must agree on one that both understand. The negotiation methods are transported through the authenticator.

o The authentication server attempts to authenticate the suppliant. If successful, the authenticator changes the port status to authorized. If unsuccessful, the authenticator keeps the port status as unauthorized.

o When the supplicant logs off or is disconnected, the authenticator changes the port status back to unauthorized. When the supplicant logs off, it sends an EAPOL-Logoff message to the authenticator.

Security Risks

o A hacker can physically insert himself between the port and the authenticated computer; and then use the authenticated port

o A DDOS attack can take place. A hacker can create EAPOL-logoff messages with the MAC address of the supplicant and send them to the authenticator, forcing the port to go into an unauthorized state. This would force the supplicant to continually go offline.

- **Extensible Authentication Protocol (EAP)** – Extensible Authentication Protocol is a system for authenticating with a wireless network.

o EAP is a framework for providing authentication, but there are more than 40 possible methods that can be used, depending on the specific vendor of the equipment.

o RFC 5247.has defined EAP

344

- Each vendor may have more specific requirements and new protocols are being developed all the time

- Within EAP are several methods, including

  - **LEAP**
    - **Lightweight Extensible Authentication Protocol**

    - Developed by Cisco

    - LEAP is not supported by Windows but is supported by many third-party applications

    - Cisco does not recommend using LEAP anymore because it does not protect user credentials

  - **PEAP**

    - **Protected Extensible Authentication Protocol**

    - Originally, EAP assumed that communications would be secure; therefore, it did not provide a mechanism to secure the data being transmitted.

    - PEAP corrects this by providing a secure TLS tunnel

    - A server-side certificate is used to create a PKI tunnel

  - **EAP-NOOB**

    - **Nimble out-of-band authentication for EAP**
    - Used by devices that do not have preloaded authentication information such as Internet of Things devices

    - The user must assist the device in connecting via an out of band channel

    - There are different connection options including QR codes and NFC

- Ephemeral Elliptic Curve Diffie-Hellman (ECDHE) exchange takes place over the in-band EAP channel. The user then provides the out-of-band channel message from the server to the device or from the device to the server, depending on what is required.

- **EAP-FAST**

  - **Flexible Authentication via Secure Tunneling**

  - Designed by Cisco to replace LEAP

  - Three parts

    o In band provisioning via Diffie-Hellman. The client is provided with a shared secret.

    o Tunnel establishment. A tunnel is established between the server and the client.

    o Authentication. The user is authenticated

- **EAP-TLS.**

  - **EAP – Transport Layer Security**

  - Uses TLS (Transport Layer Security) as its protocol.

  - All wireless manufacturers support EAP-TLS

  - Considered very secure

  - EAP-TLS requires a client-side certificate. When a system is authenticated with a certificate, a password is not required. Even if a hacker obtained the username/password, without a certificate, the hacker would not be able to connect to the Wi-Fi.

  - EAP is not implemented as widely as it should be because it requires the certificate

- **EAP-TTLS**

  - **EAP Tunneled Transport Layer Security**

  - Extends TLS so that the client does not require a certificate. Instead, the server creates a tunnel with the client. The client can then authenticate to the server using a legacy password or other authentication method. The tunnel protects the client from eavesdropping.

Finally, we must look at Risk Management, both from a security approach and a business approach. How do we evaluate risks to our infrastructure?

- **Threat Assessment** – A threat assessment is a process for evaluating potential threats. We must determine

  o Whether the threat is real

  o How serious the threat is to our organization if it takes place

  o How likely it is for the threat to take place

  We don't know what we don't know. It is not possible to determine every threat that could ever occur. We should develop a framework for brainstorming potential threats that considers the types of people who might attack our organization and their motivations.

  A threat assessment should involve subject matter experts.

- **Vulnerability Assessment** – A vulnerability assessment evaluates our systems for security risks.

  First, we should make a complete inventory of all the devices on our network. Then, we should systematically evaluate each one to determine all the ways that it can be attacked (physically, remotely, via a configuration change, via an API, etc).

- **Penetration Testing** - A **penetration test** is when an outside person is hired to find security risks in an organization. Some organizations give the penetration tester permission to attack any system and discover all possible security holes because they want to make their systems better. Others limit the penetration tester's scope because they do not want to admit to their customers, employees, shareholders, or themselves that there are security flaws in their systems.

A penetration test does not have to be electronic in nature. It can be as simple as an unauthorized person walking into a building and stealing papers from a filing cabinet.

To properly perform a penetration test, the tester must know

- o The common attack methods employed by hackers

- o The type of information and resources that a hacker would like to steal from the organization (intellectual property, financial information, etc.)

The tester should obtain written approval from the highest levels of the organization before proceeding with the penetration test. Many of the actions performed by the tester could be considered crimes (trespassing, unauthorized access to a computer system, theft, fraud, etc.). If the tester is caught in the act, local staff may report him to the police.

- **Posture Assessment** – a posture assessment shows the organization's overall security status. It shows the organization's ability to defend itself against attacks, the types of risks that the organization faces, the value of the organization's data, and the types of defences in place. The posture assessment is a tool that management can use to improve the organization's overall security.

How do we evaluate risks to our business?

- **Process Assessment** – the process assessment is a procedure for determining whether a specific business process is secure or where its vulnerabilities lie. For example, if an organization has a process for paying an invoice, the assessment will determine whether an attacker could trick the finance department into paying a fake invoice. The assessment will show the vulnerabilities and how to repair them.

- **Vendor Assessment** – a vendor assessment is a procedure for determining whether external vendors put the organization at risk. It also determines whether the vendors have security policies that are in line with that of the organization. A vendor may have remote access into our systems and may store our data on their systems. Thus, even if our own security systems are strong, an attacker could exploit a weakness in one of our vendors.

We must work with our vendors to improve their systems.

- **Security Information and Event Management (SIEM)** – SIEM stands for Security Information and Event Management. It can be a dedicated appliance, or it can be a software application. Many SIEM systems are cloud-based and share threat & intelligence data with multiple customers.

Most network devices generate and store security data. For example, a router may detect traffic from an unauthorized location or a server may detect, and log failed login attempts.

An SIEM aggregates this security data from multiple locations including routers, switches, servers, IP Phones, network storage appliances, video recorders. The SIEM may convert the logs and data into a common format. The SIEM allows a security administrator to view all security events in one place (and in one format) instead of having to log in to multiple devices.

The SIEM can also allow a network administrator to correlate events across multiple devices. For example, if a hacker gains unauthorized access to a network through the router and then fails to log in a file server multiple times, both events can be correlated as coming from the same source IP address and occurring at the same time.

The SIEM can automatically send alerts to a network administrator either via SMS or e-mail. The SIEM can be set to trigger alerts when specific events occur.

If network devices are in different time zones, the SIEM can automatically adjust the log times to the time zone of the security administrator. The SIEM can also remove duplicate events from the log.

Some examples of logged data
- o Failed log in attempt on a server or router
- o Firewall refuses traffic from a specific IP address
- o IP address is engaged in port sniffing

4.2 Compare and contrast common types of attacks

- *Technology-Based*
  - *Denial-of-Service (DoS) / Distributed Denial-of-Service (DDoS)*
    - *Botnet / Command and Control*
  - *On-Path Attack (Man-in-the-Middle)*
  - *DNS Poisoning*
  - *VLAN Hopping*
  - *ARP Spoofing*
  - *Rogue DHCP*
  - *Rogue Access Point (AP)*
  - *Evil Twin*
  - *Ransomware*
  - *Password Attacks*
    - *Brute Force*
    - *Dictionary*
  - *MAC Spoofing*
  - *IP Spoofing*
  - *Deauthentication*
  - *Malware*
- *Human and Environmental*
  - *Social Engineering*
    - *Phishing*
    - *Tailgaiting*
    - *Piggybacking*
    - *Shoulder Surfing*

Now that we have an idea of risk management, let's look at some ways that our network can be attacked.

DoS is **Denial of Service**. There are millions of servers operating on the internet (which host websites). If a hacker wants to bring down a web server, the hacker would flood that server with massive amounts of traffic. The web server would then be unable to respond to legitimate traffic, and ordinary users would be unable to visit the website. This is known as denial of service. Services other than websites exist on the internet (credit card processing, databases, etc.), and all are vulnerable to DoS.

There are many types of DoS attacks

- **SYN flooding**. Remember that when a user wants to connect to a web server, a three-way handshake (SYN, SYN/ACK, ACK) process occurs between the two computers.

    o The user sends a SYN message to the server; the server responds with a SYN/ACK message to the user, and the user responds with an ACK message to the server

    o In SYN flooding, the hacker imitates a legitimate user and sends more SYN requests than the web server can handle. The web server opens a connection for each SYN request and responds with the SYN/ACK response, but the hacker does not complete the third part of the connection by sending the SYN.

    o The server keeps a connection open waiting for an ACK message that never arrives. The server can only keep a limited number of connections open. If all of them are waiting for ACK messages that will never arrive, then the server won't be able to establish connections with legitimate users

- **Fragmenting**. When data travels over the internet, the sending computer breaks it down into pieces known as packets. The packets may take different routes to reach their destination. The receiving computer puts the packets back together. The data in each packet should not overlap.

    o In a fragmenting attack, the hacker send data to the server, but puts overlapping data into each packet

    o The server attempts to put the data back together but can't. If the operating system isn't equipped to recognize this attack and discard the bad packets, then the server will crash.

How to prevent Denial of Service

- Most DoS attacks are preventable now. Why?

- A hacker will not have enough bandwidth to bring down a large web service. Major websites such as Google, Facebook, eBay, etc. use distributed server farms consisting of millions of servers, with redundant pathways to the internet. A hacker will not have enough capacity to overload their systems.

- Most enterprise systems contain firewalls that can easily detect and block DoS attacks. If a substantial amount of illegitimate traffic appears to be originating from a single source, it can simply be turned off.

- For a small monthly fee, services such as CloudFlare offer large-scale cloud-based firewalls to protect smaller websites from DoS attacks (which they normally could not afford).

- A company should never be a victim to the same attack twice. After the first attack, they must investigate and rewrite their systems so that it never happens again. The most common types of attacks are well documented, and systems are available to prevent them.

Distributed Denial of Service was invented after DoS stopped working (due to improvements in internet infrastructure).

With **DDoS**, a hacker infects thousands (or hundreds of thousands) of computers (or other IP devices such as cameras) and uses all of them to send traffic to a web server that he wants to crash. These computers are known as **bots**, and together they are known as a **botnet**. Since the traffic appears legitimate (and is in fact originating from hundreds of thousands of different sources, in different geographic locations, different internet service providers, and different computer types), it is difficult to filter or prevent.

The botnet operator will continue to acquire additional bots, to grow his botnet. The operator will lease his network of bots to a person or organization that wants to bring down a website (for revenge, competition, or other reasons).

Examples of bots

- Mirai. Most web-accessible routers and IP cameras come preconfigured with default usernames and passwords. Most home users of routers and IP cameras neglect to change the default usernames/passwords (in some cases, it is impossible to change the default username/password).

Mirai scanned IP addresses at random and located web-accessible routers and IP cameras. It then attempted to log in using default usernames/passwords. Once successful, it infected the devices. Once infected, the devices are added to the botnet and used to launch attacks.

How to prevent

- Services such as CloudFlare use large scale cloud-based firewalls to mitigate DDoS attacks. They set up a server farm with a large amount of bandwidth that can be "donated" to a website facing a DDoS attack. CloudFlare's bandwidth can accept some DDoS attacks.

- Users should use antivirus and firewall programs to prevent their computers from becoming infected and turned into bots.

- Users should ensure that they change the default username and password on their IoT devices.

- Manufacturers of IP cameras and wireless routers should put in the effort to make their devices more secure (so that they do not become infected and used in DDoS attacks).

In a **Man-in-the-Middle attack**, a hacker inserts himself between the sender and recipient of an electronic communication. Keep in mind that more than 60% of internet traffic is machine generated (one computer talking to another with no human interaction).

Consider that Alice and Bob are two hypothetical internet users having an encrypted conversation. They could be two humans, or it could be that Alice is an online banking user and Bob is the bank. Consider that the hacker, Eve, wants to spy on them.

Alice and Bob's messages pass through a central server. Depending on Alice and Bob's geographical locations, the messages may pass through many servers, routers, switches, fiber optic cables, and copper lines. The internet is fragmented, and different parts are owned by different companies. If Alice is in New York and Bob is in Los Angeles, the traffic must pass through many states, and many internet service providers.

- If the traffic between Alice and Bob is unencrypted, and Eve can obtain access to one of the servers, routers, switches, or physical connections, then Eve can spy on the conversation.

- If the traffic is unencrypted, but Eve does not have access to one of the servers in the connection, Eve could trick Alice into sending messages addressed to Bob to her instead (by corrupting/modifying Alice's address book). Eve would do the same to Bob.

  In Alice's address book, Eve replaces Bob's address with her own.

  In Bob's address book, Eve replaces Alice's address with her own. Alice sends messages to Eve thinking she is sending them to Bob, and Bob sends messages to Eve thinking he is sending them to Alice.

  Now Eve can read Alice's messages and forward them to Bob. Eve can also read Bob's messages and forward them to Alice. Neither Alice nor Bob is aware that Eve is reading their communications.

- If the communication is encrypted and uses public key cryptography (such as Apple iMessage or WhatsApp), a man-in-the-middle attack is more difficult.

  o Consider how public key cryptography works

     - Alice and Bob each creates a private key which they keep secret. A private key can only decrypt a message

     - Alice and Bob use the private key to generate a public key, which they distribute to potential senders. A public key can only encrypt messages.

     - If the keys are long enough, they cannot be reversed. As long as the systems and algorithms are secure, it would be practically impossible to decrypt a message without the private key.

     - If Alice wants to send Bob a message, she finds his public key. She encrypts the message using his public key, and then send him the encrypted message. Bob receives the encrypted message and uses the private key to decrypt it.

     - Apple iMessage and WhatsApp automatically generate the keys for each user. If Bob is using an iPhone, his iPhone will generate a private key, which it will store on the phone. It will also generate a public key, which is stored in Apple's central directory.

     - If Alice wants to send you Bob a message via iMessage, her iPhone checks the Apple directory for his iPhone's public key, which it uses to encrypt the message.

- What if Eve wants to intercept an iMessage or WhatsApp communication between Alice and Bob?

  - Eve generates her own public and private keys

  - She hacks into the central directory and changes Bob's public key to her own. She records Bob's original public key.

  - Alice decides to send a message to Bob. She checks the directory for Bob's public key, and receives what she thinks is Bob's public key (but is in fact Eve's public key)

  - Alice sends the message to Eve (thinking she is sending it to Bob)
  - Eve decrypts the message, reads it, and then encrypts it with Bob's original public key

  - Eve sends the message to Bob

  - Bob receives the message, thinking it came from Alice and decrypts it with his own private key

  - Eve repeats the same process with Alice's public key so that she can intercept messages that Bob is sending to Alice

How to prevent

- The best way to prevent a man-in-the-middle attack is to encrypt all communications with a reliable encryption algorithm (one that uses a long enough key length and is generated through open-source methods)

- Second, ensure the integrity of the public key. Do not trust applications with "key directories" such as Apple iMessage or WhatsApp, especially for sensitive communications.

  Apple controls all the public keys in iMessage and a rogue operator could inject their own public keys, creating the man-in-the-middle attack illustrated above. The best way to ensure the integrity of the public key is to personally distribute it to the person that you want to communicate with.

What is **DNS**? Recall that every computer on the internet has a unique IP address. That means, every website's server has a unique IP address. Humans are not good at remembering IP addresses. If you had to remember and type in the IP address for every website you visited, the internet would not be very useful. Instead, you type in a domain name, such as google.com.

The DNS (Domain Name System) knows what every domain name is, and what its corresponding IP address is. When you type in a Domain Name, your computer queries the DNS to find the correct IP address for that website's server.

Who operates DNS

- There are many online public DNS servers such as Google DNS (8.8.8.8 and 8.8.4.4). These provide records for publicly-available websites.

- Many ISPs operate DNS servers for their own customers. These provide records for publicly-available websites and are only accessible to their own customers. For example, Comcast might operate a DNS for their own customers. A customer can choose to bypass Comcast's DNS and use Google's DNS.

- Many companies operate their own DNS servers for their own offices. These provide DNS for internal systems and internal websites and may also provide DNS for publicly-available websites. A public DNS would not be able to provide a DNS record for an internal device.

- Each Windows machine operates its own DNS to keep track of the most recently visited websites.

An authoritative DNS server (or nameserver) holds the original records for the hostname in question. Different DNS servers can be authoritative for different websites. A recursive (non-authoritative) DNS server is one that requests DNS data from the authoritative DNS server.

- For example, AWS Route 53 DNS Servers are authoritative for amazon.com because they hold amazon.com's original DNS records

- If a user queries the AWS server, he will receive an authoritative answer about the location of the amazon.com servers

- After querying the AWS DNS server, DNS servers at the user's ISP and office cache the DNS data. Now, DNS servers closer to the user know the IP address of amazon.com.

- The user (or other users) can go back to these servers to perform DNS lookups, but the answer will be non-authoritative. They don't have to query the authoritative DNS server, which is far away.

In **DNS Poisoning**, a hacker corrupts the DNS records. The hack can take place at the top-level DNS servers, at the ISP level, at the office level, or at the computer level. The corrupted DNS can force a user to visit a fake server.

- For example, Bank of America's web server is located at IP address 11.11.11.11

- A hacker sets up a server at 9.9.9.9 and then corrupts the local DNS server to point users to Bank of America's website at 9.9.9.9. The users' computers visit the website at 9.9.9.9 thinking they are accessing a legitimate Bank of America server.

How to prevent

- Use an authoritative DNS server. An authoritative DNS server is one that provides original DNS data. An authoritative DNS server can be hacked, but it is less likely.

- Use **Domain Name System Security Extensions (DNSSEC)**. DNSSEC uses digital signatures to authenticate DNS information.

  Each domain name server digitally signs the response it provides. The recipient can validate the signature to ensure that it received a legitimate record.

VLAN Hopping is a trick where a device can gain access to traffic on VLANs that it is not entitled to. Recall that a VLAN can be used to segment network traffic. Remember that a switch can have "access" ports, which transmit traffic on only one VLAN, and "trunk" ports, which transmit traffic on multiple VLANs.

When we connect a device (such as a laptop for example) to an access port, the device can access the network on the VLAN that is specified on that port.

We would normally connect two switches together on switches configured as trunk ports. If we didn't explicitly configure the ports as trunks, when we connect two switches together, those switches may attempt to negotiate a "trunk" and agree to exchange traffic on multiple VLANs.

A malicious device connected to a switch can pretend that it is also a switch, with a trunk port. The other switch would then establish a trunk and exchange traffic on multiple VLANs. We can prevent this by configuring our switch ports explicitly – that means telling each port to act as either an access port or as a trunk port. A device connected to an access port will not be able to move to another VLAN.

If we don't explicitly set a VLAN, then the default VLAN on an access port is VLAN 1. The default VLAN is also known as the native VLAN. The switch will ignore any frames tagged with the native VLAN of the port.

A malicious device can tag a frame with two VLANs – the native VLAN, and the VLAN of a device that it wants to exploit. This is known as a **double-tagged frame**. The switch will ignore the native VLAN tag and forward the frame with the second tag. If the trunk port has a native VLAN, then the trunk port will not attempt to retag the frame. If the device to be exploited is connected to a second switch, then that second switch will accept that frame on the VLAN.

For example,

- A legitimate device is connected to Port 1 of Switch 2, VLAN 2

- A malicious device is connected to Port 1 of Switch 1, VLAN 1 (the native VLAN)

- The two switches have a trunk that passes traffic from VLAN 1 and VLAN 2

- The malicious device should not be able to communicate with the legitimate device because they are on different VLANs

- If the malicious device double-tags a frame with VLAN 1 and VLAN 2, and addresses it to the legitimate device

  o Switch 1 will receive the frame and ignore the tag for VLAN 1

  o It will send the frame to Switch 2 over the trunk port

  o Switch 2 will see that the frame is tagged for VLAN 2 and addressed to the legitimate device

  o Switch 2 will forward the frame to the legitimate device

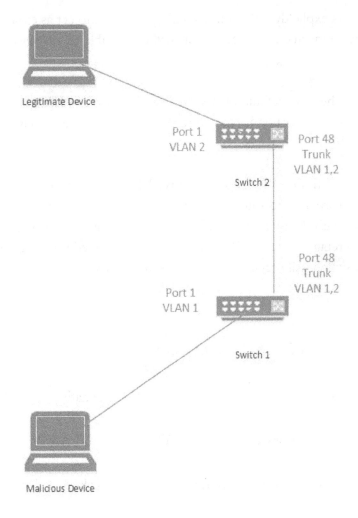

Legitimate Device

Port 1
VLAN 2

Port 48
Trunk
VLAN 1,2

Switch 2

Port 48
Trunk
VLAN 1,2

Port 1
VLAN 1

Switch 1

Malicious Device

How can we stop this from happening?

- We should make sure not to use VLAN 1 for anything.

- We should explicitly configure each access and trunk port VLAN

- We should ensure that the native VLAN on a trunk port is changed to one that is not used.

ARP is **Address Resolution Protocol**. Remember that every network device has a unique MAC address, set from the factory. A MAC address is kind of like a serial number. When a device connects to a network, it announces its MAC address.

360

Every device is assigned (or should be assigned) a unique IP address. On a LAN (Local Area Network), devices communicate by addressing data to the each other's MAC addresses.

If the sender knows the recipient device's IP address, but not it's MAC address, it uses ARP to discover the MAC address. It does so by flooding the network with a request for the MAC address. Since the device doesn't know who it is looking for, every device on the network receives the request. It sends the electronic equivalent of a "hey if this is your IP address, reply with your MAC". The device in question replies with its MAC address.

The opposite is also possible. A device can flood the network with a request for an IP address when the MAC address is known. This is known as reverse ARP or RARP.

Each network device stores common MAC addresses and their corresponding IP addresses in a table known as the ARP table, so that it doesn't have to look them up each time it needs to send data (too many ARP lookups can overload the network).

There is no authentication mechanism for the ARP table. Each device simply adds/updates the ARP table when data is received. A device will update the ARP table with new data even if it did not create an ARP request. There is no way to check if a device has lied about its MAC address.

ARP Poisoning is when a hacker sends wrong data to corrupt the ARP table.

- Let's say our office has a printer with an IP address of 10.10.1.1 and a MAC address of AB:CD:EF:12:34:56

- Bob wants to print some sensitive documents. His computer knows that the printer's IP address is 10.10.1.1 but doesn't know its MAC address. It sends out an ARP request to 10.10.1.1, and the printer responds with AB:CD:EF:12:34:56

- Bob's computer stores this data in its ARP table

- Bob's computer sends documents to be printed to AB:CD:EF:12:34:56

- A hacker comes along and plugs a laptop into an open ethernet port in Bob's office. The hacker's laptop has an IP address of 10.10.1.2 and a MAC address of AA:BB:CC:11:22:33

- The hacker sends out an ARP message saying that 10.10.1.1 belongs to AA:BB:CC:11:22:33, the hacker's computer

- Bob's computer picks up this unsolicited ARP message and stores it in the ARP table

- Bob's computer sends all printed documents to the hacker's computer instead of the printer

- The hacker can forward Bob's documents to the printer, so that they print correctly, and Bob doesn't suspect that his documents have been stolen

How to prevent

- Obviously, the hacker should never have been able to plug his laptop into an open ethernet port in Bob's office.

  o Somebody should have noticed that there was an intruder and called the police

  o An open ethernet port should never be patched into a switch

  o The hacker's laptop should never have been permitted to access the network, even if the port was open

  o But many offices do not have adequate security

- Use ARP spoofing detection software. The software can perform cross-checking of ARP entries against a DHCP server or switch, which has accurate information.

- Critical system components should have static ARP entries that cannot be changed. This could require a substantial amount of maintenance for hosts use DHCP.

A hacker who found an open ethernet port could connect a **rogue DHCP** server (any small router will have a DHCP server built in) and attempt to take the other network devices offline. Each time a device attempts to obtain an IP address via DHCP, the rogue DHCP server responds faster than the legitimate server.

Eventually, many devices receive IP addresses issued by the rogue DHCP server and are unable to access the internet or other devices on the network.

The hacker can take this one step further and specify his own default gateway as part of the DHCP configuration. Now devices receiving DHCP configuration from the rogue server will forward their external traffic to a rogue default gateway.

We can prevent a rogue DHCP server from operating by enforcing MAC address filtering on the network. We can also use DHCP snooping.

There are many types of wireless attacks.

- **Evil Twin**. A wireless client will connect to the access point that has the highest signal (typically the one that is nearest to the client). In an Evil Twin attack, the hacker deploys a wireless access point with the same SSIDs as the legitimate access points, but with a higher signal strength. Clients that are preconfigured to connect to the SSIDs will connect to the evil twin.

  The evil twin attack can be prevented by authenticating all wireless connections through certificates. The client should be configured to verify the identity of the network that it is connecting to. A rogue access point will not be able to prove its identity.

- **Rogue AP**. A Rogue AP is an evil twin that forwards traffic to the main network. The Rogue AP allows a hacker to act as a man-in-the-middle and intercept all traffic.

  Preventing Rogue APS can be done by

  - Using access points that detect Rogue APs (for example, Cisco Aironet APs have optional Rogue AP detection modules)

  - Using MAC address filtering on the network to prevent unauthorized devices from connecting

- **Jamming**. Wireless Access Points operate on a specific band of the electromagnetic frequency spectrum (2.4 GHz and 5 GHz). A hacker can flood the air with useless signals in the same frequency. If these signals are more powerful than those put out by the access point, they will prevent legitimate users from connecting. Signal jamming has applications in other types of networks (cell phone jamming, radar jamming).

- **Disassociation**. In a disassociation attack, a hacker forces a client to disassociate from an access point. A hacker can force a client to disassociate from an access point by sending a "disassociation" message to the client.

  - The disassociation message is a standard message that an access point could sent to a client to disconnect it

  - It contains the MAC address of the client and the SSID of the access point

  - If a hacker intercepts communication between the client and the access point, he could learn the MAC address of the client, and then create a fake disassociation

363

message

- The hacker must send these messages to the client constantly, or it will try to reconnect. This creates a cycle where the client is constantly stuck between connecting to and disconnecting from the wireless network.

Crypto-malware and **ransomware** are closely related. Crypto-malware is a type of virus or malicious program that encrypts data on a computer.

The malware can be introduced through e-mail or downloaded files. The malware usually encrypts user documents, videos, photos, and music. It does not usually encrypt system files.

The distribution of crypto-malware is usually automated, although people or organizations can be specifically targeted. It should be noted that after the crypto-malware has infected the computer, then the author is able to view the contents of the computer. At that point, he can make an assessment as to how high of a ransom to charge. For example, if an ordinary person was targeted, the ransom might be low, but if a hospital was targeted, then the ransom might be high.

After infection, the computer operates as normal, but the user is provided with a message that their files have been encrypted. The malware usually instructs the user to pay a ransom to unlock the files. The ransom must typically be paid in bitcoin or another cryptocurrency that can't be traced.

There are two types of crypto-malware

- Crypto-malware that pretends to encrypt the files. They change the file extension to something random, but do not encrypt the file. A non-sophisticated user will assume that the files are encrypted because an error message will be encountered when the file is opened. If the extension is changed back to the original, the files revert to normal. These forms of crypto-malware are extremely rare.

- Crypto-malware that encrypts the files. After the files are encrypted, the decryption key is sent to a central server maintained by the hacker. The user receives the decryption key after paying the ransom.

  Files encrypted by some forms of crypto-malware cannot be decrypted, either because the crypto-malware is misconfigured, or because the hacker's intention is to permanently encrypt the files.

Ransomware is an extension of crypto-malware, in that it instructs the user to pay a ransom in exchange for unlocking the files.

Typically, the user is instructed to visit a TOR website, where they are provided further instructions. TOR websites are generally able to hide the location of their servers, although law enforcement agencies have developed methods to identify them. The user is instructed to pay the ransom with cryptocurrency (untraceable currency) such as bitcoin.
In most cases, the hackers provide the victim with the tool to decrypt their files upon receipt of payment. In some cases, the hackers do not.

The ransom amounts have ranged from the equivalent of $500 to $20,000 depending on the person or organization that was affected. Many organizations pay the ransom and don't publicly admit that they have been hacked.

How to prevent ransomware

- Proper user education to teach users how to identify potential ransomware delivered via e-mail, and to not open unusual attachments.

- Block e-mail attachments that contain macro-enabled Microsoft Word and Excel documents.

- Regularly install Windows operating system security updates

How to defeat ransomware once infected

- Attempt to restore data from backup or from the Volume Shadow Copy. This only works if the organization has backed up their data, and only the data that was backed up can be restored. Newer versions of ransomware delete the Volume Shadow Copy.

- Attempt to decrypt the ransomware. Police forces in the EU have been able to provide victims with assistance in decrypting some forms of ransomware. Some versions of ransomware use weak encryption that can be broken through brute force or other techniques.

- Pay the ransom. In earlier cases, it was almost certain that the hackers would automatically (or manually) provide the decryption key upon payment of the ransom. In more recent cases, this is not guaranteed because there are many copycat ransomware viruses created by people with very little knowledge or infrastructure. Ransomware developers have franchised their operation to "script kiddies" who are simply distributing the ransomware and collecting payments. There are also versions of ransomware that have been put out by nation-states to cause political disruption; this type of malware only destroys data but is disguised as ransomware.

Notable infections

- In 2019, Jackson County, Georgia paid $400,000 to remove ransomware from their computers.
- University of Calgary paid $20,000 to decrypt computers infected by ransomware in 2017. The FBI later charged two people in Iran with spreading the virus, which infected computers at health care providers and other organizations.

Notable ransomware

- CryptoLocker was transmitted over e-mail as a ZIP file. Inside the e-mail was an executable disguised as a PDF. The decryption key was sent to a remote server. A victim could pay a ransom and receive a decryption key automatically. The creators of CryptoLocker made an estimated $27 million. In 2014, security firm FireEye was able to obtain the database of decryption keys, allowing victims to decrypt their files for free.

- WannaCry took advantage of a zero-day exploit in the Windows Server Message Block. WannaCry infected computers that had not patched the Windows Server Message Block vulnerability. The average ransom amount was $600. Over 200,000 computers were infected, with losses estimated at over $4 billion.

- Unlike other forms of ransomware, Petya encrypted the master boot record of a Windows computer. This caused the entire computer hard drive to be encrypted. Another version, known as NotPetya was targeted towards Ukrainian government entities and critical infrastructure. NotPetya quickly spread to other computers worldwide and could not be decrypted. It is believed that NotPetya was created by the Russian government.

Some ways that a hacker can attempt to decrypt a password

- **Rainbow Tables**. It is bad security practice to store passwords in plain text. Passwords are typically hashed, and the hash is stored (the hash is not reversible). A hash is a one-way mathematical function. Thus, when the password is created, the hash is generated and stored. Each time the user logs in, the password entered is hashed; this hash is compared against the stored hash to determine whether it is correct.

  If a database of hashed passwords is leaked, the hackers will only see the hashes, which cannot be reversed back to the original passwords. The hash can't be used to log in.

But a hacker could generate a dictionary of passwords (common and uncommon) and calculate the corresponding hash for each one. This reference is known as a **rainbow table**. The hacker could then steal a database of password hashes and look up the corresponding password for each one.

Rainbow tables are readily available on the internet for passwords up to eight characters (every possible combination!) and rainbow tables of even longer passwords can be computed.

To prevent the use of rainbow table attacks, modern password hash functions incorporate a 'salt'. The salt is a random set of characters appended to the end of each password before the hash is calculated. The hash and the salt are stored in plain text. If the hash database is compromised, the hacker would have to regenerate each rainbow table incorporating the salt into every password to make any sense of it. This would be practically impossible.

- **Dictionary**. A Dictionary attack uses a list of predetermined passwords and brute force to guess the password. The dictionary could consist of common words in the English language, especially common passwords such as "password", "12345678", and "abcd".

   A hacker could create a custom dictionary based on the user account that he is trying to hack into. For example, the dictionary could be customized to include the names of the user's children, pets, vehicles, etc..

   Many organizations force users to choose complex passwords. Password complexity could include

   o   Not reusing the same password

   o   Including upper case letters, lower case letters, numbers, and special characters

   o   Ensuring that the password meets a minimum length

   o   Not using a person's name, address, or username in the password

   Yet, it is still possible to create a custom dictionary based on the password complexity requirements. For example, if the user's password was 'donkey', then a complicated password might be 'D0nkey!'. Users tend to substitute @ for a, 0 for o, 1 for l, and so forth in a predictable manner.

   A dictionary attack can be prevented by limiting the amount of password attempts a user has before his account is locked out. Of course, the dictionary attack could occur offline, or the hacker may have a way to bypass the incorrect password attempt count.

- **Brute Force**. A brute force attack is like a dictionary attack, except that the system attempts every password combination possible (based on the character set), starting from the letter a and working its way up until the password is guessed. For example, the system will guess the password 'sdfsfgdgsdfsdfd', and then the next password would be 'sdfsfgdgsdfsdfe'.

  The length of time for a brute force attack to be successful depends on the computing power available (how many passwords can be attempted every second) and the length of the password (how many passwords need to be attempted).

  An online brute force attack is when the brute force occurs against a live computer. For example, consider Active Directory, a Microsoft system that stores user accounts on a central server. When a user attempts to log in to an Active Directory-based computer, the computer validates the login credentials with the server. On a successful login, the computer caches the correct credentials on the local computer. If the computer is later offline (or off the local network), the user can still log in (the computer validates the login with the cached credentials).

  o In an online attack, the hacker would brute force the computer's login while it is connected to the Active Directory server. This attack would likely be unsuccessful because the server would notice the incorrect logins and disable the account.

  o In an offline attack, the hacker would brute force the computer's login while it is not connected to the Active Directory server. This attack may or may not be successful depending on the length and complexity of the password.

  How to prevent

  o Offline attacks can't be prevented. Where possible, secure equipment so that it is not stolen. Stolen equipment is more susceptible to offline attacks.

  o Enforce stronger password requirements (including special characters, numbers, upper/lower case letters).

  o Enforce a timer that delays the entry of passwords. This can be accomplished at the software or hardware level, by hashing the password multiple times.

  o Offline data can be encrypted with a strong algorithm that takes several seconds to validate the password. This would be a minor inconvenience to a user entering an incorrect password but would substantially slow down a brute force attack.

- o If the computer is secured with a password but the data on the computer is not encrypted, the hacker might have other ways to compromise the device. Then the password is ineffective regardless of its length or complexity.

Recall that each network device is manufactured with a unique, unmodifiable (in theory) MAC address. On a LAN, one security measure to prevent rogue devices is to only allow traffic between trusted MAC addresses. If an intruder attempts to connect a new device to the network, it will not be permitted to communicate because its MAC address is not on a list of authorized devices.

If a hacker learns the MAC address of a legitimate network device, he can change his device's MAC address and gain access to the network (and to the traffic originally directed to the legitimate device).

How to prevent

- Require additional user authentication before allowing a device to access the network

- Use port security on switches. A switch can remember which MAC address sent traffic on which port. If the switch detects the same MAC address on a different port, it can either shut down the port or alert an administrator of the discrepancy.

Recall that each network device is assigned a unique IP address. Two network devices can communicate over a LAN or public network if they know each other's IP addresses. A hacker can intercept their communication by changing his machine's IP address to match that of one of the devices. This method takes special skill and control/modification of network routers, because

- Most network devices/computers will detect the IP address conflict.

- The device whose IP address is spoofed will not receive any traffic because it is being intercepted by the hacker's computer. The hacker's computer would pretend to be the legitimate computer and carry on the communication.

- To remain undetected, the hacker will have to intercept the IP traffic through the router and then forward it to the legitimate recipient.

A broadcast IP address is a special type of IP address that exists in every network. The broadcast address allows a device to send a single message to all the IP addresses on that network. One type of broadcast message is known as an "echo". Devices receiving the "echo" message reply to the sending device.

In a Smurf Attack, the hacker forges the "from" portion of the echo message so that it appears to have come from another system (the system that he wants to attack). The device whose address appears in the "from" portion will receive all the replies. Depending on the size of the network, and the number of echo messages sent, that device could receive hundreds or thousands of replies. A Smurf Attack is like an internal DDoS attack.

How to prevent

- Encrypt all traffic. An IP spoofing attempt will not allow a hacker to read encrypted traffic.

- Set firewalls to drop traffic that originates from outside the network but appears to come from inside the network (could indicate that the address has been spoofed).

Malware is a general term given to programs that are illegitimate. They include viruses, trojans, and worms.

A **virus** is an unauthorized program that causes undesired activity. A virus is not a standalone program, but instead it latches on to another legitimate program. When the legitimate program runs, so does the virus.

Viruses typically infect executable programs such as programs with extensions of .exe. Viruses can also infect documents, such as Microsoft Word documents or Microsoft Excel spreadsheets. These are known as macro viruses. Current versions of Microsoft Office disable macros by default (a user can open a Microsoft Office document file without allowing the macro to execute).

Viruses can enter automatically through vulnerabilities. A user could inadvertently introduce a virus by clicking on attachments or downloading files from the internet.

The damage that a virus does is called the **payload**. Viruses can cause a wide range of effects from being simply a nuisance to deleting files. Viruses that infect industrial control systems can cause millions of dollars in damage. Viruses that infect medical equipment can put lives at risk.

A virus can be detected and prevented using an **antivirus program**. An antivirus program has two methods of detecting viruses

- **Definitions**: A definition is a specific "fingerprint" of the virus. An antivirus program may contain hundreds of thousands of virus definitions. It scans each new file introduced into the computer against the definitions. If the attributes of a file match a definition, then the antivirus program knows that it has located a virus (and knows which virus it has located).

To develop the antivirus definitions, the antivirus software manufacturer must first obtain copies of the virus and create the definition. That means that some computers have already been infected with the virus by the time the definition has been created. Thus, definitions do not provide complete protection against viruses.

A **polymorphic virus** is one that attempts to change its code. Each time the virus runs, the code changes slightly, but the damage that it causes remains the same. A polymorphic virus attempts to hide from antivirus definitions.

- **Heuristics**. A heuristic is a type of artificial intelligence. It allows the antivirus program to determine whether a specific program is legitimate or not, based on its behavior. For example, a program that attempts to modify critical system files is likely not legitimate.

  The latest generation antivirus programs share data with the cloud. For example, Norton Antivirus automatically collects data regarding suspicious applications from users. This data is sent to a response center for further analysis. Norton Antivirus then updates all user programs with the results. By sharing data with the cloud, antivirus programs are able to detect viruses faster.

The most famous computer viruses have been

- ILOVEYOU. Released in 2000, ILOVEYOU was transmitted via e-mail with a subject line of "I love you". It overwrote system files and personal files, before spreading through e-mail. It caused $15 billion in damage.

- MyDoom. Similar, to ILOVEYOU, MyDoom spread via e-mail in 2004. It is estimated that 25% of all e-mails sent in 2004 were infected with MyDoom. It caused $38 billion in damage.

- Stuxnet. Stuxnet is a special kind of virus because it infected the firmware of a USB drive. The firmware of a USB drive is not typically accessible to the computer or to an antivirus program – it's considered "read only" memory and allows the USB drive to read/write data from/to the computer.

  The Stuxnet virus contained a second virus inside of it. When the USB drive was inserted into a PLC (an industrial control system), the second virus infected the PLC. Stuxnet only infected Siemens S7 PLCs.

Stuxnet was used to infect industrial control systems that were "air gapped" (not connected to the internet or to any network).

Stuxnet was unusual because

- o It took advantage of multiple zero-day exploits (security holes that are unknown to the software manufacturers). A zero-day exploit is considered valuable to a virus manufacturer/hacker, and to use several in the same virus is highly unusual. Zero-day exploits are quickly patched by manufacturers once discovered and can't be reused. A zero-day exploit could be worth up to a million dollars. To use several million dollars worth of zero-day exploits in a virus that brings the creator no financial reward is highly unusual.

- o It limited its infection to only specific types of computers and PLCs. Most virus manufacturers do not want to limit the damage that they cause.

- o It is estimated that Stuxnet took between three man-years and fifteen man-years to prepare. Development of Stuxnet required advanced knowledge of the Windows operating system, USB firmware, and Siemens PLCs.

The difference between a **worm** and a virus is that the worm replicates by itself, whereas the virus must attach itself to a legitimate file. The virus only runs when the legitimate file runs.

Worms can generally spread over a network from computer to computer, by themselves. They take advantage of security holes.

Examples of worms

- • SQL Slammer took advantage of a buffer overflow bug in Microsoft SQL Server. The worm would randomly generate IP addresses and then send itself to those IP addresses. If the IP addresses belonged to computers that were running an unpatched version of SQL Server, then the worm would be successful in infecting them. The worm caused many internet routers to crash, and reboot. Each time the routers rebooted, they would resend routing updates to each other, which would cause internet traffic congestion. SQL Slammer was exceptional in that it fit inside a single data packet.

A **trojan** is a legitimate program that hides an illegitimate program. A user must install the trojan and/or give it permission before it can take effect. Trojans are named after the Trojan horse.

Trojans can hide in many programs including toolbars, screensavers, games, and other applications. Examples of Trojans

- FinFisher (FinSpy), which is developed by Lench IT Solutions plc. This trojan is used to infect Windows computers and all brands of phones. It travels through e-mail, links, and security flaws in popular programs. Many antivirus programs are unable to detect it.

    FinFisher is sold to law enforcement agencies and dictatorships, some of which are accused of numerous human rights violations.

A **rootkit** provides unauthorized administrative level access to a computer by changing its operating system and attempting to bypass its security functions.
There are five types of rootkits

- **Firmware**. A firmware rootkit hides inside the device firmware (such as the BIOS, video card controller, router, network card, or hard drive controller). The device firmware is not typically scanned by (and is out of reach of) antivirus programs. While manufacturers such as HP have introduced BIOS integrity features that check for changes to the BIOS firmware, rootkits can infect other components such as the graphics card or hard drive.

- **Virtual**. A virtual rootkit is also known as a hypervisor rootkit. It operates between the processor and the operating system. It intercepts calls made by the operating system, like a "man-in-the-middle" attack. The result is that the processor believes that it is talking to the operating system and the operating system believes that it is taking to the processor, but, both are talking to the rootkit. The rootkit sends everything it learns to a central server.

- **Kernel**. A kernel rootkit runs on a computer with the highest privileges (the same privileges as the operating system) by replacing parts of the operating system core and device drivers. A kernel rootkit can't be detected by an antivirus program because the rootkit is acting like part of the legitimate operating system.

- **Library**. A library level rootkit replaces legitimate operating system DLLs with fake ones. A library is a set of code/functions that an application can reference (a software developer will include different DLLs with their application so that they don't have to rewrite thousands of lines of code for common functions). When an application references code in an infected DLL, the rootkit will also run.

- **Application Level**. An application level rootkit replaces application files with fake versions. The application may need to run at an elevated level in order to cause damage.

Examples of rootkits

- LoJack. LoJack is a legitimate rootkit that comes preinstalled in the BIOS of some laptops. If the laptop is lost or stolen and later connected to the internet, LoJack will report the location of the laptop to a server. LoJack is designed to remain on the laptop even if its hard disk drive is erased or replaced.

- Sony BMG. In 2005, Sony installed a rootkit known as XCP (Extended Copy Protection) on music CD's that it released. When users attempted to play the CD's through their computer, the rootkit created security vulnerabilities. The intention of the rootkit was to prevent people from copying music off the CD's, but the rootkit created security holes and hid in the background.

  Sony was forced to recall all unsold music CDs and faced multiple class-action lawsuits.

A **keylogger** records each key that a user presses. It may also take screenshots, activate the webcam, or activate the microphone without the knowledge or consent of the user.

The keylogger reports all data back to a central source or records the data on the computer for further retrieval. Data may be sent via

- Email

- FTP

- Wireless/Bluetooth to a nearby receiver

A keylogger may have legitimate purposes if installed by an employer or law enforcement agency. Some antivirus programs will detect keyloggers created by law enforcement and some will deliberately ignore them.

A keylogger may be used to invade the privacy of another person (stalking) or it may be used for financial gain (the logged data is analysed to obtain online banking passwords, e-mail passwords, etc.).

The keylogger may be introduced into a system through another type of malware such as a virus or trojan.

Whether the keylogger can be detected by an antivirus program depends on where it runs. Keyloggers that run in the operating system kernel or through a hypervisor may be undetectable.

Keyloggers can also be hardware-based

- Keyboard keylogger device (USB device that sits between the keyboard cable and the computer). A keyboard's circuitry can be covertly modified to include a keylogger.

- Wireless keyboard sniffer (device that can intercept signals between a wireless keyboard and the dongle; this device functions when the connection is not encrypted or where the encryption method can be easily broken)

How to prevent keyloggers

- It is difficult, if not impossible to detect a hardware based keylogger, especially one that is embedded into the device circuitry. Keeping computer hardware physically secure is the best defense.

- The use of multi-factor authentication methods can keep accounts secure even when the usernames and passwords are compromised.

- Most software-based keyloggers are detectable by antivirus programs. Some software-based keyloggers that take advantage of zero-day exploits or that operate on the firmware, kernel, or hypervisor level cannot be detected.

Adware is software that shows advertisements. The advertisements may appear as pop-ups, videos, or audio. Adware may be included in legitimate software programs such as games, music applications, or other applications. Typically, adware is bundled with low-quality applications. The advertisements are also of low quality as most legitimate advertisers do not want to be associated with this type of exploitation.

Adware can also be installed without the user's consent when introduced as part of a computer virus or trojan.

Adware can hijack legitimate website advertisements. When a user visits a legitimate website, the adware swaps advertisements placed by the website owner with advertisements sold by the adware publisher. Thus, the revenue from the advertisements is diverted to the adware publisher without the knowledge of the user or website owner.

It may be difficult or impossible to remove adware. Adware may spy on a user's activity or browsing history. The adware publisher may sell this data to market research firms or use it to show the user more relevant advertising.

It is illegal to install or distribute adware without the consent of the user. In addition, the user must have an opportunity to remove the adware. There is no specific anti-adware law, but in the United States Section 5 of the Federal Trade Commission Act prohibits "unfair or deceptive acts". The Federal Trade Commission (FTC) is empowered to commence civil actions against publishers who distribute adware.

Social engineering is the attempt to use psychological methods to manipulate individuals into providing confidential information or access to systems.

Unlike malware, social engineering relies on human emotion. People fall victim because they have the following feelings

- Wanting to be liked

- Fear

- Wanting to help

- Intimidation

- Familiarity

- Hostility

A good book on social engineering is *Social Engineering: The Art of Human Hacking* by Christopher Hadnagy.

Why do social engineering attempts work? There are many reasons.

- **Authority**

    o The person on the other end of the phone call/in person acts with authority. People are afraid to challenge those who appear to be in a position of authority (such as members of senior management).

    o Authority can be established by confidence, tone of voice, clothing, and/or uniforms.

- People are afraid to challenge authority because of perceived negative consequences (getting fired)

- The consequences do not have to be explicitly stated by the thief. They can be implied, or the user might simply assume what they are based on the alleged authority.

- Social engineering authority attacks can be prevented by enforcing policy against all users, regardless of their position. The company must create a culture where verifying the identity of another person is encouraged, regardless of that person's position.

- For example, the thief could pretend to be a member of senior management and convince the victim that she could lose her job if she does not comply. The thief could demand that the victim provide him with corporate financial information, or wire money to a third party.

- **Intimidation**

  - Intimidation uses the threat or idea of negative consequences if the person fails to comply.

  - The thief does not have to make any direct threats, but instead may cause the victim to believe that negative consequences will occur (or the victim may assume that negative consequences will occur if they fail to comply).

  - For example, the thief could pretend to be a police officer and convince the victim that she will be arrested if she does not comply. The thief demands that the victim disclose sensitive data relevant to an investigation.

- **Consensus**

  - Consensus involves a group-decision.

  - If a social engineer is unable to convince a specific person to perform an action, he could attempt to convince others in that person's social circle. Those other people could convince the victim to proceed.

  - For example, the thief could convince the victim that her co-workers completed the same action.

- **Scarcity**

    o Scarcity means that something is unavailable or in limited supply.

    o If the victim values something that is scarce, they may forgo normal procedures and fall into the trap to obtain that item.

    o For example, the victim wants a rare (sold out) toy at Christmas time. The thief convinces her that he can supply the toy if she provides him with her credit card/banking information (which he uses fraudulently). The victim never receives the toy.

- **Familiarity**

    o The victim feels familiar with the situation and proceeds because nothing seems out of place.

    o The thief can convince the victim to focus on ideas that are familiar, by dropping familiar names, projects, or other tasks into the conversation.

    o Although the victim does not know the thief, she is led to believe that he is a legitimate co-worker because he has knowledge of the workplace or business.

- **Trust**

    o The victim trusts the thief and proceeds with their own free will.

    o The victim believes that the person they are talking to or the site that they have visited is legitimate.

    o The thief may take time to build this trust, especially with a high-value target. The greater the victim trusts the thief, the more the victim will be willing to do.

- **Urgency**

    o Urgency is like scarcity

    o Urgency builds on the idea that there is a limited time to act.

    o People hate losing money more than they hate not making money.

- For example, the victim could be told that money is about to be withdrawn from their bank account and they only have a few minutes to stop it (by providing their banking information to the thief). Normally, the victim would take their time to check that the person they are speaking with is legitimate but bypasses these risk controls because of the urgency.

Phishing is the attempt to obtain sensitive data by pretending to be a trusted entity. Phishing usually occurs through e-mail or telephone. Phishing is usually sent as a mass e-mail to thousands or millions of people.

Typically, a user will receive an e-mail asking them to sign in to their bank account or other account (such as PayPal, eBay, Amazon). The e-mail is fake, and the website that the e-mail leads to is fake (but appears to be real).

Typical phishing e-mails will say

- Your account has been compromised and you must log in to correct the issue

- Your account will be suspended if you don't log in

- You have received a large payment (Interac eTransfer) and you must log in to accept the money

The hacker may register a domain that looks like the legitimate one. For example, the user may register www.paypal.com instead of www.paypal.com. Or the hacker may register a domain that is completely unrelated to the original website and attach a subdomain that looks like the legitimate site. For example, the hacker registers fakewebsite.com and attaches the "www.paypal" subdomain to it, making www.paypal.com.fakewebsite.com. The users will see the first part of the URL "www.paypal.com" and think they are on a legitimate site, even though the user's browser went to fakewebsite.com.

Update Required!!

Recently, there's been activity in your PayPal account that seems unusual compared to your normal account activities. Please log in to PayPal to confirm your identity.

This is part of our security process and helps ensure that PayPal continue to be safer way to buy online. Often all we need is a bit more information. While your account is limited, some options in your account won't be available.
How to remove my limitation?
You can resolve your limitation by following these simple steps:

- **Log in here**.

- Provide the information needed. The sooner your provide the information we need, the sooner we can resolve the situation.

"If this message sent as Junk or Spam, its just an error by our new system, please click at Not Junk or Not Spam"

Sincerely,

PayPal

How do we prevent phishing?

- Proper user education to identify suspicious e-mails.

  o Knowledge that legitimate e-mails from banks and other sites will contain the user's full name while phishing e-mails will not (unless the sender has access to the user's data)

  o Phishing e-mails and/or websites may (but not always) contain poor grammar or spelling

  o Phishing websites will not contain the correct URL. Users should always check that they have visited the correct URL.

- Automated systems that detect and filter phishing e-mails. These systems are built into most web browsers and e-mail systems and verify that the e-mails originated from legitimate sources and that the websites are legitimate.

Spear Phishing is like phishing, but it targets specific groups or people who have lots of money and/or are more likely to respond. The more precise the target, the higher the response rate.

A normal phishing attack could target millions of users. For example,

- A hacker could send a fake e-mail appearing to be from Bank of America to 1,000,000 e-mail addresses

- From those 1,000,000 addresses, only 250,000 might be valid

- The SPAM filter would block 200,000 from those 250,000

- From the 50,000 only 10,000 might have accounts at Bank of America

- 80% of those users might be smart enough to detect the phishing scam, in which case only 2,000 people respond

- The attack is shut down early on (because some users report the scam leading the website to be blacklisted by web browsers), and many subsequent users are warned, so the hackers only collect data from 500 users

- Thus, the success rate is about 0.005%. Although it is low, the return on investment might be high. It may cost the hackers a few hundred dollars to send out the e-mail, but if they are able to collect at least $100 from each user, they could collect $50,000.

In spear phishing, the hackers identify specific customers of Bank of America for example. They may use a list stolen from the bank. The hackers customize the e-mail to include the name and other personally identifying information of each recipient. As a result, the SPAM filter will be less likely to identify the e-mail as SPAM, and the user will be more likely to respond. The hackers send out fewer emails but may collect more money.

Whaling is like Phishing, but targets high-value individuals such as celebrities, CEOs or other executives. Whaling is specifically targeted to the high-value individual. Whaling takes more effort to execute, but the response rate is higher, and the amount of money stolen from each user is higher. Many high-net worth individuals have access to credit cards with high limits.

Another scheme involves a scammer visiting a store such as Best Buy and attempting to illegally purchase expensive electronics in the name of a celebrity on credit. The scammer disappears with the electronics and the store is never paid. The store should have verified that the buyer legitimately represents the celebrity.

How do we prevent whaling?

- Proper user education

- 100% identity verification of the person who is seeking information.

- A high-net worth individual should understand that he is at much higher risk of exploitation either through fraud or extortion schemes. This person should employ people who specialize in detecting and preventing these threats.

Vishing is like Phishing but uses the telephone (VoIP) network. The thieves will place phone calls that appear to come from legitimate entities such as the IRS, a bank, or a credit card company. The thieves will attempt to obtain sensitive data such as credit card numbers or bank account numbers.

Common features

- The scammer will threaten the victim with legal action or arrest if they do not comply

- The scammer will ask the victim to purchase gift cards from a store and send them the numbers

- The scammer will speak with a foreign accent or bad grammar (but not always)

How to Prevent?

- If a user receives a telephone call from somebody who is seeking sensitive information, they should

  o Verify that the number is in fact legitimate

  o Hang up and call the number back (as caller IDs can be spoofed)

- Verify that the caller will require the information (for example a bank will never ask a client for his/her PIN)

- Provide the required information through the legitimate online website of the purported requester (such as IRS.gov)

Tailgaiting is an attempt to obtain unauthorized access to a physical facility.

Many offices, industrial facilities, and data centers are controlled via electronic proximity card and/or biometric locks. When a legitimate user unlocks an entrance with their access card and/or biometric lock, an intruder can follow them into the building. Tailgaiting works because

- A person might hold the door open for a person who is walking behind him (doing otherwise might be considered rude)

- A person might not wait to verify that the door closed and locked behind him, and another person might follow him. The door lock might not work properly, in which case the door does not fully close.

When a user deliberately allows another user to follow him through the secure entrance, it is known as **piggybacking**. An attacker might try to gain access to a secure facility by convincing another user that he is a legitimate employee or vendor and forgot his keycard.

How to prevent

- Proper user education to enforce the use of access cards and prohibit tailgating. Users should know that not holding the door is not considered rude.

- Install a security guard at each entrance or monitor entrances with security cameras

- In more extreme cases, installation of man trap doors might be necessary. A man trap door allows only one person to enter at a time. The man trap door contains cameras with artificial intelligence to detect the number of people inside and permits entry to only one individual at a time.

Shoulder Surfing is when a thief looks over the shoulder of a victim. Shoulder surfing can occur at a computer or at an ATM. The thief may watch the screen or the keyboard. The thief might also watch the reflection of the screen on another surface.

Shoulder surfing happens at offices, in airports, and on public transportation.

How to prevent

- Install shields at ATMs and debit/credit card terminals

- Install privacy screens on computers/laptops.

- If using a laptop on an airplane or other public place, the user should avoid doing anything sensitive and/or be wary of his/her neighbors/surroundings.

4.3 Given a scenario, apply network hardening techniques

- *Best Practices*
  - *Secure SNMP*
  - *Router Advertisement (RA) Guard*
  - *Port Security*
  - *Dynamic ARP Inspection*
  - *Control Plane Policing*
  - *Private VLANs*
  - *Disable Unneeded Switchports*
  - *Disable Unneeded Network Services*
  - *Change Default Passwords*
  - *Password Complexity/Length*
  - *Enable DHCP Snooping*
  - *Change Default VLAN*
  - *Patch and Firmware Management*
  - *Access Control List*
  - *Role-Based Access*
  - *Firewall Rules*
    - *Explicit Deny*
    - *Implicit Deny*
- *Wireless Security*
  - *MAC Filtering*
  - *Antenna Placement*
  - *Power Levels*
  - *Wireless Client Isolation*
  - *Guest Network Isolation*
  - *Preshared Keys (PSKs)*
  - *EAP*
  - *Geofencing*
  - *Captive Portal*
- *IoT Access Considerations*

Now that we've described some of the bad things out there, how can we keep them from getting into our network? We will talk about physical security later, but let's look at some software configuration

- Use the most secure version of the protocol that is available. For example, use secure SNMP instead of normal SNMP; use secure FTP instead of regular FTP, etc.

- Use **Router Advertisement (RA) Guard**. Remember that when we connect a bunch of routers together, they start communicating and figure out who each other's neighbors are? That way, we can build a network with multiple routers regardless of the make or model.

  The problem is that a malicious user could
    o send out rogue router advertisement messages to our legitimate router which would confuse our routers and disrupt our network
    o install a rogue router that listens to the router advertisement guard messages

  Thus, we can configure a guard on the router that filters the messages based on their source IP address, source MAC address, and other factors.

- Use **Port Security**. Remember that a switch remembers the MAC address of every device that is connected to each port? We can force the switch to block traffic from devices with MAC addresses that it doesn't recognize. Some ideas

    o We can force the switch to accept traffic from only one MAC address per port. This makes sense if a security camera, wireless access point, or other fixed device is connected to that port.

    o We can limit the number of unique MAC addresses per port to a specific quantity. For example, we might allow up to five unique MAC addresses on a port that is used by multiple people. We can set a timer so that if the switch doesn't see traffic from a unique MAC address for some time, then that MAC address stops counting towards to the total.

    o We can decide whether the switch shuts down the port (blocks all traffic) after detecting a violation, or whether it just logs the issue.

    o We can configure the setting and response on a port by port basis.

    o The specific way that this setting is configured depends on the make and model of the switch.

- Enable **DHCP Snooping**. Remember that a hacker could install a rogue DHCP server on our network and give out invalid IP addresses or force devices to forward their external traffic to the wrong gateway?

That is because when a device requires an IP address, it sends out a DHCP message. If the rogue DHCP server responds with IP address information prior to the legitimate DHCP server, then the device will be compromised.

What we do is tell the switch which port is connected to the legitimate DHCP server. This is known as a trusted port. All the other ports are untrusted. The switch will assume that any DHCP Offer messages entering an untrusted port have originated from a rogue DHCP server, and it will not forward them.

On an untrusted port, the switch will accept DHCP messages from clients. These messages include the DHCP Discover message. Thus anybody can ask for an IP address, but only the legitimate DHCP server can reply.

The switch creates a table called the **DHCP Snooping Binding Table**. Each time a client accepts a DHCP Offer, the switch creates an entry in that table. It records the MAC address of the client and the IP address that was assigned to it. It also records the VLAN and interface that the client is connected to.

Say your computer's IP address is 10.5.5.5, and I'm a hacker. I want to kick you off the network, so I send the DHCP server a release message saying, "release IP address 10.5.5.5". The DHCP server will normally release the IP address and try to assign it to somebody else, which will disrupt your network connection.

DHCP snooping can protect against this kind of attack as well. When the switch sees a new DHCP Release message, it checks that message's sender's MAC address against the table. It will see that the request to release 10.5.5.5 came from my MAC address instead of yours. It knows that the message isn't valid and doesn't let it through.

A hacker might try to lease many hundreds or thousands of DHCP addresses so that nobody else can get any. The switch can protect against this as well. If a client sends a Discover or Request DHCP message, the switch checks its MAC address (the MAC address inside the Ethernet header) against the MAC address inside the actual message. Remember that a DHCP message is something like "hey, my MAC address is aa:bb:cc:dd:ee:ff, can I please have an IP address". This message is encapsulated inside an IP packet which is encapsulated inside an Ethernet frame. If the MAC address sending the message is different from the MAC address inside the message, then the switch knows something is wrong, and doesn't let it through.

- Use **Dynamic ARP Inspection**. Remember that a rogue device can send out false ARP messages. For example, if I want to intercept documents going to the printer, I plug in a fake device and pretend that it is a printer. I send out ARP messages with the MAC address of the printer.

  If we turn on the DHCP Snooping, then the switch knows which IP address belongs to which MAC address (due to the binding table). We can also turn on the Dynamic ARP Inspection and force the switch to block any ARP messages that don't match what is in the table.

  If a device has a static IP, then it won't make a DHCP request and neither its IP address nor its MAC address will appear in the table. Thus, devices such as cameras and printers, which have static IP addresses, can be subject to ARP spoofing.

  A good countermeasure is to set up DHCP reservations for such devices in the DHCP server. These devices will then continue to receive the same IP addresses, but their MAC address and IP address will be recorded in the DHCP table.

- **Control Plane Policing**. Remember that a switch or router sends traffic through the "data" plane and management traffic through the "control" plane. A hacker wanting to disrupt the device might attempt to send a large amount of traffic through the control plane.

  Control Plane Policing allows us to protect the switch and router control planes from attacks. It does so by reducing the amount of traffic that the control plane can accept through a QoS policy. When the switch receives, on its data plane, a packet with a destination of the control plane, it will decide whether to forward or drop that packet.

- **Change Default VLAN**. The default VLAN should always be changed. This prevents VLAN hopping.

- **Private VLANs**. A private VLAN is an idea where we can break a single VLAN into multiple sub VLANs. The main VLAN is called the **primary VLAN**. A port belonging to the primary VLAN is known as the **promiscuous port** and can talk to all other ports. The sub VLANs can be of two types

  o **Isolated VLAN** – a port assigned to an isolated VLAN can not talk to any other port except the promiscuous port

  o **Community VLAN** – a port assigned to a community VLAN can talk to any other port in that same community and with the promiscuous port

The advantage of the private VLAN is that we can separate traffic from devices within the same VLAN. It also reduces the number of VLANs and IP subnets that are required.

- **Disable Unneeded Switchports**. It goes without saying that if a switch port is not used (not physically connected to a device), then we should turn it off. That way, if somebody tries to connect a device to it, no traffic will flow.

- **Disable Unneeded Network Services**. Many services may be enabled by default on your switch, router, computer, or server. Turn off any services that you aren't using such as DHCP servers, web servers, FTP, SMTP, etc. Sometimes these services are installed and operational by default.

  Every running service is a potential for a security vulnerability because if you aren't using it, then you likely aren't monitoring or patching it.

- **Change Default Passwords**. I mentioned this many times. It is important to change the default username and password on every device, and to not use devices that do allow you to change the default password.

- **Password Complexity/Length**. You must enforce a password that is complicated so that it cannot be easily guessed. Some rules for password complexity

  o Includes at least eight characters

  o Includes special characters, capital letters, and numbers

  o Does not include the user's name or other personally identifying information

  o Does not reuse old passwords

- **Patch and Firmware Management**. You should make sure to patch all devices when patches become available. Some devices are configured to automatically download and install patches. When there are many devices of many makes and models, an automated system should be used. The system will

  o Determine when a patch is available for a given device

  o Automatically deploy the patch onto the device

o Verify that the device has been successfully patched or report the failure to patch to an administrator

- **Access Control List**. The Access Control List is a set of rules for what traffic is permitted to pass and what traffic is not permitted. There are many types of rules, based on

  o Source IP address. Where is the traffic coming from? The source IP address could be on the LAN or on the WAN. It could be a specific IP address or a range of addresses.

  o Destination IP address. Where is the traffic going? The destination IP address could be on the LAN or on the WAN. It could be a specific IP address or a range of addresses.

  o Source Port Number. What is the port number of the source traffic? The source port could be on the LAN or on the WAN. It could be a specific port or a range of ports.

  o Destination Port Number. What is the port number of the destination traffic? The destination port could be on the LAN or on the WAN. It could be a specific port or a range of ports.

  o Username. Access Control Lists can be user-based. Permissions can be granted or denied to specific users based on their needs in the organization. For example, guests can be permitted to access only the internet and not resources such as remote desktop or SQL servers.

  o Rules can be specific or could combine a combination of parameters

    ▪ For example, a rule could say 'Allow traffic from 10.1.1.1, port 5 to the range of IPs 192.168.3.0 to 192.168.3.255'. All traffic received from 10.1.1.1 port 5 will be permitted to access destinations in the range of 192.168.3.0 to 192.168.3.255. Traffic from other source IP addresses and/or ports will be rejected. Traffic from 10.1.1.1 to destinations outside of 192.168.3.0 and 192.168.3.255 will be rejected.

    ▪ **Always Allow**. An Always Allow rule allows all traffic matching a rule. For example, "always allow traffic from the source IP 10.1.1.1". All traffic from 10.1.1.1 will be permitted regardless of the port number or destination.

- **Always Deny**. An Always Deny rule denies all traffic matching a rule. For example, "always deny traffic from the source IP 10.1.1.1". All traffic from 10.1.1.1 will be denied regardless of the port number or destination.

  This is also known as an **Explicit Deny**. If we create a bunch of rules to allow traffic from specific sources, and then tell the firewall to block any traffic that doesn't match those rules, that is known as an **Implicit Deny**. In other words, Implicit Deny means that the traffic is blocked until another rule is created to allow it, whereas Explicit Deny blocks the traffic regardless of any other rules.

- Order of Operations

  - A firewall could have dozens or thousands of rules. The rules are ranked in order of priority.

  - When the firewall receives a piece of traffic, it starts checking the rules in order until it finds one that matches the traffic's source and destination. It then applies that rule to the traffic.

  - The firewall will only apply one rule to a piece of traffic. Once that rule is applied, the firewall stops checking additional rules.

  - It is important to put the rules in logical order so that traffic is not accidentally accepted or rejected. When a firewall receives a piece of traffic that does not match any rules, it will either allow or reject the traffic based on its configuration.

  - Many firewalls are preconfigured with two default rules

    - Always allow traffic with a source inside the network (LAN)

    - Always reject traffic with a source outside the network (WAN)

  - The two default rules should be put at the bottom of the list.

    - The first rule (allowing all traffic from inside the LAN) is dangerous because users cannot be trusted to access only safe resources on the internet. It should be modified (broken down) into two rules.

- o Always allow traffic with a

  - Source inside the network (LAN)

  - Destination outside the network (WAN)

  - Limited to specific ports outside the network (port 80, port 443, port 3306, etc.). The specific ports should be based on resources that users need to access.

- o Always deny traffic

  - Source inside the network (LAN)

  - Destination outside the network (WAN)

  - This rule applies second; any traffic not matching the previous rule will be denied

- **Role-Based Access** – Permissions are not assigned to individual users or to objects. Instead, permissions are assigned to operations/actions (known as roles)

  - o A user can be assigned to a specific group (the user is given a role); the user inherits the permissions assigned to the role

  - o The organization can define the operations and actions that are relevant to their organization. For example:

    - Sales person (can access sales data)

    - Accountant (can enter data into the accounting system)

  - o Accounts payable clerk (can approve invoices and issue payments)

How can we enforce security on wireless networks?

- **MAC Filtering**. We can enforce a rule where only devices with specific MAC addresses are permitted on our wireless network.

This rule works if we have an accurate inventory of all the wireless devices that may connect. It is not practical if we allow users to bring their own devices and connect them to the wireless network. It can also be bypassed by a hacker who spoofs his device MAC address to match that of one that is authorized.

- **Antenna Placement**. We can adjust the position and type of antennas so that our wireless signal does not exit our building. This would prevent hackers outside the building from connecting.

- **Power Levels**. We can adjust the power level on the device so that the wireless signal does not propagate outside of our building. This would prevent hackers outside the building or in neighboring suites from connecting.

- **Wireless Client Isolation**. A wireless client can normally communicate with another wireless or ethernet client (and vice versa) provided they are on the same VLAN or WLAN. Traffic from a wireless device destined to another device on the same VLAN travels through the wireless access point to the switch and then back through the switch (or another switch) or wireless access point as applicable.

  Wireless Client Isolation prevents different wireless clients from communicating with each other, even though they are on the same VLAN and subnet (and possibly connected to the same wireless access point).

  This is important when we have a wireless network open to guests or unrelated users. For example, devices connected to the guest Wi-Fi at a hotel or student Wi-Fi at a University should not be able to reach to each other. A guest in one hotel room should not be able to see devices belonging to a guest in another hotel room.

  The isolation may be enforced by the router.

- **Guest Network Isolation**. If we have a guest Wi-Fi and a corporate Wi-Fi, we should physically or logically isolate the guest Wi-Fi network.

  o Physically isolating the network requires us to construct and configure a physically separate guest network. That means separate wireless access points, switches, routers, and wiring. This measure might be too expensive for most customers.

  o Logically isolating the network allows us to map the guest Wi-Fi SSID to a separate VLAN that can reach the internet, and no other devices. This VLAN should also enforce wireless client isolation.

- As mentioned earlier, we can use **Preshared Keys** and EAP to enable wireless security. **Extensible Authentication Protocol (EAP)** is a system for authenticating with a wireless network.

  - EAP is a framework for providing authentication, but there are more than 40 possible methods that can be used, depending on the specific vendor of the equipment.

  - Each vendor may have more specific requirements and new protocols are being developed all the time

  - Within EAP are several methods, including

    - **LEAP**

      - **Lightweight Extensible Authentication Protocol**

      - Developed by Cisco

      - LEAP is not supported by Windows but is supported by many third-party applications

      - Cisco does not recommend using LEAP anymore because it does not protect user credentials

    - **PEAP**

      - **Protected Extensible Authentication Protocol**

      - Originally, EAP assumed that communications would be secure; therefore, it did not provide a mechanism to secure the data being transmitted.

      - PEAP corrects this by providing a secure TLS tunnel

      - A server-side certificate is used to create a PKI tunnel

    - **EAP-NOOB**

- **Nimble out-of-band authentication for EAP**

- Used by devices that do not have preloaded authentication information such as Internet of Things devices

- The user must assist the device in connecting via an out of band channel

- There are different connection options including QR codes and NFC

- Ephemeral Elliptic Curve Diffie-Hellman (ECDHE) exchange takes place over the in-band EAP channel. The user then provides the out-of-band channel message from the server to the device or from the device to the server, depending on what is required.

- **EAP-FAST**

  - **Flexible Authentication via Secure Tunneling**

  - Designed by Cisco to replace LEAP

  - Three parts

    o In band provisioning via Diffie-Hellman. The client is provided with a shared secret.

    o Tunnel establishment. A tunnel is established between the server and the client.

    o Authentication. The user is authenticated

- **EAP-TLS.**

  - **EAP – Transport Layer Security**

  - Uses TLS (Transport Layer Security) as its protocol.

  - All wireless manufacturers support EAP-TLS

- Considered very secure

- EAP-TLS requires a client-side certificate. When a system is authenticated with a certificate, a password is not required. Even if a hacker obtained the username/password, without a certificate, the hacker would not be able to connect to the Wi-Fi.

- EAP is not implemented as widely as it should be because it requires the certificate

- **EAP-TTLS**

  - **EAP Tunneled Transport Layer Security**

    o Extends TLS so that the client does not require a certificate. Instead, the server creates a tunnel with the client. The client can then authenticate to the server using a legacy password or other authentication method. The tunnel protects the client from eavesdropping.

- **Geofencing**. Geofencing allows us to track the physical location of a wireless device and send an alert if it leaves the building or if it is taken to a portion of the building where it is nor permitted. This ensures that secure devices such as laptops or mobile readers are not removed from the building.

- **Captive Portal**. A Captive Portal is a web page that a user sees when they first connect to the wireless network. The Captive Portal allows the user to authenticate with the wireless network. It may also inform the user of the terms and conditions that he must adhere to when using the network. Captive Portals are common on guest Wi-Fi networks.

What about IoT devices? What if IoT devices such as HVAC sensors, alarm sensors, etc. need to connect to our network?

- We should determine how we will identify each IoT device uniquely

- We should determine how we will authenticate that IoT device. How do we know that the connected device is legitimate?

- Can we ensure that the device will establish a secure end-to-end communication with the server?

- Can we ensure that the device will securely connect to the network?

- Can we encrypt the data that is stored on the device?

- Can we ensure that the device is not compromised by hackers?

400

4.4 Compare and contrast remote access methods and security implications

- *Site-to-Site VPN*
- *Client-to-Site VPN*
    - *Clientless VPN*
    - *Split Tunnel vs Full Tunnel*
- *Remote Desktop Connection*
- *Remote Desktop Gateway*
- *SSH*
- *Virtual Network Computing (VNC)*
- *Virtual Desktop*
- *Authentication and Authorization Considerations*
- *In-Band vs Out-of-Band Management*

How do we keep the network secure but still allow external users to connect? As mentioned earlier, we can use a VPN or Virtual Private Network.

A Remote Access VPN allows users to connect back to a corporate network, typically through their computer. A Site-to-Site VPN allows two offices to connect to each other and pretend like they are part of the same physical network. A Site-to-Site VPN typically applies to the site's router and not to individual devices on the network.

- The performance on a VPN is affected by the quality of the user's internet connection, by the quality of the corporate network's internet connection, by the number of active users, and by the type of resources being accessed.

- When there are multiple sites that need to be connected, a site-to-site VPN should be replaced by a WAN

A VPN can be secured with IPSec – a set of protocols that allow hosts to exchange packets securely. IPSec has several modes of operation, including

- **Tunnel Mode**. The Tunnel Mode encrypts the source, destination, and contents of every packet. Essentially, it establishes a secure tunnel between two network devices where data can travel securely. The devices that are establishing the tunnel are not necessarily the devices that are creating the traffic. For example, a router could be sending traffic on behalf of a server inside the network. An outsider will not be able to examine the source, destination, or contents of any traffic.

- **Transport Mode**. The Transport Mode only encrypts the contents of the packet. It does not encrypt the source or destination. An outsider will be able to examine the source and destination. Transport Mode is established by the two network devices who are communicating, and not by the routers on the edges of the network.

- **SA**. An SA, or Security Association is an algorithm and key that are used to encrypt traffic in an IPSec tunnel. Each direction of communication requires a separate SA. Therefore, most IPSec tunnels will require two SAs.

- There are four methods of connecting a tunnel. Consider that two computers (each inside a separate network and behind a router) would like to communicate securely across the internet. How can an IPSec tunnel be established?

  - **Machine-to-Machine**. Two computers (or smartphones) establish a tunnel and communicate. This is not practical because each computer will expend a substantial amount of computing power encrypting and decrypting the IPSec traffic.

- **Router-to-Router.** It is assumed that the connection between the computer and the router (on the internal network) is secure. The routers establish an IPSec tunnel. The computers no longer encrypt traffic between themselves and the routers. The routers encrypt all traffic between themselves.

- **Machine-to-Machine and Router-to-Router.** This combines the previous two scenarios. Each machine establishes an IPSec tunnel with the router on its network, and the routers establish an IPSec tunnel between themselves.

- **Remote User.** A remote user connects to a router through an IPSec tunnel, and then establishes a secondary IPSec tunnel to connect to a device deeper in the network.

- **Tunnel Mode Encryption.** The tunnel mode is the method for encrypting the traffic. Consider that two routers have created an IPSec tunnel and that behind each router is a computer that wants to communicate. What is the order of operations?

  - The computer generates some data and places it in a packet.

  - The computer puts the address of the remote computer in the header of the packet (or the address of the network that it is sending it to, when the network employs NAT – more on this later).

  - The computer sends the packet to the router (through the switch)

  - The router encrypts this packet, including the headers

  - The router encapsulates this packet inside a larger packet and adds the recipient's router address to the header

  - The router sends the packet to the destination router

- The destination router removes the outer header, decrypts the packet, and forwards it to the computer inside its network

- Neither computer is aware of the existence of the IPSec tunnel

- Tunnel encryption works through the following security protocols

  - AH. **Authentication Header**. When AH is used, the original IP header (created by the computer that generated the data) is visible to outsiders, but the contents are protected. AH protects the integrity of the data. That is, the recipient can be sure that the sender listed on the packet is in fact the true sender.

  - ESP. **Encapsulating Security Payload**. ESP encrypts the contents of the data, but it does not guarantee integrity.

  - It is recommended to use both AH and ESP, thereby providing privacy and integrity.

- IPSec algorithms

  - IPSec is a framework for exchanging data, but the contents of the framework vary from vendor to vendor and network to network. Just like there can be many different models of vehicles on a road, all following the same traffic rules, there can be many different types of algorithms to exchange data within a tunnel.

  - Many different encryption algorithms can be used. This flexibility allows an algorithm to be replaced when it is discovered to be weak.

  - Methods include
    - Diffie-Hellman key exchange with public key signing
    - MD5 and SHA-1 hashing algorithms to ensure data integrity

- IPv4 vs IPv6. IPSec is integrated into all IPv6 packets by default, but not IPv4 packets. When IPv4 was designed, security was not a primary consideration. As the internet grew, the design of IPv6 required security to be integrated into all communications. A device can use IPv6 and not activate the IPSec feature however.

In a **Full Tunnel VPN**, all traffic is routed through the VPN, but in a **Split Tunnel VPN**, only specific traffic is routed through the VPN.

The advantage of a split tunnel is that it reduces bottlenecks. Consider a corporate user working from home. The user needs to access network resources such as a shared drive and corporate finance applications. This traffic must go over the VPN. The user is also watching YouTube videos in the background. There is no reason to route YouTube videos over the corporate network (requiring encryption on both sides). YouTube traffic can travel over the user's home internet connection.

In addition to providing internet security, Transport Layer Security is an alternative to IPSec VPN. A TLS VPN is useful when the network uses NAT.

An Always-On VPN is just like it sounds. It is a VPN that is always on. Typically, an Always-On VPN is part of a hardware appliance, but it could also be software-based. When the VPN detects an active internet connection, it automatically attempts to re-establish the VPN.

For security purposes, an Always-On VPN can block traffic from travelling over the internet when the VPN is not running. This would prevent a user from inadvertently disclosing his true location to websites that shouldn't know it.

If a user requires access to a specific computer or device on the network, we can use the **Remote Desktop Connection (RDC)**. RDC allows a user to have remote keyboard, mouse, and video control of a computer. It also allows a user to share printers and files. It can be established via the Microsoft Remote Desktop Protocol, or via another application such as Team Viewer or Log Me In.

A remote user wanting to connect to a computer might need to have the following

- Connect to the computer via RDC using the computer's public IP address, if it has one

- Log in to the computer with the user's credentials. The user must have permission to log in to that computer.

If the computer that we want to connect to does not have a public IP address, then the user might need to do the following

- Connect to the corporate network via a VPN.

- Connect to the computer via RDC using the computer's LAN IP address. The computer must have RDC enabled.

- Log in to the computer with the user's credentials. The user must have permission to log in to that computer.

Using third party software

- The remote user will not need to connect to the VPN.

- The computer on the corporate network will need to have the Team Viewer, Log Me In, or other software installed.

- The software establishes a connection to a server. The remote user also installs the connection client, which connects his computer to the same server, which allows him to reach the device.

Clearly there is a problem. If we want a remote user to be able to connect to a Windows server or computer on the internal network, then that device must have a public IP address (i.e we are exposing the remote desktop connection to the entire internet, which is bad), or we must force the user to use a VPN, which may not be practical, or we must force a user to install third party software.

There is another way. It is called the **Remote Desktop Gateway**. The Gateway is a server that allows an external user to connect to internal devices without any third-party software and without forcing those devices to carry public IP addresses. It does three things

- Create an SSL tunnel between the remote user and the Remote Desktop Gateway on the corporate network

- Authenticate the remote user via Active Directory, RADIUS, or another system

- Connect the remote user to the network resource (the server or computer that must be accessed)

There are other ways to remotely connect and control a computer. They include

- **SSH**. SSH is a protocol that allows a user to securely connect to a remote device via a terminal like PuTTY.

  SSH is used for remotely configuring network equipment and servers running Linux. SSH originally did not provide a graphical user interface but there are some add on Linux applications that will do so.

  SSH by default encrypts all data.

- **Virtual Network Computing (VNC)** is a system that allows a user to remotely control a computer via the Remote Frame Buffer Protocol. The protocol is open source and works with Windows, Mac, and X Window (a GUI system for Linux).

  An administrator must install an application on the server or computer, which accepts incoming connections from remote users. A remote user installs a client application that connects to and controls the server.

  VNC is not secure by default, but there are add on applications that can make it secure. We can also tunnel the VNC connection over an existing SSH connection.

These connections that I've talked about are all considered "in bound" management. That is, we have one network and we are trying to administer our network equipment over the same network that those devices are running.

What if there is a problem with the router that brings down the network we can no longer access it remotely? Or what if we need to perform an operating system upgrade on a switch or server, which causes it to reboot? We need a back up method to get in. This is called **out of band management**.

Looking at a piece of network equipment like a Cisco Router or Cisco Switch, there are three ways to get into it

- The physical console port. The physical console port looks like an ethernet port, but requires you to connect the device to your computer via a special cable known as a console cable, which has a special pin out. To use the console port, an administrator must be physically present at the device.

- The management port. The management port allows you to connect an ethernet cable to the switch. We should set up a management VLAN and connect the various management ports to it. The management port will then be configured to have an IP address on that VLAN.

- Remote access through SSH or Telnet. Telnet is not secure and not recommended. Telnet and SSH operate over the existing physical network that the devices are connected to.

So what?

- If we have only one network device, we can connect the console port to a special 56K dial-up modem. The most popular modems are made by US Robotics and are still quite common. The modem allows us to connect to the network equipment even if the network is down or the internet connection is down. Only a phone line is required.

- When we have many devices, we can install what is known as a **console server**. The console server looks like a normal switch. We connect a normal ethernet cable between the console port on each device and the console server. The console server can be configured to communicate with each console port.

We connect the console server to the internet, and now we can remotely connect to the console server, and then use it to connect to and configure the network devices. It is recommended that we use a separate internet connection.

This can get tricky when the network is large and widespread because the various IDFs may not connect via copper, only fiber. Thus there may not be a copper link between the location where the switch is and the location where the console server is.

The perle console servers include the following features

o   Modular design, which allows us to substitute ethernet style ports for USB ports. That means we can have remote USB access to a device.

o   Built in cellular modem that provides remote access to the server without having to connect a separate modem.

• We can set up a separate physical network for the management. This might take a substantial amount of equipment to create. And the question becomes, how do we manage the devices on the management network?

That covers network devices. But what about servers? What if we need to remotely upgrade the operating system of a server or want to remotely change the BIOS settings? On the back of many servers, you will find a "remote access" port. On a Dell server, it is known as an iDRAC port, and on an HP server, it is known as an iLO (Integrated Lights Out) Port.

This "port" is actually a card that fits inside the back of the server. The card is a small modular computer, like a server within a server. It connects to the ethernet network (which can be the same network, a separate management VLAN, or a separate physical network) and allows us to remotely connect to the server.

If we have many servers, we can configure the remote access port to connect to a central server where we can manage the equipment. iLO and iDRAC are not free and require licenses to use more advanced features.

We've talked about Authentication and Authorization before, but how can we make sure that only legitimate users are able to connect to our network?

- It is most practical to assign each user a single account. This is usually a Microsoft Active Directory account.
- When a user is also an administrator, we may assign him a second account, which provides administrative access.

- We can enforce different roles and permissions on each account or group of accounts. Each user should have access to only the devices that he needs to do his job, and each user should only be given the exact privileges he needs within those devices. For example, an administrator may be given remote access to the server to view content but not be given permission to make any changes.

- The users will connect to the corporate VPN or other remote access tool and authenticate with their Active Directory accounts.

- Use two-factor authentication where possible.

- We can configure TACAS+ on most network devices. The TACAS+ system allows the switch to verify an administrator's credentials with the Active Directory Server. This allows an administrator to log in to the device with his AD credentials.

- We should enforce individual or group user permissions on network equipment as well. This will ensure that administrators only have the specific permissions that they require to do their job.

Here is a typical set up

- On the left, we have a server.

- The server's ethernet port is connected to the switch port one, which is configured for VLAN 21 (remember that we should change the default VLAN to prevent VLAN hopping).

- The server's iLO port is connected to the switch port two. We set up VLAN 25 as the management VLAN. Thus, we can configure the server as long as we are connected to the network (either locally or remotely). We can also use Remote Desktop to access the server via VLAN 21.

- The switch and router connect to a console server via their console ports. Even if the primary internet connection stops functioning, we can still configure those devices because the console server connects to the internet via a cellular modem.

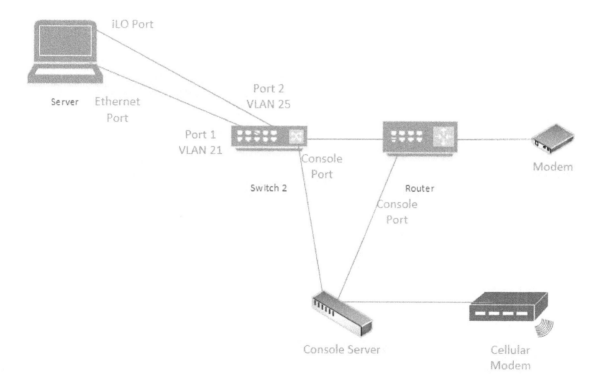

4.5 Explain the importance of physical security

- *Detection Methods*
  - o *Camera*
  - o *Motion Detection*
  - o *Asset Tags*
  - o *Tamper Detection*
- *Prevention Methods*
  - o *Employee Training*
  - o *Access Control Hardware*
    - ▪ *Badge Readers*
    - ▪ *Biometrics*
  - o *Locking Racks*
  - o *Locking Cabinets*
  - o *Access Control Vestibule (mantrap)*
  - o *Smart Lockers*
- *Asset Disposal*
  - o *Factory Reset / Wipe Configuration*
  - o *Sanitize Devices for Disposal*

All our security- measures are pointless if we don't have good physical security. A hacker with physical access to our network infrastructure can cause significant damage or disruption. Just like the software configuration, we must also ensure that our physical security comes in layers.

Proper **lighting** is important for

- Physical safety of people walking. Hazards can be illuminated. It is important to provide bright lights on all entrances and walkways

- Making things visible. Intruders and criminals are more tempted to access buildings at night.

- Emergencies. Emergency lighting is necessary and may be required under various building codes. Emergency lighting is battery-operated and activates in the event of a power outage.

Bad people can hide in dark corners and then sneak into the building or mug people walking by.

A Camera System is important for physical security. **Cameras** in sensitive places can be hijacked. It is important that

- Each camera is physically secure so that it cannot be removed or manipulated

- The connection between the camera and its monitoring station is encrypted

- The camera software is secured. Cameras connected to the internet can be exploited by botnets.

A **Fence** or **Gate** or **Cage** keeps people out or keeps people in. For example, a tool storage area inside a building/warehouse might be fenced in.

Consider

- Who you are trying to stop. A chain-link fence can be cut with wire cutters easily. Even a barbed wire fence can be cut. Fences are good for slowing down random people who are trying to climb over but are not so good for vehicles or sneaky people. In those cases, a concrete wall may be required.

    o An electric fence is more effective at keep people out but may introduce unwanted legal liability. An electric fence must have clear signage that identifies it as such. It should also be separated from the public by a normal fence so that people cannot inadvertently contact it.

- Whether the fence is opaque or transparent (chain link). The fence may need to be opaque so that people can't see inside.

- The height of the fence. A tall fence may stop people from climbing or seeing over it, but it is irrelevant if people can cut through the fence or fly drones into the facility.

- Fences can be used in combination with other security measures. The fence provides a buffer zone. It slows people down. By the time a person has penetrated the fence, security will have been able to intercept them. The fence can be monitored with cameras, security patrols, and sensors.

Inside a building, chain link fencing can be used to set up cages for controlled physical access. It is cheaper to build a cage than a physical room.

A **security guard** is a human who provides security. The security guards may be stationed in key areas, may walk around, or may drive patrol vehicles.

Proper training is important. A security guard who is not vigilant will not be effective. Security guards who use excessive force, are disrespectful, or are perceived to be incompetent, will cost the company money, introduce legal liability, and damage its reputation.

Security guards may be outsourced from a company like G4S or Garda. There is no good reason to outsource, except for cost. When renting security guards, it is important to ensure that the security company sends the same people each time, so that they become familiar with the premises. Many companies outsource security so that they do not have to risk legal liability in the event that a security guard acts inappropriately.

A larger organization may be able to better train an internal security force, even with as few as 50 security guards.

The security guard's most important tool is his brain. Security guards also have other tools like guns, handcuffs, batons, and pepper spray, depending on the state/province that they are in. The organization must decide if it should risk the liability and cost of training to supply security guards with weapons.

Artificial intelligence is no substitute for a human brain. It is important to ensure that the security guard is aware of his surroundings. A security guard who is complacent may be worse than no security guard at all. Security guards are human and can be manipulated through social engineering techniques.

In general, a security guard is not a law enforcement officer. A security guard is entitled to

- Enforce the law when seeing an actual commission of a crime on the organization's property

- Use reasonable force to protect himself or another human being from physical harm or death

- Use reasonable force to protect the physical property of his organization

- Detain an individual who the security guard knows has committed a felony (an indictable offense in Canada), and promptly turn him to a law enforcement agent

- Use reasonable force to prevent a trespasser from entering a secured facility

Security guards may also have dogs that can detect for food, drugs, or explosives. Like a weapon, the use of a dog can also subject the organization to serious legal liability.

A security guard also keeps track of visitors

- Signs visitors in and out

- Verifies that the visitors are legitimate

- Ensures that visitors have been briefed on the organization's security and safety policies and that they are wearing appropriate personal protective equipment (PPE), if required

- Escorts visitors to the appropriate locations

An **alarm** is necessary to protect critical assets. The two main types of alarms

- Intruder alarm – detects intrusions

- Environmental alarm – detects a fire, flood, high temperatures, etc.

The alarm will have multiple components

- **Sensor**. The sensor detects an event

  - Motion Sensor detects motion, which could indicate the presence of an unauthorized person

  - Glass Break Sensor detects if glass has been broken based on the specific sound frequency that broken glass makes

  - Door/Window Contact detects if a door/window is closed or if has been opened. The sensor consists of a magnet that sits on the door/window and a contact that sits on the door/window frame. This creates a closed circuit. When opened, the door/window breaks the circuit, and an alarm activates

  - Smoke Detector detects for the presence of smoke but can also sound a false alarm. It can be triggered by dusty conditions.

  - Flood Detector detects moisture content. This may be installed in a server room.

  - Thermostat detects temperatures that are too high or too low. High temperatures can lead to equipment damage. Cold temperatures can cause water pipes to burst.

- **Controls**. The controls allow the alarm to be programmed. The controls collect data from the sensors and decide if an abnormal event has occurred, in which case the alarm is triggered. The controls send an alert to another device.

- **Alerts**. The alarm must make an alert, or else it will have no purpose. It must notify somebody that an abnormal condition is present. Some forms of alerts

  - Siren/Flashing Lights can scare intruders but are by themselves just a nuisance. Some intruders will ignore the alarms, especially when there are many false alarms. A police department will probably not respond to an audible alarm unless they are specifically notified that a crime is in progress.

  - Alert on a control panel. The alarm can notify a monitoring station so that the responsible people can verify that the alarm is real and take additional action such as calling the police, calling for emergency services, or dispatching a security guard to investigate.

  - Automated phone call/email/SMS alert to an on call person, who may or may not respond.

When an alarm is triggered, a security guard might first review the surveillance cameras in the relevant areas to determine if there is a problem. The security guard would then physically investigate the areas and act as appropriate. If nothing out of the ordinary is present, the security guard may turn off the alarm and record his findings.

An alarm system can be divided into multiple zones. Each zone is subject to its own rules. For example, a zone can be always armed, or it can be armed at night. A server room might always be armed unless somebody needs to access it. An office might only be armed at night when nobody is present.

When an alarm is in an armed state, any sensor activity will trigger an alarm. When an alarm is disarmed, then sensor activity will not trigger an alarm.

The control system for an alarm must be in a physically secure room. The control system must itself be alarmed (connected to a tamper-detecting sensor), so that any attempt to disable it is detected.

Protected distribution ensures that the cables are physically secure. An intruder could physically penetrate a data cable and hijack a connection to a device such as a camera or a printer. This is an unlikely scenario, but still possible and has been demonstrated.

Cables should be protected against damage. They should be installed inside conduit and cable trays.

It is important to physically secure devices such as cameras and wireless access points (which can be hidden inside the ceiling space).

Biometrics are used in combination with other devices to provide an additional layer of authentication. These include

- Facial recognition

- Finger print reader

- Voice recognition

- Palm reader

- Retinal scan

The biometric devices take a photograph of a human body part and then converts it into a mathematical model. For example, a fingerprint reader understands the bumps and ridges on a fingerprint and compares their relative sizes. There are many different algorithms and each one is different.

Not every scan is perfect. Most biometrics have a false positive because of the algorithm. The false positive rate is approximately 1 in 50,000.

A biometric reader does not (and cannot) create a pixel-by-pixel comparison of a person. Imagine taking a photograph of your face 100 times. Each photo will be slightly different. The lighting, the reflection, the angle of your head, and the position of your hair will be slightly different each time. The computer needs a way to understand that it is still you despite the changes. It does so by, for example, measuring the distance between your eyes or the width of your lips.

A biometric reader is part of an access control system. An access control system is used to track and restrict access to different buildings or rooms. It typically has four parts

- A card reader and/or biometric reader – this device is installed next to each doorway and scans user proximity cards or biometrics

- A door lock – an electronic door lock that allows the door to be unlocked automatically. This might be known as a door strike.

- A controller – the controller connects to both the card reader and the electronic door lock. When a user scans a card at a card reader, the card reader reports the user's information to the controller. The controller checks the time and decides whether the user is permitted to access that door at that particular time. If the user is permitted, then the card reader sends a signal to the lock to unlock the door.

- The wiring between the controller and the card reader.

The access control system can be wired as follows (depending on the make and model of the system)

- The controller is connected directly to the network and power. The controller powers the card reader and door lock. The controller connects to each card reader and door lock via a proprietary cable. The door lock and card reader communicate with the controller via the proprietary cable. The controller may have a software program or web-based interface where it can be programmed.

- The controller is connected directly to the network. Each card reader and door lock are also connected to the network and receive power via PoE. The card reader and door lock use the network to communicate with the controller. They might be on a separate VLAN or on a separate physical network.

We might label each device with an **asset tag**. The asset tag tells people that this device belongs to our company. We would record this number in a central database. If the device is lost or stolen, the thief will probably just remove the asset tag.

But more advanced devices such as Cisco Meraki Switches and Routers, computers, Android phones, Apple iPhones, etc. only work after they are activated through an internet server. If the device is registered to a specific organization and then is lost or stolen, the organization can deactivate it. When the device is reconnected to the internet, the thief will not be able to use it.

LoJack is a legitimate rootkit that comes preinstalled in the BIOS of some laptops. If the laptop is lost or stolen and later connected to the internet, LoJack will report the location of the laptop to a server. LoJack is designed to remain on the laptop even if its hard disk drive is erased or replaced.

There are physical devices that can connect to the system board of a router or switch and intercept the traffic on a binary level without detection. These are complicated devices that are generally available only to nation-state actors, but it is important to protect the infrastructure anyways. We can also use **tamper detection** methods to determine whether a device has been physically opened. A tamper detection method might be as simple as a sticker that is damaged when peeled off.

Proper physical security can only be achieved through proper employee training

- Employees should be trained to recognize and report unusual activity

- Employees should be trained to challenge any individual they do not recognize, any individual attempting to tailgate through the mantrap or secure entry, and any individual who is not wearing an ID badge.

We might also have Locking Racks and Locking Cabinets. When we have a small MDF or IDF and must share the space with other members of the organization then we should have all of our equipment stored in a locking cabinet. For example, if our IDF is also a storage room, then we must have a locking cabinet so that unauthorized users do not accidentally or deliberately unplug or tamper with the equipment.

If the MDF or IDF is a separate room with separate keys or an access control system, then it is not always necessary to use locking racks. Using open racks may be more cost effective. If the organization is large, and many different departments have equipment in the MDF, and only specific people have access to each set of equipment, then we might use locking racks to enforce access.

In general, server racks come with cheap locks that are easily picked or broken. You might consider purchasing racks or cabinets with combination locks or racks that accommodate external padlocks.

Smart Lockers are becoming more popular. A smart locker is a set of lockers that is connected to a computer system. Each locker has an electronic lock that can be unlocked remotely. Smart Lockers are being used for the following

- Mail delivery and package delivery. A user lives in an apartment building. FedEx attempts to deliver a package but the user is not home. FedEx leaves the package in a locker and provides the occupant with a code. The occupant returns home and enters the code into the locker's computer. The locker's computer unlocks the locker containing the user's package.

- Online purchase pick up. A user places an order online at Home Depot. Home Depot gathers the product and places it inside the locker, which is located outside the store. The store provides the user with a combination that he can use to pick up his purchase. The user visits the locker and enters a combination into the locker's computer. The locker's computer unlocks the locker containing the user's purchase.

- Spare parts. We might install a set of lockers in our office and fill them with spare parts such as RAM, ethernet cables, etc. When a user requires a spare part, he visits the locker, and enters his credentials into the computer. The computer opens a locker containing the spare parts that he requested. The computer can keep track of which user took which item.

- Key retrieval. When our organization has many physical keys, we must identify a reliable way to keep track of all of them.

  o Assign each key or set of keys to a different person. This is a bad idea because if only one person has keys to a resource, and he is away, then nobody else will be able to gain access.

o Leave keys with security. Security keeps track of the keys. When a user needs keys, the security guard verifies that the user is permitted to take them. The security guard keeps track of the request in a log.

o Use a key locker. A smart key locker can contain locking compartments or hooks. When a user needs keys to a specific resource, he logs in to the locker with a username/password combination or with an access control card. The user can request a specific set of keys from the locker. The locker verifies that the user is permitted access and either unlocks the correct set of keys or denies access. The locker keeps track of each access attempt. The locker also verifies when the user has returned the keys.

A locker might be better than a security guard because it is automated and can keep track of hundreds of different keys.

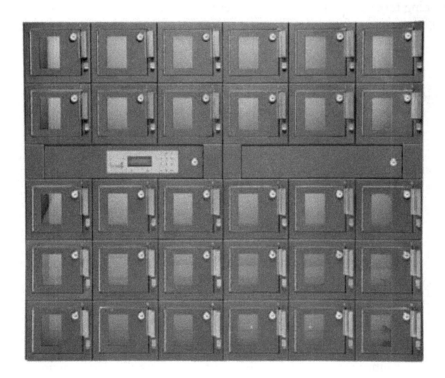

Finally, it is important to destroy sensitive data. The best method depends on the medium in which the data is stored, and whether the organization needs to reuse the media. When it is time to recycle or sell a device that has reached the end of its life, we must make sure that all sensitive data has been removed.

Some people might be tempted to "factory reset" a device and call it a day. The problem is that many modern devices are closed systems and so it is not always possible to determine how they operate or whether a factory reset procedure truly removes user data.

For example, an iPhone encrypts all user data. When the iPhone is reset, the iPhone does not actually wipe the user data; it just deletes the encryption key. If something went wrong with this process or if an exploit is discovered later, it may be possible for a hacker to retrieve this key, and thus some of the user data.

When we know that a device stores user data on a hard disk drive or SSD, the best way to reset the device is to physically remove the hard disk drive and shred it. We must be careful to ensure that the device only stored user data on that specific drive.

If the system is a closed system, such as an iPhone, then the only reliable way to erase the device is to physically destroy it.

Let's look at how the government does it

- Shred all paper documents to size of less than 5 mm x 5 mm or burn them at a temperature of at least 233 °C. We might pulp the paper (convert them to paper fiber with a detergent) after shredding.

- Smash all computer monitors to a size of less than 5 cm x 5 cm. This applies to computer monitors that have images burned in to them

- Degauss any hard disk drive or magnetic tapes. If degaussing is not available, then you can burn them at a temperature of at least 600 °C.

- Many hard disk drives are now hybrid (that is, they contain a magnetic portion and a solid-state portion). The solid-state portion must be shredded to a size of less than 2 mm x 2 mm and the hard disk drive must be degaussed or burned.

- After degaussing a hard disk drive, the physical platters must also be physically damaged.

- CD's, DVDs, and Solid State Drives must be burned at a temperature of at least 500°C, or shredded to a size less than 2 mm x 2 mm.

Part F: N10-008 5.0 Networking Troubleshooting

5.1 Explain the network troubleshooting methodology

- *Identify the Problem*
  - *Gather Information*
  - *Question Users*
  - *Identify Symptoms*
  - *Determine if Anything Has Changed*
  - *Duplicate the Problem, if Possible*
  - *Approach Multiple Problems Individually*
- *Establish a Theory of Probably Cause*
  - *Question the Obvious*
  - *Consider Multiple Approaches*
    - *Top-to-Bottom/Bottom-To-Top OSI Model*
    - *Divide and Conquer*
- *Test the Theory to Determine the Cause*
  - *Once the theory is confirmed, determine the next steps to resolve the problem*
  - *If the theory is not confirmed, re-establish a new theory or escalate*
- *Establish a Plan of Action to Resolve the Problem and Identify Potential Effects*
- *Implement the Solution or Escalate as Necessary*
- *Verify Full System Functionality and, if Applicable, Implement Preventative Measures*
- *Document Findings, Actions, Outcomes, and Lessons Learned*

Identify the Problem

Every problem has a solution. How do we find the solution? We need to focus on a framework for approaching each problem, no matter the cause or who it affects. Having a framework will help us solve each problem better.

Before we can solve the problem, we need to know what it is.

First, we must **gather information** about the problem. What is the problem? What systems does it affect? How often does it happen? Does it happen randomly or at specific time intervals? What are the symptoms?

We should attempt to **duplicate the problem**, if we can do so safely and without causing damage. If we can replicate the problem in a controlled environment, we can observe it and possibly determine its cause.

We can **ask users** for advice. Even non-technical users have good information about the problem. They can explain their observations. We should be non-judgemental and approachable when speaking with users.

Next, we can **identify the symptoms** of the problem. Symptoms can give us clues as to what is causing the problem.

We should also **ask if anything has changed**. We can review our change management log and our patch management software to see if updates were installed prior to the problem taking place. Did the user install a new program or change a configuration?

Multiple problems should be approached individually. We should not assume that multiple issues have the same cause, but we should not rule it out either.

If you go to the doctor and your stomach hurts and your leg hurts, the doctor is going to consider them separately. He will ask you if anything changed. Have you eaten something different today? Did you take any new medications? How bad does your stomach hurt? All the time? Sometimes? In the morning? After you eat? Your leg and stomach are probably not connected but they might be.

Establish a Theory of Probably Cause

Second, we must come up with a **theory for the cause** of the problem. We should look for obvious causes. Sometimes they are overlooked, but an obvious cause can be quickly investigated, and if correct, it will save a lot of trouble. Having a second set of eyes on the problem is also good.

Many times, a problem is caused by a typo in the configuration. The person who wrote the configuration can't "see" the typo because he wrote it and no matter how many times he stares at it, he won't find the problem. A second set of eyes helps because another user will quickly see what is wrong.

We can divide the problem into multiple smaller problems and solve each one separately. It is possible that multiple issues contribute to the same problem. For example, if your basement is flooding, it could be caused by a leaky bathtub or a leaky toilet, or both. If you only find and plug one leak, your basement will continue to flood.

We can use the OSI model to help us solve the problem, either starting at the top or at the bottom. The OSI model can help us rule out issues. For example, if a user is having trouble connecting to the internet, but their computer has obtained a valid IP address and can connect to the router, then the physical, data link, and network layers are working. We can start investigating at the next layer. This is a top-to-bottom approach.

Remember that the layers are

- **Layer 1 – Physical**
- **Layer 2 – Data Link**
- **Layer 3 – Network**
- **Layer 4 – Transport**
- **Layer 5 – Session**
- **Layer 6 – Presentation**
- **Layer 7 – Application**

If your stomach hurts, the doctor will come up with a theory for the cause. Is it muscle pain? Is it nerve pain? Is it a chemical imbalance in your blood? Something you ate?

Test the Theory to Determine the Cause

We **test our theory**. The theory is what we think caused the problem. We can test the theory by removing the source of the error. For example, if a software update caused the error, we should roll back the update.

If the problem is solved, then the theory is correct. Otherwise, the theory is wrong, and we must find a new theory. If we find that the cause is beyond our control, we should escalate to another expert.

If you have a stomach ache, the doctor might give you medication. If the medication makes your stomach ache go away, then the theory is proven. Otherwise, the doctor needs to find a new medication or treatment option.

Establish a Plan of Action to Resolve the Problem and Identify Potential Effects

If the theory is correct, we should develop a **plan** to resolve the problem. Remember that a problem may affect multiple users. If we rolled out a software update across the organization, and it caused errors, and our theory was that the software update caused the error, we could test our theory by rolling back the update on a single user's computer.

The plan of action would be to roll back the update across the entire organization. Before we execute a plan of action, we should identify its potential effects. The effects can include disruption to the organization's systems, and financial risk. What if the software update was necessary to patch a security vulnerability? Rolling it back would open the organization to risk.

If the doctor gives you stomach medication, that medication may give you side effects that are worse than the illness you're trying to treat.

Implement the Solution or Escalate as Necessary

Finally, we must **implement the solution**. If we don't have the ability to implement the solution (don't have permission, don't have approval for the cost of the solution, don't have approval to implement a solution that causes downtime, etc.), we must seek approval from a higher level. This is known as an **escalation**.

Verify Full System Functionality and, if Applicable, Implement Preventative Measures

After we have **implemented the entire solution**, we should verify that everything is working and that no new problems have been caused. We should consider implementing **preventative measures** to keep the problem from happening again. That is, we don't want to resolve just the symptoms with a "band aid" fix; we want to resolve the root cause of the problem.

If you've been taking your stomach medication, the doctor will verify that your stomach ache went away. He might recommend that you go on a diet or stop eating spicy foods so that the stomach ache doesn't come back. You don't want to stay on stomach medication for your entire life.

Document Findings, Actions, and Outcomes

Finally, we should fully **document the problem**. Our documentation should include the symptoms of the problem, the actions we took to resolve it, and the outcome. This documentation can be used by other technicians who encounter the same problem in the future. We might call this documentation **lessons learned**.

5.2 Given a scenario, troubleshoot common cable connectivity issues and select the appropriate tools

- *Specifications and Limitations*
  - *Throughput*
  - *Speed*
  - *Distance*
- *Cable Considerations*
  - *Shielded and Unshielded*
  - *Plenum and Riser-Rated*
- *Cable Application*
  - *Rollover Cable/Console Cable*
  - *Crossover Cable*
  - *Power Over Ethernet*
- *Common Issues*
  - *Attenuation*
  - *Interference*
  - *Decibel (dB) Loss*
  - *Incorrect Pinout*
  - *Bad Ports*
  - *Open/Short*
  - *Light-Emitting Diode (LED) Status Indicators*
  - *Incorrect Transreceivers*
  - *Duplexing Issues*
  - *Transmit and Receive (TX/RX) Reversed*
  - *Dirty Optical Cables*
- *Common Tools*
  - *Cable Crimper*
  - *Punchdown Tool*
  - *Tone Generator*
  - *Loopback Adapter*
  - *Optical Time-Domain Reflectometer (OTDR)*
  - *Multimeter*
  - *Cable Tester*
  - *Wire Map*
  - *Tap*
  - *Fusion Splicers*
  - *Spectrum Analyzers*
  - *Snips/Cutters*
  - *Cable Stripper*
  - *Fiber Light Meter*

Now that we have an idea of the problem-solving framework, let's look at some physical cable issues.

When a network connection is not working, what can you check for?

- Throughput – how much bandwidth are you getting? If you aren't getting enough bandwidth, then maybe the entire system is lagging because too many people are downloading too many things. Or maybe the ISP is not giving you as much bandwidth as you are paying for. You need to identify the bottleneck.

- Speed – how fast is the connection? 10 Mbps? 100 Mbps? 1 Gbps? If your equipment is rated for 1 Gbps on both sides (the device port and the switch port) but your speed is 100 Mbps, you must investigate. Are the devices configured for the wrong speed? Is there damage to some of the pairs in the ethernet cable that prevent the devices from using its full capacity? Is there interference on the cable that is causing errors?

- Distance – how long is the cable? Does it exceed the recommended distance of 100m for copper or the manufacturer's recommended distance for fiber? If the cable is too long, errors will result in the transmission.

Some ideas about cable types

- Is the cable shielded or unshielded? If there are sources of interference near the cable, then a shielded cable is necessary to prevent errors.

- Is the cable plenum rated or riser rated? A plenum rated cable is the only type of cable that is suitable for installation in a plenum space. What is a plenum space? It is the space above the ceiling where there is ventilation. Local building codes dictate that plenum cable must be used in the plenum space. A riser rated cable can be installed between floors but not in a plenum space. The plenum rating won't affect the quality of the data being transmitted.

Are we using the correct type of cable?

- Check the pin out of the cable to ensure that it is correct for the application. Most applications will accept a straight-thru cable or a crossover cable. Remember that modern switches will detect and use either a straight-thru or crossover cable, so mixing them won't usually cause an issue (unless the feature is disabled). Having said that, it is a good practice to only use straight-thru cables.

- A console cable is used for connecting to a switch or router. You must make sure that the console cable has the correct pin out for the device. Although console cables look alike, different manufacturers use different pin outs for their devices.

- If the device uses Power Over Ethernet, is the device's PoE type compatible with the switch's PoE type? Is the switch capable of PoE? Does the switch have PoE enabled on the port that the device is connected to? You might connect a PoE injector to the device and see if it boots up.

Some areas of concern in physical cable transmission

- **Attenuation**. Attenuation means that we have a physical loss of the signal power. The loss may be low or high. A small loss is expected over copper or fiber optic cable, but a large loss may indicate damage to the cable. The amount of attenuation can be measured in dB, and might be known as Decibel Loss.

- **Interference**. Interference means that we have some electromagnetic noise on the cable. It is common when the cables are installed parallel to high voltage power lines but does not typically cause data loss on cat6 or cat6A cable.

- **Incorrect Pinout**. When an ethernet jack is miswired, data cannot be transmitted. A commercially manufactured patch cable won't typically have an incorrect pinout, but an ethernet jack installed in the field might.

- **Bad Port**. A bad ethernet port on a switch or device will result in errors, dropped connections, or no connection at all. A bad port on high quality switches is rare.

- **Open/Short**. An open means that the circuit is not a complete loop. In other words, a wire in the circuit has been cut and now the electrical signal has nowhere to go.

  If you plug in a light bulb, electricity flows from the wall outlet, to the light bulb and back into the wall outlet. If you cut the wire or remove the light bulb, the electricity has no pathway, and now you have an open.

  A short is caused when a wire touches another wire. It means that the electrical signal is flowing back to the source without passing through the device that needs it.

  If you plug in a light bulb but cut the wires coming out of the wall and twist them together, you now have a short. In a high-voltage system, a short will activate a circuit breaker.

  A cable tester can tell us whether we have an open wire or a short wire in an ethernet cable.

- **Light-Emitting Diode (LED) Status Indicators**. We can check the LED status on an ethernet port to determine what it is doing. Typically, there are two lights: one tells us if we have a link (that is the two devices see each other) and the other one tells us if we have activity (the two devices are talking). The color of the lights and the pattern at which they blink can tell us

  - Whether there is activity

  - What speed they are connected at

  - Whether there is PoE

  - Whether there is half duplex or full duplex

  The pattern and color vary from manufacturer to manufacturer. But in general, a green light indicates a faster connection than an orange light, which indicates a faster connection than a red light. No lights mean that there is no physical connection.

  If you connect two devices (a computer and a switch for example) via an ethernet cable, and you don't see any link lights, then you have a problem. What might be the cause?

  - Test the cable end to end to make sure that it has continuity and that the pin out is correct

  - The ethernet port on the switch and/or the computer might be disabled. Check the configuration.

  - The switch or computer might not be powered on

  - The switch port is bad

  - The ethernet port on the computer is bad

  If you only see link lights on one device, that usually means that one device can transmit and receive but the other one can't. This is usually caused by damage to some pairs in the cable. If it is a fiber optic connection, then one of the fiber strands may be damaged.

- **Incorrect Transreceivers**. Remember that a transreceiver allows a cable to talk to a switch or router. If we use the wrong transreceiver (for example we use a multi mode transreceiver and a single mode fiber), then no communication can take place. We must make sure to use the correct transreceiver for the correct fiber. We must also make sure that the transreceiver we use is compatible with the switch or router that it is installed into.

- **Duplexing Issues**. A duplexing issue happens when we have two devices trying to talk at the same time on the same wire. The result is that the data is transmitted down the wire and collides in the middle. A connection with a duplex issue will appear to be connected properly but will perform poorly with lots of errors.

  The cause is usually that the devices have mismatched duplex settings. For example, one device is set to full duplex and the other is set to half duplex or to autonegotiate.

- **Transmit and Receive (TX/RX) Reversed**. Remember that a switch transmits data on one pair of copper wires and receives data on another pair. It is not possible to reverse the pairs unless we use a crossover cable. The likelihood that this will happen is low since most switches can detect whether a straight-thru or crossover cable has been used.

  When we have a fiber optic connection, the switch transmits data on one strand and receives data on another strand. If the strands are reversed, then the switch will not see a connection, because both devices are trying to transmit data on the same strand.

- **Dirty Optical Cables**. Dirty Optical Cables are the most common cause of transmission errors over fiber. We can examine the end of the cable with a measuring tool to verify if it is clean. If it is dirty, we should clean it with the appropriate cleaning tool.

At the beginning of this book, I told you about some tools you should have. When you come to work with the right tools, the job becomes much easier. The right tools are often high quality.

Some of the tools that you should have are below.

A **crimper** is used to fix a cat6 or cat5e male end onto a cable. This crimper below can crimp a cat3 male end (a 6-position plug) onto a cable as well. We would use this crimper to terminate a cable to a male end. It costs about $80.

Male ends are used in the field when we are directly connecting an ethernet cable to a device such as a surveillance camera or an access point. In general, at a server room, we should terminate the cable to a patch panel instead of a male end that is connected directly to a switch. Male ends are less reliable, and I do not recommend using them in the field either. I prefer to terminate my cables to female jacks. If I need to connect a camera or access point, I can plug it into the jack with a patch cable.

A **cable tester** tells us whether a cable has **continuity**. Remember that a cat6 cable contains eight wires. We connect the main part of the tester to one end of the cable being tested, and we connect the remote part to the other end. The tester tells us whether all eight wires are continuous (intact) from end to end.

This particular tester shows us the status of all eight wires at the same time. Some testers are only capable of testing one wire at a time. It also tells us if a wire is continuous but punched down on the wrong position of a jack. Finally, it can test coaxial cable and shielded cat6 cable. It costs about $150.

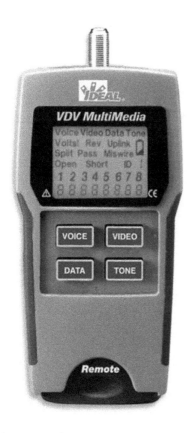

A more advanced device is a **cable certifier**. The cable certifier takes additional measurements in the cable to ensure not just that it has continuity but also that it is not subject to interference. It can save thousands of tests and generate a PDF report. Some customers require the use of a cable certifier after installation, which proves that the cabling was installed and terminated correctly.

Below is the Fluke Versiv cable certifier, which I use to certify copper and fiber optic cables. The certifier must be calibrated each year. It costs about $25,000 for a full package that includes modules for testing copper and fiber.

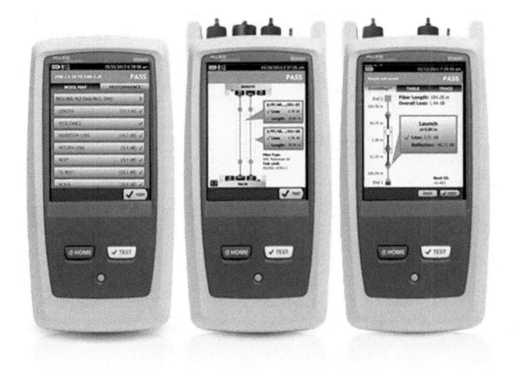

A **punch down tool** inserts wires into a jack and cuts off the excess. Punch down tools come with replaceable blades (such as BIX, Krone, 110, and 66). I recommend a punch down tool with a spring-loaded action, which is much easier to operate. It costs about $80.

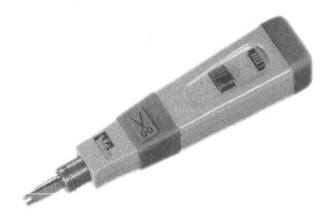

If you are terminating a large quantity of jacks, consider buying a tool that can punch down all eight wires at the same time. Below is the Fluke JackRapid Punch Down Tool. The tool has repeatable heads for different makes and models of jacks. You must buy the head that is compatible with the jacks that you are installing.

The tool can reduce termination time by up to 50%, reduce errors, and reduce the risk of hand strain. It costs about $150.

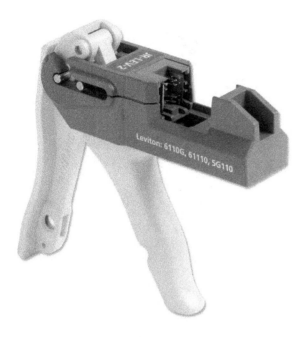

A **tone generator** (also known as a fox and hound) helps us find cables. Say we have a big mess of cables like in the photograph below. We found one end of the cable, and we're trying to find the other end in this mess. We can use the tone generator.

One end generates the tone. We connect it to the cable that we are trying to identify. The tone generator creates an audible tone that passes down the cable. We take the other end (called the wand) and wave it around in the mess of cables. It will create an audible alert when it is touching the correct cable.

I recommend the Fluke IntelliTone Pro 200 because it works well even with long cables. When using other brands of toners, I find that the signal can bleed to other adjacent cables, causing inaccurate results. This toner also has a built-in cable tester, which makes it good for finding and terminating cables in a single trip.

Another good toner is made by Greenlee. The Fluke toner is better at finding cat5e/cat6/cat6A wiring, but the Greenlee is better at finding cat3 wiring. What is interesting is that the Fluke tone generator is compatible with the Greenlee wand, and vice versa. The Fluke toner costs about $300 and the Greenlee toner costs about $200.

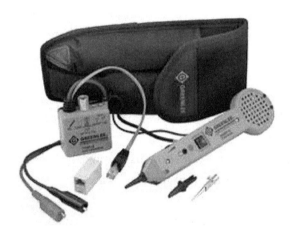

A **loopback plug** or **loopback adapter** is a device for testing a signal. If I have a DSL line or fiber optic cable coming from an ISP, how can I test it? I can't take the other end of my cable tester to the ISP and plug it in there because the cable might be 10 km long!

But if the ISP has terminated their cable to a jack in my building, I connect a loopback plug like the one below. The ISP sends a signal down the wire, and the loopback plug sends the signal back to the ISP. If the signal arrives intact at the ISP, then the ISP knows that the line is working.

The loopback connector below is designed for a Smart Jack. We can use two standard fiber optic cables to create a fiber optic loop. You can buy a T1 loop for a few dollars, or you can make it yourself using a crimper, a male cat6 termination, and a small piece of cat6 cable.

An **OTDR** or **Optical Time Domain Reflectometer** is a device that measures defects in a fiber optic cable. Think about if we installed a 2km long fiber optic cable and we later notice that there is a problem. Maybe a mouse chewed through it. How do we know where the damage is? We use the OTDR. It shines a light down the cable. If the light encounters some damage, it bounces back. The OTDR can measure how long it took for the light to bounce back and how much of the light bounced back. Based on the time it took to bounce back, we can determine where the damage is.

The OTDR has advanced algorithms for processing the signal and can show us graphically how long the fiber is and where the damage is (even when the cable is damaged in multiple places).

The OTDR is only testing the glass strands inside the fiber. If OTDR won't be able to detect physical damage to the cable jacket.

The cost of an OTDR varies between $2000 and $30,000. If you buy the Fluke Versiv, you can buy the OTDR module for an additional $10,000.

A **light meter** shines a light down the fiber optic cable and measures the brightness on the other end. If the light is bright enough, then we know that the cable is suitable for transmitting a signal. It doesn't tell us whether the cable was terminated correctly or where it is damaged. It costs about $200.

A fiber optic strand that has some damage may still transmit enough light for the receiving device to process the signal.

A **multimeter** allows us to measure the voltage, resistance, or wattage on a pair of wires. It may be suitable for diagnosing issues with DSL or phone lines, although I rarely use such a device. It can also tell us if a pair of wires has continuity. It costs between $50 and $500.

A **fiber optic fusion splicer** melts two fiber optic cables together. You can use this when terminating a fiber optic cable with a pigtail. You can also use it to repair a damaged fiber optic cable.

A fusion splicer can cost between $1000 and $25,000. I found that some of cheaper Chinese ones available on Amazon work just as well as the expensive Japanese ones.

I used to use the **Corning Unicam 2 fiber termination kit**, which allowed me to mechanically terminate fiber optic cables. This kit cost $2500. For reasons discussed previously, we no longer mechanically terminate fiber optic cables.

Before terminating a fiber optic cable, you will need to strip the jacket off it. You must use a cable stripper that is designed for the fiber cable that you are using. This costs about $50, but also comes with most fusion splicers.

You will also need a cleaver. The cleaver precisely cuts the fiber optic cable strands so that they line up perfectly when placed inside the fusion splicer. The cleaver usually comes with the splicer. You can buy one for about $200.

I also carry a Klein tools cable stripper for stripping copper cables and for stripping the outer jacket of a fiber optic cable. You must be careful when stripping copper cables because different cables have different outer jacket diameters. If you are not careful, you might nick the wires inside the cable. It costs about $80.

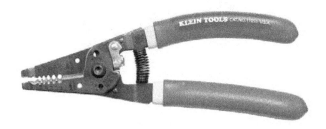

I also recommend a pair of cutters. The ones I like to use are made by Wiss, specifically the W7T model. This pair of cutters cost about $50 and can cut through almost anything.

A **spectrum analyser** is a device that measures Wi-Fi signals. The spectrum analyser may be a physical device or may be incorporated into a software application such as inSSIDer. The Wi-Fi spectrum analyser tells us what frequencies different access points are broadcasting on.

A **handheld network analyser** such as the JDSU T-BERD below is a more advanced tool that can test fiber and copper cables from 1 Mbps to 100 Gbps. You can connect an SFP to it as well. It is very expensive but very useful especially for testing advanced internet connections including SONET and 5G. This device costs upwards of $40,000.

A tool that I have but rarely use is the sidekick meter below. It can test a phone line to determine whether it has the appropriate voltage under stress. Sometimes, a phone line appears to have a dial tone but does not work when you actually pick up the phone. This device costs about $1500, but I found a used one for $200.

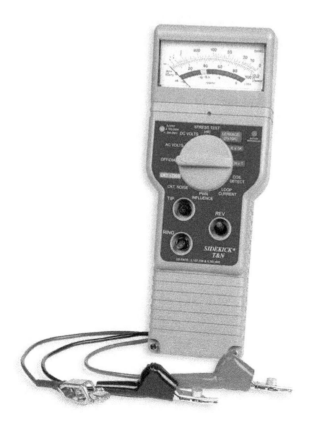

Another tool that I have but rarely use is the QAM meter. I use this for testing coaxial cable transmission systems. This device costs about $2500, but I also found a used one for $200.

5.3 Given a scenario, use the appropriate network software tools and commands

- *Software Tools*
    - *Wi-Fi Analyzer*
    - *Protocol Analyzer / Packet Capture*
    - *Bandwidth Speed Tester*
    - *Port Scanner*
    - *iperf*
    - *NetFlor Analyzers*
    - *Trivial File Transfer Protocol (TFTP) Server*
    - *Terminal Emulator*
    - *IP Scanner*
- *Command Line Tool*
    - *ping*
    - *ipconfig / ifconfig / ip*
    - *nslookup / dig*
    - *traceroute / tracert*
    - *arp*
    - *netstat*
    - *hostname*
    - *route*
    - *telnet*
    - *tcpdump*
    - *nmap*
- *Basic Network Platform Commands*
    - *show interface*
    - *show config*
    - *show route*

We mentioned the hardware tools that you should carry. Now let's look at some software tools. Some of these tools are integrated into hardware like the network analysers that I mentioned previously, but you may also install their respective software components onto a laptop.

- **Packet Sniffer/Protocol Analyzer**. It might also known be known as a packet analyzer or network analyzer. This lets us intercept packets on a wired or wireless network so that we can analyse them. We may also be able to generate traffic so that we can test our network. We can also determine whether traffic is being encrypted or if it sent in plain text. A good packet sniffer is called WireShark. Packet sniffing another person's network without permission might be illegal.

- **Port Scanner**. A port scanner tells us which ports are open on a given network or device. We can use it to test the effectiveness of our firewall and to detect rogue devices.

- **IP Scanner**. An IP Scanner tells us which devices on our network are active. We give it a range of IP addresses, and it scans through them to see which ones return a response. It will identify each device by its IP Address, MAC Address, Hostname, and Open Ports. It may also be able to tell us the manufacturer of the device (or at least the manufacturer of its network card).

  The Port Scanner and the IP Scanner may be integrated into the same software, such as the Advanced Network Scanner, which is available for free.

  A properly configured device should only respond to requests made by devices authorized to access it. Thus, we can use the scanner to determine whether

  o A device is present on our network, but shouldn't be

  o A device is not responding to anybody, even those who are permitted to access it, in which case it may be offline or misconfigured

  o A device is responding to people who have no authorization to access it, in which case its security settings are misconfigured

  o A device is responding but has open ports that should be closed and/or closed ports that should be open.

- **Wi-Fi Analyser**. A Wi-Fi analyser can measure wireless signals and networks. Ekahau and Air Magnet SurveyPro are examples of Wi-Fi analysers.

- **Bandwidth Speed Tester**. A speed tester can tell us the upload and download speed of a connection. It may also tell us about jitters, latency, and packet loss.

  Speed testers are available on the internet and can include speedtest.net and fast.com. The results of the speed test are only as good as the speed test website; if the server is slow, then the results might be slow.

  One of the best speed testing applications is iperf. You can use iperf to create an end to end speed test between a client and server.

- **Net Flow Analyser**. A Net Flow Analyser allows us to determine which the traffic on our network is coming from, and where it is going. This way, we can identify where the sources of congestion are.

  Many software defined networks have this tool built in to their administrative applications. For example, Cisco Meraki allows you to analyse and shape traffic via an online interface.

- **TFTP Server**. A TFTP Server is an application that you can run on your laptop. The most common purpose you will use it for is to upgrade the operating system on a switch or router. You can download an image of the router's operating system onto your laptop and then use the TFTP software to upload it to the switch. This is useful when the organization does not have a reliable repository for the switch or router operating systems.

- **Terminal Emulator**. A common Terminal Emulator is called PuTTY. PuTTY allows us to connect to and communicate with a server, switch, or other device, via console, SSH, or Telnet. PuTTY is an important program to have and it is free.

We can also perform testing from a command line. Some of the commands are in the table below.

ping	ping tests the availability of a network host
	The ping protocol sends a small packet to the host, and the host responds
	Ping measures the round-trip time that the packet travelled, which can help identify bottlenecks
	A user could ping a hostname or an IP address; in the event of pinging a hostname, the user's device will contact a DNS server to obtain the IP address and then ping the IP address

A ping could fail if

- The host is offline

- The host is online but has a firewall that is blocking the pings (a good secure host will not respond to pings)

- The user's computer is offline (no pathway to the host)

- The DNS server could not translate the hostname to an IP address or translated it to an incorrect IP address

The command is
ping *hostname*

```
Pinging 8.8.8.8 with 32 bytes of data:
Reply from 8.8.8.8: bytes=32 time=32ms TTL=56
Reply from 8.8.8.8: bytes=32 time=33ms TTL=56
Reply from 8.8.8.8: bytes=32 time=30ms TTL=56
Reply from 8.8.8.8: bytes=32 time=35ms TTL=56

Ping statistics for 8.8.8.8:
    Packets: Sent = 4, Received = 4, Lost = 0 (0% loss),
Approximate round trip times in milli-seconds:
    Minimum = 30ms, Maximum = 35ms, Average = 32ms
```

netstat   Netstat lists all the active network connections on a computer

This includes

- Whether the connection is TCP or UDP

- The local address and port of the connection

- The remote address and port (protocol) of the connection

- The state of the connection

The connections can be filtered by status or connection type.

The command is
netstat

Connection states

- Listening – a program is listening. A software program can listen on a socket (a socket is a combination of a port and protocol). For example, a web server may listen on TCP port 80 for incoming HTTP requests.

- Close_Wait – the remote host has closed the connection, but the local host is still waiting for some packets to arrive (the command to close the connection may have arrived prior to all of the packets, if they took different routes)

- Time_Wait – the local host has closed the connection, but the local host is still waiting for packets to arrive

- Established – an active connection

To show only sockets, a user can type

netstat a

```
C:\Users\xxy401003>netstat

Active Connections

  Proto  Local Address          Foreign Address        State
  TCP    10.0.0.168:56744       ec2-52-6-197-42:https    ESTABLISHED
  TCP    10.0.0.168:56745       ec2-52-2-221-190:https   ESTABLISHED
  TCP    10.0.0.168:56746       ec2-18-215-111-224:https ESTABLISHED
  TCP    10.0.0.168:57051       72.21.91.29:http         CLOSE_WAIT
  TCP    10.0.0.168:58607       relay-0e394848:http      ESTABLISHED
```

**tracert /
traceroute**

tracert shows the route from the local host to the remote host. A user can run a tracert on an IP address or on a hostname; in the event of running a tracert on a hostname, the user's device will contact a DNS server to obtain the IP address and then tracert the IP address.

Since data must typically travel through multiple computer networks before it reaches its final destination, the tracert command will send three packets to each router in the route, and then display the round-trip travel time.

459

Each destination in the trip is known as a hop. The route that a packet takes may vary from network to network and from time to time. Just like there are multiple pathways to fly an airplane from one city to another, data packets may have multiple routers that they can pass through. The pathway that is selected depends on current network congestion, and the route that the user's ISP has negotiated with downstream carriers.

Tracert can be used to identify if routers along the pathway are correctly configured. If the ping test fails, but the remote host is online, then the next step would be to run a tracert and see how the packet is travelling (and why it is not reaching its destination).

```
Tracing route to google.ca [172.217.14.195]
over a maximum of 30 hops:

  1    <1 ms    <1 ms    <1 ms   192.168.1.99
  2     2 ms     1 ms     1 ms   10.0.0.1
  3    11 ms    12 ms    11 ms   68.151.192.1
  4    15 ms    16 ms    12 ms   rc2ar-be125-1.ed.shawcable.net [64.59.184.185]
  5    14 ms    13 ms    14 ms   rc2we-be7.ed.shawcable.net [66.163.70.129]
  6    18 ms    18 ms    16 ms   rc3no-be6.cg.shawcable.net [66.163.64.69]
  7    32 ms    32 ms    31 ms   rc2wt-be100.wa.shawcable.net [66.163.75.233]
  8    30 ms    32 ms    29 ms   72.14.242.90
  9    34 ms    33 ms    30 ms   216.239.51.73
 10    32 ms    33 ms    30 ms   209.85.254.171
 11    33 ms    30 ms    30 ms   sea30s01-in-f3.1e100.net [172.217.14.195]

Trace complete.
```

nslookup/dig   nslookup provides the name of the name server associated with a specific domain name, or the domain name associated with a specific IP address.

The command is
nslookup *ip address or hostname*

For example, when running nslookup on dns.google, the server will return the following results

```
C:\Users\xxy401003>nslookup dns.google
Server:  nsc4.ar.ed.shawcable.net
Address:  2001:4e8:0:4004::14

Non-authoritative answer:
Name:    dns.google
Addresses:  2001:4860:4860::8844
            2001:4860:4860::8888
            8.8.4.4
            8.8.8.8
```

nslookup allows a user to determine if the name server for a specific hostname is correctly configured.

arp   ARP or Address Resolution Protocol

Each network device keeps a table (known as the ARP table) of other network devices on its network; the table contains the device's physical (MAC address), IP address, and whether the address is static or dynamic. Each time a device receives data from another network device, it creates a new entry in the table (or updates an existing entry if the MAC address matches).

When a device chooses to send data packet over the network, it uses the MAC address of the device (provided that both devices are on the same network segment).

The ARP command is
arp -a

The ARP command lists all of the entries in the ARP table. A user can troubleshoot a network connection on a local network segment by checking the ARP table. If a remote host is not reachable and does not appear in the ARP table, then the local host does not see it.

```
Interface: 10.0.0.168 --- 0x8
  Internet Address       Physical Address        Type
  10.0.0.1               bc-9b-68-aa-90-50        dynamic
  10.0.0.27              44-00-49-af-7a-e7        dynamic
  10.0.0.62              02-0f-b5-7f-23-54        dynamic
  10.0.0.210             94-53-30-b6-74-e3        dynamic
  10.0.0.255             ff-ff-ff-ff-ff-ff        static
  224.0.0.22             01-00-5e-00-00-16        static
```

ipconfig/ifconfig   ipconfig shows the network interface configuration of the device. A device may have multiple network interfaces, including an ethernet interface, a wireless interface, and VPN interfaces

The ipconfig command will show the

- DNS Suffix

- IPv4 addresses

- IPv6 addresses

- Subnet mask

- Default gateway

- DNS Server IP address

- DHCP Server IP address

Additional functions of ipconfig

- flushdns – erases current DNS cache

- release – released currently set DHCP addresses

- renew – renews the currently set DHCP addresses

The command is
ipconfig /a

The ipconfig command allows a user to see if the computer's network interface is configured correctly. Some problems

- There is no IP address – an IP address is not configured, the device is not reaching the DHCP server, or the network interface is disconnected or not functioning

- The assigned IP address is a link-local address – the device did not reach the DHCP address

- The IP address is in the wrong subnet – the wrong static IP address may have been set or the device is connected in the wrong VLAN

hostname   hostname tells us the hostname of the device

telnet   telnet is a command that allows us to launch a telnet session. Newer versions of Windows no longer include Telnet.

tcpdump	tcpdump lists the packets being transmitted and received over a network interface. It only functions on UNIX. The packets can be saved to a file.
nmap	nmap is an open-source application that provides network scanning. You can install nmap on UNIX and then run the command. nmap has many functions • Scan a single IP address or host for open ports • Scan a range of IP addresses and/or port ranges for open ports • Scan TCP or UDP protocols • Detect malware • Detect the operating system version of a remote host
netcat	netcat reads from and writes to TCP/UDP connections. It only works on UNIX. netcat can • Intercept inbound and outbound TCP/UDP connections • Check forward and reverse DNS settings • Scan for open ports on a remote host or range of IP addresses • Dump intercepted data to a text file
iptables	On UNIX, iptables can provide us with a list of rules for how packets are handled
pathping	Pathping combines the tracert with the ping command
route	On UNIX, route can provide us with the IP routing table for that system.

When we're logged in to a router or switch, there are some commands we can run. Across the multiple makes and models of routers, switches, firewalls, and wireless access points you will encounter, there can be thousands of commands. It is not possible to list all of them here, but they generally follow a pattern.

show

show tells the device to show us something. We would add the description of what we want it to show us at the end, so that it looks like this

show *details*

The three most common show commands

- show interface – this gives us a list of interfaces and their status (whether they are connected, how fast they are, what they are connected to, whether there are any errors, etc.)

- show config – this gives us a copy of the device's configuration

- show route – this gives us a list of the routes and their status. It only works on a router.

- Show vlan – this gives us a list of VLANs configured and their status

For example, I ran the show ip interface brief command on a Cisco switch and below is what I got. Notice that the command on the Cisco switch is slightly different than just "show interface".

```
Switch>show ip interface brief
Interface              IP-Address      OK? Method Status                Protocol
FastEthernet0/1        unassigned      YES manual down                  down
FastEthernet0/2        unassigned      YES manual down                  down
FastEthernet0/3        unassigned      YES manual down                  down
FastEthernet0/4        unassigned      YES manual down                  down
FastEthernet0/5        unassigned      YES manual down                  down
FastEthernet0/6        unassigned      YES manual down                  down
FastEthernet0/7        unassigned      YES manual down                  down
FastEthernet0/8        unassigned      YES manual down                  down
FastEthernet0/9        unassigned      YES manual down                  down
FastEthernet0/10       unassigned      YES manual down                  down
FastEthernet0/11       unassigned      YES manual down                  down
FastEthernet0/12       unassigned      YES manual down                  down
FastEthernet0/13       unassigned      YES manual down                  down
FastEthernet0/14       unassigned      YES manual down                  down
FastEthernet0/15       unassigned      YES manual down                  down
FastEthernet0/16       unassigned      YES manual down                  down
FastEthernet0/17       unassigned      YES manual down                  down
FastEthernet0/18       unassigned      YES manual down                  down
FastEthernet0/19       unassigned      YES manual down                  down
FastEthernet0/20       unassigned      YES manual down                  down
FastEthernet0/21       unassigned      YES manual down                  down
FastEthernet0/22       unassigned      YES manual down                  down
FastEthernet0/23       unassigned      YES manual down                  down
FastEthernet0/24       unassigned      YES manual down                  down
GigabitEthernet0/1     unassigned      YES manual down                  down
GigabitEthernet0/2     unassigned      YES manual down                  down
Vlan1                  unassigned      YES manual administratively down down
Switch>
```

configure

confiure tells the device that we want to make a change

On a switch or router, we might enter the configure command to configure general settings, or we might enter some details after it to configure specific items.

For example

- configure interface *interface name* – allows us to configure a specific interface on a switch or router

- configure vlan *vlan name* – allows us to configure a VLAN on the switch

- configure terminal – allows us to configure remote access to the device

Help When you type help, the switch or router will give you some hints about how to use a particular command.

The type of help that you will see will depend upon what you are doing. For example, if you are configuring a VLAN, and you type help, the switch will show you information about configuring a VLAN.

5.4 Given a scenario, troubleshoot common wireless connectivity issues

- *Specification and Limitations*
  - *Throughput*
  - *Speed*
  - *Distance*
  - *Received Signal Strength Indication (RSSI) Signal Strength*
  - *Effective Isotropic Radiated Power (EIRP) / Power Settings*
- *Considerations*
  - *Antennas*
    - *Placement*
    - *Type*
    - *Polarization*
  - *Channel Utilization*
  - *AP Association Time*
  - *Site Survey*
- *Common Issues*
  - *Interference*
    - *Channel Overlap*
  - *Antenna Cable Attenuation / Signal Loss*
  - *RF Attenuation / Signal Loss*
  - *Wrong SSID*
  - *Incorrect Passphrase*
  - *Encryption Protocol Mismatch*
  - *Insufficient Wireless Coverage*
  - *Captive Portal Issues*
  - *Client Disassociation Issues*

Let's look at some common Wi-Fi issues.

Older Wi-Fi access point typically sends signals (radio waves) in all directions, in the hope that some of them will land on devices that need to connect. Newer Wi-Fi access points use a technique called beam forming to make sure that they get to where they need to go.

What happens to these signals? Some of them hit reflective surfaces. A **reflection** means that the signal bounces back. Surfaces that cause reflection include metal and glass. A device may pick up a reflected signal, but the range of the signal will be reduced when reflection is involved.

Refraction is when a signal passes through a surface but bends. Surfaces that cause refraction include walls and doors. A device may be able to pick up a refracted signal.

Absorption is when the signal is absorbed by a surface. The signal simply disappears. Very few signals completely consume Wi-Fi signals, but most surfaces absorb a portion of the Wi-Fi signal. An absorbed signal becomes weaker.

We can improve the signal strength by installing antennas. If we install an antenna, we could improve the access point so that the signal strength is -10 dBm at the access point, -40 dBm about 100 ft away, and -70 dBm about 200 ft away.

Remember that there are different types of antennas. A wireless access point will come with a built-in internal antenna, but we might need to add some external ones to improve the signal. Each type provides a signal of a different shape. If we choose the wrong antenna, we will not have the correct coverage. Even if we choose the correct type of antenna, if we point it in the wrong direction, then we won't have the correct coverage.

For example, if we have a warehouse with tall metal shelves and long aisles, putting access points in the ceiling won't give us a good signal. Instead, we should install antennas at the end of each aisle and point them down the aisle.

In office buildings, schools, and hospitals, we should avoid putting access points in the hallways. Instead, we should put them inside the classrooms and large open areas where the signal can spread out. If we put an access point in a hallway, the signal will tend to bounce down the wall left to right until it runs out of power.

In a wireless network, latency and jitter can be caused by poor quality access points. If the access point takes a long time to process or transmit the signal, significant latency can develop.

When the access points form a mesh network, a signal may need to travel between several access points to get from the main network to the user's device. This also increases latency.

We also have latency due to the WAPs advertising themselves (letting users know about their SSIDs). The actual data transmission rate is called throughput. The actual beneficial throughput from an access point is called **goodput**.

Another item we can measure is **RSSI** or **Received Signal Strength Indication**. The RSSI value tells us how strong the wireless signal is at the device that is receiving it. Each manufacturer will use a different scale for the RSSI measurement, so we must check the score against the device's operating manual to be able to interpret the results.

Effective Isotropic Radiated Power measures the actual power transmitted by an antenna. Consider the following. On the left, I have a Cisco wireless access point, which has four connectors for antennas. On the right, I have a Cisco directional antenna, with four antenna cables.

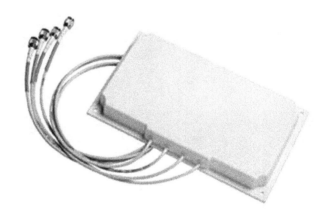

The actual radio signal generated by the wireless access point leaves those four holes, travels down the antenna cables, and is outputted by the directional antenna. If we didn't have an antenna, the signal from the access point's transmitter would spread across a large area and would be low. The antenna takes the signal and allows us to focus it in a specific direction.

If the access point has 10 Watts of power, and the antenna has a gain factor of 3 (it multiplies the signal by 3), then the antenna has an effective power of 30 Watts in a specific direction. That is not to say that the system has multiplied the power, since it is impossible for an antenna to create energy. Instead, what we are saying is that the antennas is focusing the power in a specific direction such that a transmitter would have required 30 Watts to accomplish the same task by itself.

It should also be noted that we will lose some power through the antenna cables. The longer the antenna cables, the greater the loss.

Let's take a look at some antennas

Dipole Antenna

A dipole antenna radiates power in a circle around the antenna.

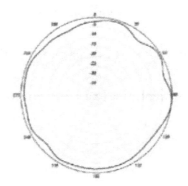

A dipole is a good antenna for a classroom or other large open area.

When we have multiple dipole antennas connected to the same wireless access point, we can take advantage of MU MIMO because each antenna will transmit the same signal in a slightly different direction. This allows the wireless access point to use beamforming and ensure a high-quality signal at the destination.

Omni Antenna

An Omni Antenna provides a signal in a circular direction. It offers less gain and distance than a dipole antenna.

It is good when we have a smaller room that requires Wi-Fi coverage.

Omni Antennas come in different shapes so that they can be mounted either to a wall or to a ceiling.

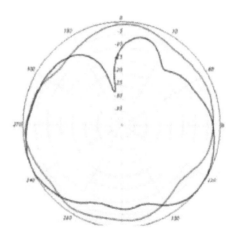

Directional or Patch Antenna

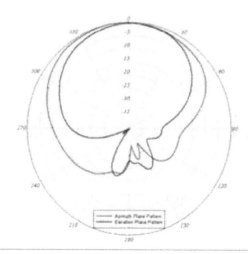

A directional antenna provides a strong signal in one direction. The antenna is good when we want to focus the signal in a specific direction.

Stadium Antenna

A stadium antenna is a directional antenna that is even more focused.

The directional antenna provides about 120 degrees of coverage whereas the stadium antenna only provides about 30 degrees of coverage.

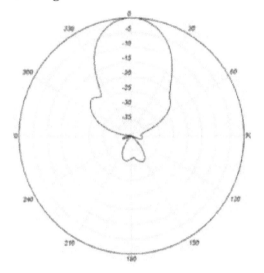

When choosing an antenna, decide

- Does the wireless access point have adequate built-in antenna coverage, or do I need an external antenna?

- If I need an external antenna, what type do I need. In other words, where do I need to focus the signal?

- How much gain do I need? Different antennas have different gains.

- How will I mount the antenna?

- Make sure that the antenna supports both 2.4 GHz and 5 GHz. An antenna may have different patterns/gains for each frequency or may only support one frequency.

You must also consider how the antenna is polarized. The **polarization** is the direction that the signal leaves the antenna. If we have a directional antenna and we don't know the polarization, then we won't know how to mount it correctly. The signal may leave the antenna at a completely wrong angle.

We should make sure that all the antennas in our system have the same polarization. Most antennas have a linear (flat) polarization that is oriented horizontally or vertically.

Attenuation is when the signal strength is reduced. The further we get from an access point, the weaker the signal. The signal strength is also reduced by surfaces that reflect, refract, or absorb the signal.

For example, if the signal strength is -40 dBm (a good strength) at the access point, it might be -70 dBm (an average strength) about 100 ft away, and -100 dBm (a weak strength) about 200 ft away.

Interference is when two Wi-Fi signals cancel each other out. Consider the following access points, both of which are broadcasting on Channel #1. The signal is good, except where it overlaps, where it cancels out.

A device in the red area will see a weak signal because the access point signals are cancelling each other out. The solution is to change the channel on one of the access points.

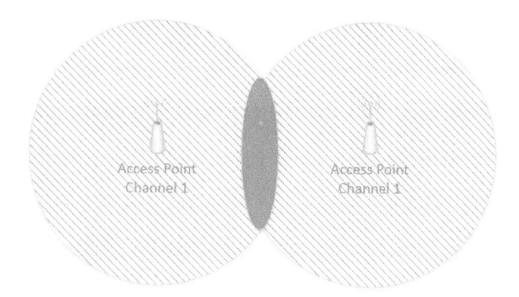

Remember how I said that a Wi-Fi channel is 22 MHz wide and that the channels are spaced 5 MHz apart? That means that on the 2.4 GHz range, the first channel is 2.412 GHz, but it actually ranges from 2.401 GHz to 2.423 GHz. The second channel is 2.417 GHz, but it actually ranges from 2.406 GHz to 2.428 GHz. That means that channels one and two overlap. Thus, we should pick two channels that are far enough apart so that interference does not take place. The sixth channel ranges from 2.426 GHz to 2.448 GHz. In the above example, I should set one access point to Channel 1 and the other access point to Channel 6. Now the signals won't interfere.

There are two other things we need to consider. An access point may only be able to handle fifty connections – this is an estimate for a high-quality access point; a poor-quality access point may only be able to handle twenty. If I have a conference room or theater with 200 or 400 occupants, even if the access point provides a good signal across the entire room, it may not have the capacity to connect to all the devices. We should install multiple access points to ensure that we have enough capacity. We should spread them out and give each one a different channel. We should also reduce the transmit power on each access point so that it only covers a small portion of the room.

We should install access points to ensure that the signal is at least -67 dBm everywhere. In the past, we used to aim for a -70 dBm signal strength, but as more advanced applications such as streaming video emerged, the requirements grew to -67 dBm.

We should also verify that our **Signal to Noise Ratio (SNR)** is at least 24. Noise is caused by wireless signals that are outside of our network. Devices such as cell phones, cordless phones, microwaves can cause noise. Other wireless networks can also cause noise. If our SNR ratio is too low, we might need to add additional access points, move the existing access points, install shielding in the building, or remove the sources of noise.

On the 2.4 GHz network, only four channels don't overlap – 1, 5, 11, and 14. Where possible, we should limit our design to these four channels.

Consider this small rectangular room, which requires six access points due to accommodating many users.

476

If I space out the access points evenly and set them as best as I can so that there are no neighboring channels, they might look like this.

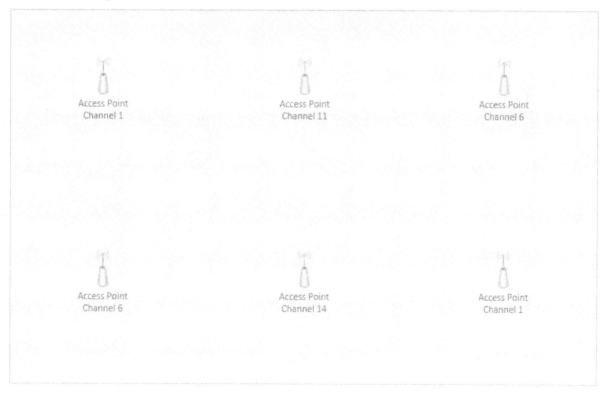

The access points that are on Channel one are in the top left corner and bottom right corner. If we highlight the coverage area of just those two access points, we can see that there is a significant overlap in the middle of the room (shown in red). The red area will have poor coverage due to interference – there will be signals from two access points on Channel one. What can we do?

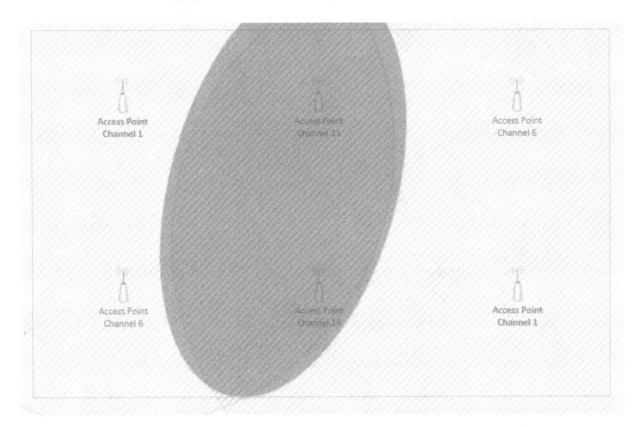

We can reduce the transmit power of each access point, so that the signal range is weaker. This way, the signals don't overlap, but we can still cover the entire room with an adequate Wi-Fi signal.

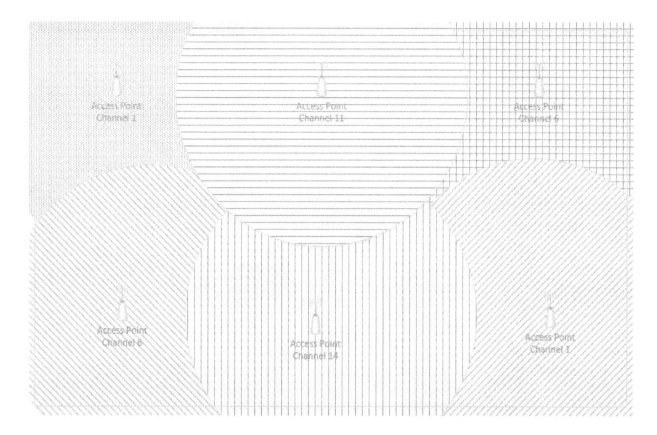

I still have overlapping signals. But the overlap doesn't extend across the entire room. The access points that overlap are broadcasting on slightly different frequencies; therefore, their signals do not interfere.

Before we install a wireless network, we should first complete a **wireless site survey**. The site survey allows us to identify the following

- The areas that require wireless coverage

- The type of material that the walls are made of

- The shape and size of the room and buildings

- Any other factors that would affect Wi-Fi coverage

- How the wireless access points will be mounted

- The type of antennas required

- The type of ethernet cabling present; if no ethernet cabling is present than we can determine the best way to install new ethernet cabling

- The distance from the wireless access points to the IDF or MDF

- Whether the existing network equipment will support the addition of new wireless access points. In other words, are there available Gigabit (or 2.5 Gigabit) PoE switch ports?

At the end of the survey, we should have a plan for exactly how we are going to install the new Wi-Fi network, and where they will go.

I use a software tool called ekahau. I used to use Air Magnet Survey Pro. Ekahau comes with a tool called a "side kick". The sidekick is a device that collects Wi-Fi signals.

Let's say we have a new building and we want to install a new wireless network. What will we do?

- We start by gathering basic information – the building floor plan, the areas that need Wi-Fi coverage, the user requirements, the security requirements, the way that the building was constructed, the types of vendors that the customer will permit (do they want Cisco, Meraki, HP, Aruba, etc.?)

- We walk around the facility to confirm the data that we gathered. We determine if there are area where wireless access points cannot be installed.

- Once we have an idea, we can import the floor plan into our survey software. We can draw out the areas that need coverage and tell the software where there are areas that will reduce coverage (such as metal shelves, concrete walls, etc.)

- We also tell the software the type of access points and antennas that we want to use

- The software runs a simulation that predicts the best spot each wireless access point. This is just a preliminary design. The software will show us a heat map that demonstrates the coverage. We can this adjust this design to add more wireless access points where there are many users (such as in conference rooms or classrooms). We can also move the wireless access points to more practical installation locations. The software adjusts the heat map each time we make a change.

- We then complete a Passive site survey. The passive site survey involves us walking around the building and collecting wireless signals automatically. The passive survey gives us a baseline idea of the noise in the environment. It should be completed during the day when many people and devices are active.

- We then complete an Active site survey. This is known as an AP on a Stick. Basically, we get a telescoping pole and mount an AP to the top, facing down. Then we power up the AP and place the stick at the first spot identified by our survey software.

  We walk around and take measurements to determine whether the AP is providing adequate coverage. In other words, did the software correctly predict a good spot for the AP where we have at least -67 dBm and an SNR of at least 24?

  Once we have gathered enough data, we move the AP on a Stick to the second location and take additional measurements. We continue to do this until we have placed the AP on a Stick at every location predicted by the software.

- The software takes all the data that we collected and stiches it together. Then we can compare it against the original prediction. If the coverage determined during the survey is adequate, then we can proceed with installation. If not, we must make changes to the design and take additional measurements. This might be an iterative process until we get it 100% correct.

- Once we have the system installed and operational, we perform a final survey to verify that the system is operating in accordance with the original plan.

We can also survey an existing Wi-Fi network to determine whether it is operating correctly. At the end of that survey, we will have a plan to correct any issues we found.

On the user's side a Wi-Fi connection can fail if the user attempts to connect to the wrong SSID, if the user has entered the wrong passphrase, or if he has selected the wrong type of security. The user's computer and the Wi-Fi network must agree to the same security setting. If not, this is known as an **encryption protocol mismatch**.

Typically, a failure to connect will return a generic error on the user's device but may return a more detailed error to the network administrator.

We should verify that the credentials are correct. We should attempt to clear or forget saved Wi-Fi networks and credentials. We should also update the network adapter drivers on the client device.

5.5 Given a scenario, troubleshoot general networking issues

- *Considerations*
  - *Device Configuration Review*
  - *Routing Tables*
  - *Interface Status*
  - *VLAN Assignment*
  - *Network Performance Baselines*
- *Common Issues*
  - *Collisions*
  - *Broadcast Storm*
  - *Duplicate MAC Address*
  - *Duplicate IP Address*
  - *Multicast Flooding*
  - *Asymmetrical Routing*
  - *Switching Loops*
  - *Routing Loops*
  - *Rogue DHCP Server*
  - *DHCP Scope Exhaustion*
  - *IP Setting Issues*
    - *Incorrect Gateway*
    - *Incorrect Subnet Mask*
    - *Incorrect IP Address*
    - *Incorrect DNS*
  - *Missing Route*
  - *Low Optical Link Budget*
  - *Certificate Issues*
  - *Hardware Failure*
  - *Host-Based/Network-Based Firewall Settings*
  - *Blocked Services, Ports, or Addresses*
  - *Incorrect VLAN*
  - *DNS Issues*
  - *NTP Issues*
  - *BYOD Challenges*
  - *Licensed Feature Issues*
  - *Network Performance Issues*

We should make sure that our network continues to operate smoothly. A few things we can review

- **Device Configuration**

  - Are all our devices configured correctly?

  - Do we have a back up of every configuration?

  - If the device received an operating system upgrade, has the configuration been reviewed to ensure that no changes were made? Has the configuration been reviewed to ensure that it takes advantage of any new features made available by the upgrade?

  - Are changes to the configuration logged and do they follow the change management procedure in our organization?

- **Routing Tables**

  - Are all our routing tables accurate and complete?

  - Are new routes being added to the routing table as required?

  - Are the weights for each route accurate or do they need to be updated?

  - Are our routing tables protocols secure?

- **Interface Status**

  - Does each router and switch interface have a detailed description about what is connected to it?

  - Is each interface operational, and at the correct speed and duplex setting? If not, we must investigate to see if any devices are offline or disconnected.

  - Are unused interfaces shut down and assigned to a VLAN that we are not using?

- **VLAN Assignment**

  - Is each interface assigned to the correct VLAN?

- o Does each VLAN have a detailed description?

- o Can larger VLANs be broken into smaller sub VLANs?

- o Can we separate the network into more VLANs or eliminate some unused VLANs?

- **Network Performance Baselines**

  - o Is the network performing at, better than, or worse than the previously established baseline?

Let's look at some other areas that can cause network disruptions.

- **Collisions**

  - o A collision happens when two devices send a packet down the same ethernet cable at the same time. The packets collide and must be resent.

  - o Collisions only happen on hubs and half-duplex links.

  - o Removing hubs and ensuring that all links operate at 1 Gbps or higher will eliminate the potential for a collision

- **Broadcast Storm**

  - o A broadcast storm happens when too many broadcast packets are sent at the same time. Remember that a broadcast packet is one that a switch forwards to all the members of the broadcast domain (all of the devices in the VLAN where the broadcast packet originated).

  - o A broadcast storm can be created by a loop in the switch.

  - o We break up larger VLANs (VLANs with many devices) into smaller VLANs. This will reduce the size of the broadcast domain.

  - o Cheaper or misconfigured network hardware such as low-end switches and hubs can create broadcast storms.

- **Duplicate MAC Address**

  - Two devices should not have the same MAC address, ever. If it happens, then one device is rogue. Or in other words, one of the devices has a spoofed MAC address. You must identify the rogue device and remove it.

- **Duplicate IP Address**

  - Two devices should not have the same IP address. If they do, then that is likely because somebody statically configured the same IP address on two devices, or statically configured an IP address that is already assigned by DHCP.

  - The solution is to change the IP address on one device.

- **Multicast Flooding**

  - A flood of multicast traffic happens because devices are sending traffic to the multicast address and because the switch is forwarding it.

  - Large volumes of multicast traffic can happen if the router forwards multicast traffic from the internet. This should be disabled.

- **Asymmetrical Routing**

  - Asymmetrical routing happens when traffic leaves the router from one interface and returns from another interface.

  - If we have an SD-WAN with multiple internet connections, the most efficient path might be different in each direction. A router may be configured to send and receive traffic using different paths.

  - However, a router or firewall needs to be able to see the traffic in both directions so that it can analyse it and so that it can enforce filtering rules. If traffic only passes in one direction, the firewall won't know which side originated the connection.

- **Switching Loops**

  - A Switching Loop happens when a physical cable is connected to two ports on the same switch, or when multiple switches are connected in a loop. A loop will cause the switch to crash.

- If we enable Spanning Tree Protocol on a switch, the switch will detect loops and shut down the affected ports. Upon receiving an alert that a port is shut down, we can physically trace the cables to determine whether a loop exists and remove them.

- When cables are neatly labelled and organized, and when access to the switches is provided only to authorized individuals, the risk of a switching loop is greatly reduced.

- **Routing Loops**

  - A Routing Loop happens because two or more routers think that the other router is the destination of the traffic.

  - Below, Router A receives a packet addressed to 10.1.3.4. The final destination is Router C.

  - There are two scenarios here. First, let's say that the routers have learned their routes from OSPF or another routing algorithm, and the link between Router B and Router C has been broken, but Router A hasn't learned about it yet. Router A checks its routing table and determines that the next hop router is Router B, so it forwards the packet to Router B.

  - Why not forward directly to Router C? Well, the link between Router A and Router C may be slow (so it may have a higher administrative cost).

  - Router B is thinks that the next hop router is Router A. It might be misconfigured, or it might know that the link between itself and Router C is down. It forwards the packet to Router A, which forwards it to Router B. The packet travels back and forth until it is dropped by one of the routers. Remember that a packet has a field that tells the router how many times it has been forwarded. A packet will be dropped after being forwarded 30 times. This prevents undeliverable packets from destroying the entire internet.

  - After a few seconds, Router A should learn the new route from Router B. Or in other words, Router A will learn that Router B no longer has a route to Router C, and then therefore, Router A must forward the traffic to Router C directly.

  - Let's think about a second scenario. Router A has a statically configured route to send Router C's traffic to Router B, and Router B has a statically configured route to send Router C's traffic to Router A. Now we will have a permanent loop between the two routers when either of them receives traffic with a destination of Router C.

this loop can be removed by deleting the static route.

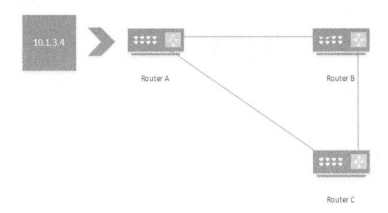

- **Rogue DHCP Server**

  o A Rogue DHCP server happens when somebody installs a rogue DHCP server on our network. We can identify that it is happening because devices will receive DHCP IP addresses that are not correct.

  o We can prevent a rogue DHCP server from being connected by enforcing DHCP snooping on all of our switches and by enforcing port security.

- **DHCP Scope Exhaustion**

  o DHCP Scope Exhaustion happens when we run out of IP addresses. It simply means that there are more devices than available IP addresses. New devices requesting DHCP addresses will be unable to connect.

  o We can fix DHCP Scope Exhaustion by ensuring that our range of DHCP addresses is wide enough.

  o If we have 10,000 potential devices, then we should have a range of at least 10,000 IP addresses. We should choose a class of network that provides us with enough addresses to accommodate all the potential devices connecting to it.

  o DHCP Scope Exhaustion can be caused by having many devices connect for brief periods. For example, the Wi-Fi at an airport sees many different devices, each for a short time. If we see 100,000 unique devices per week, we don't need 100,000 IP addresses. The average traveller only connects for a few hours. Thus, we can set a DHCP range of 10,000 IP addresses and reduce the lease time to one day, or even twelve hours. Now, used DHCP addresses will expire quickly and be returned to the pool.

- A hacker can connect to the network and request a DHCP address, change his MAC address electronically, reconnect, and request a new DHCP address. A hacker can encode these actions in a script and use up all the available addresses. Then legitimate users will not be able to connect. We can reduce the risk of this by verifying the identity of each device connecting to our network. We can also enforce a username and password on our guest Wi-Fi.

- **IP Setting Issues**

  - If our device has the wrong Gateway, Subnet Mask, IP Address, or DNS we must check why.

  - If the device is assigned these settings through a DHCP server, and they are not correct, then the DHCP server may be misconfigured.

  - If the device is assigned these settings statically, then we must configure it correctly.

  - A device might have the wrong settings if it is connected in the wrong VLAN.

- **Missing Route**

  - A missing route is when a router does not know the destination for a piece of traffic. It checks the routing table but does not have a rule matching the destination.

  - A missing route happens when the router is misconfigured or not able to learn the route via a routing protocol. We might check the settings on the routing protocol or configure a static route.

- **Low Optical Link Budget**

  - This means that the loss on our fiber optic cable is too high.

  - Remember that a fiber optic connection has a transmitter and a receiver. The transmitter operates at a certain power level and the receiver measures at a certain power level. The difference is known as the **dynamic range** and is measured in dB. It is the gain in the signal strength between the transmitter and the receiver.

- Our cable has loss. For example, if the dynamic range on our fiber optic transmitter/receiver is 10 dB and our fiber optic cable has a loss of 5 dB, then our loss budget is 5 dB, which is acceptable.

- But if our cable loss is 15 dB and our dynamic range is 10 dB, then our loss budget is -5 dB, which is not acceptable. That means that we do not have a good enough transport medium to send the signal.

- When our budget is too low, we need to either use more powerful transmitters, more sensitive receivers, or repair the fiber optic cable so that it performs better.

- A good fiber optic cable installation requires proper planning to ensure that all the components will perform within the recommended range.

- **Certificate Issues**

  - A certificate issue will prevent a device from connecting securely or from connecting at all. Without valid certificates, a client and a server cannot negotiate a secure connection.

  - Reasons why a certificate issue could occur and how to correct them

    - The certificate is not present on one of the devices – it must be reinstalled

    - The certificate has expired – a new certificate must be installed

    - The date or time on the device is not correct and now the device incorrectly thinks that the certificate has expired – the date and time should be corrected

    - The certificate has been revoked by the issuer – the administrator should verify the cause of the revocation and correct it

- **Hardware Failure**

  - A hardware failure happens when a device fails. When it fails, we must replace it.

  - We should ensure that our network has been configured so that critical hardware devices are redundant. That is, there should not be a single point of failure.

o We should adequately inspect and maintain network hardware so that we can reduce the risk that a component will fail while in use.

o We should replace aging hardware to reduce the risk that one will fail while in use.

- **Host-Based/Network-Based Firewall Settings**

  o A misconfigured firewall will could block legitimate traffic, or worse, allow malicious traffic through.

  o We should verify that each firewall allows only the permitted traffic through, and no other traffic.

  o The firewall on the Windows computers should be configured automatically through a group policy so that local users are unable to change its settings.

  o We should regularly audit the firewall rules to ensure that they are working correctly.

- **Incorrect VLAN**

  o When a device is on the wrong VLAN, it will not be able to reach the resources that it requires, and other devices will not be able to reach it.

  o A device that has an ethernet connection but has an IP address in the wrong subnet might be in the wrong VLAN.

  o We might have misconfigured the VLAN on the switch port that the device is connected to, or we might have connected the device to the wrong switch port.

- **DNS Issues**

  o If we are unable to reach a specific website or hostname from a device, but we can ping its IP address, then the DNS might not be correct or functional.

  o We must verify that the device has the correct DNS configuration. If not, we must configure the correct DNS server address on the device.

  o We must verify that the DNS is reachable from the device. We should verify that it is not blocked by a firewall. If it is blocked, we should unblock it or try a new DNS server.

o   We must verify that the DNS has an entry for the hostname that we are trying to reach, and that it is replying with the correct information. If the DNS server does not have the correct information, we should attempt to correct it. If we are not able to correct the issue, we should choose a more authoritative DNS.

- **NTP Issues**

  o   NTP allows network devices to synchronize their time.

  o   When a device does not have the correct time, then it is either set to ignore the NTP server or it cannot reach the NTP server.

  o   We can check whether the NTP server is reachable or whether it is blocked by a firewall or router.

  o   We should also verify that the device is configured to obtain the time from an NTP server that is reachable. An NTP issue can be caused by a DNS misconfiguration, if the device is unable to resolve the hostname of the NTP server.

- **BYOD Challenges**

  o   BYOD means Bring Your Own Device.

  o   If you allow users to bring their own devices to work, you must ensure that those devices have adequate security measures to protect your network. That might mean enforcing security policies and data compartmentalization on them.

- **Licensed Feature Issues**

  o   Many advanced routing and switching features are available with the purchase of an additional license.

  o   For example, if you purchase a Cisco switch, like a Cisco 3750, it will function as a normal switch right out of the box. If you want to use it as a layer 3 switch (to be able to route packets between VLANs without a separate router), then you need a license. If you want it to manage your wireless access points, then you need a license. If you want advanced security features, then you need a license.

  Once you purchase the license, you can activate it on the device and start using the features right away. Some features may be available for a limited time as a trial. Once the trial expires, the features are deactivated.

You should not activate a feature as a trial in a production network. If you do, then the network will be disrupted once the trial is over.

o   Cisco Meraki hardware is Cisco's line of cloud-managed hardware. Each Cisco Meraki switch, router, and wireless access point comes with a one-year license that allows you to connect the device to the cloud. To continue using Cisco Meraki hardware, you must renew your license each year. If your license expires, your hardware stops working.